ROYAL OCCASIONS

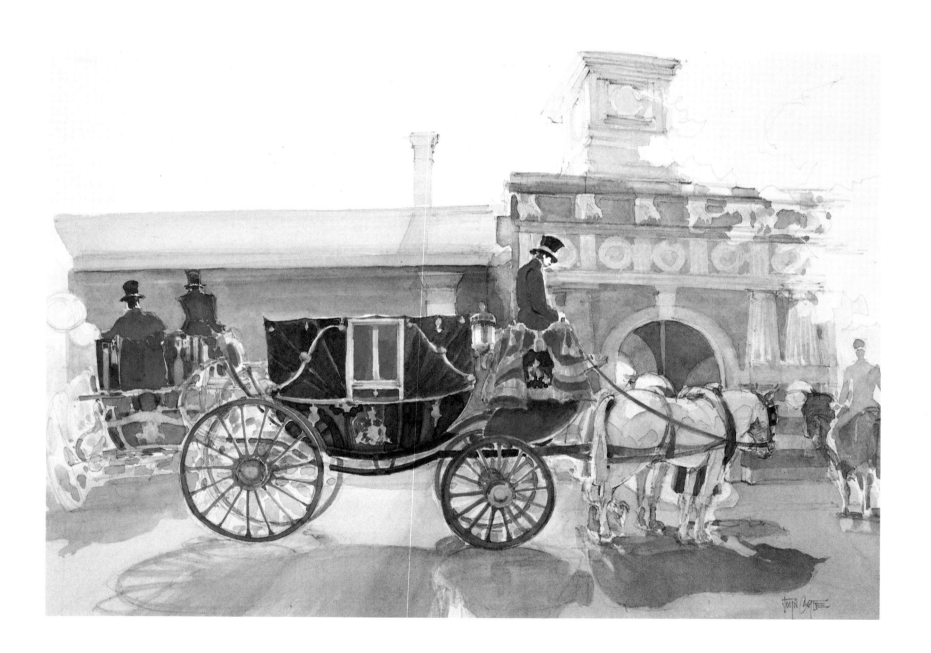

ROYAL OCCASIONS

Watercolours and Drawings

JOHN CASTLE
F.R.S.A.

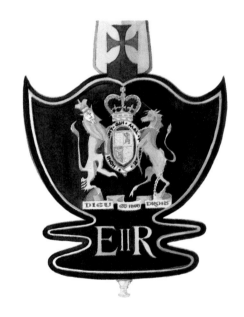

MICHAEL O'MARA BOOKS LIMITED

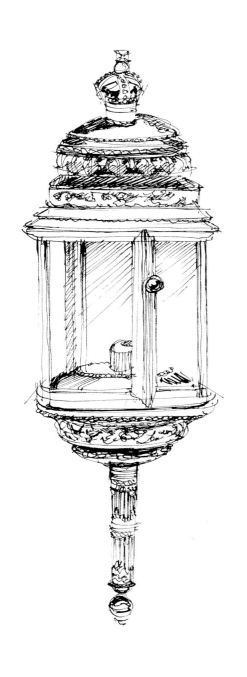

CONTENTS

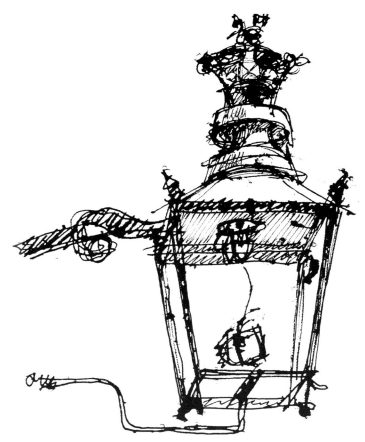

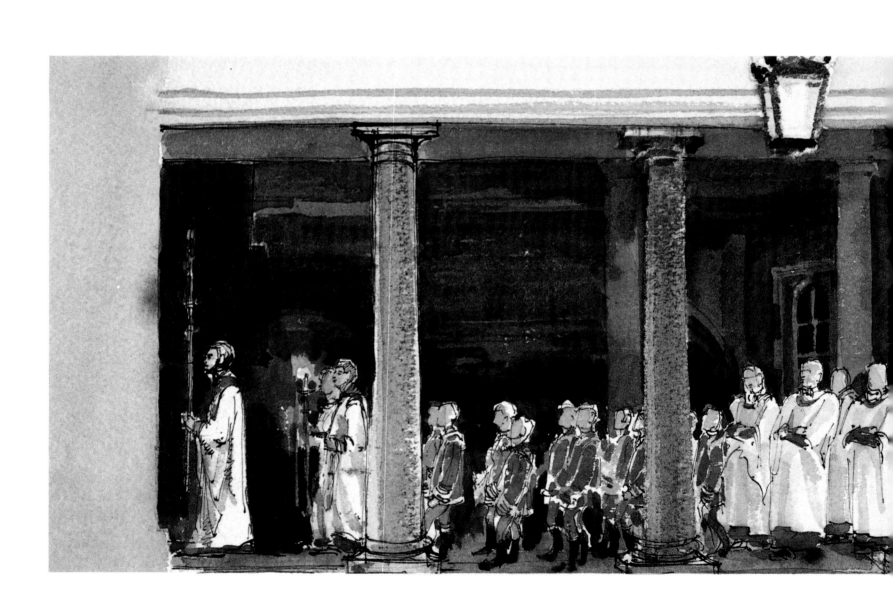

In memory of my daughter Jacqueline

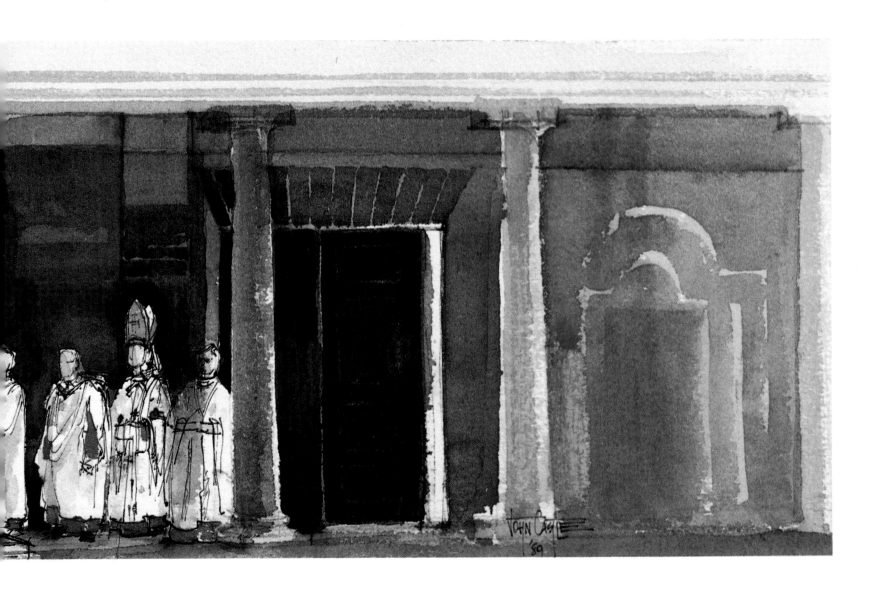

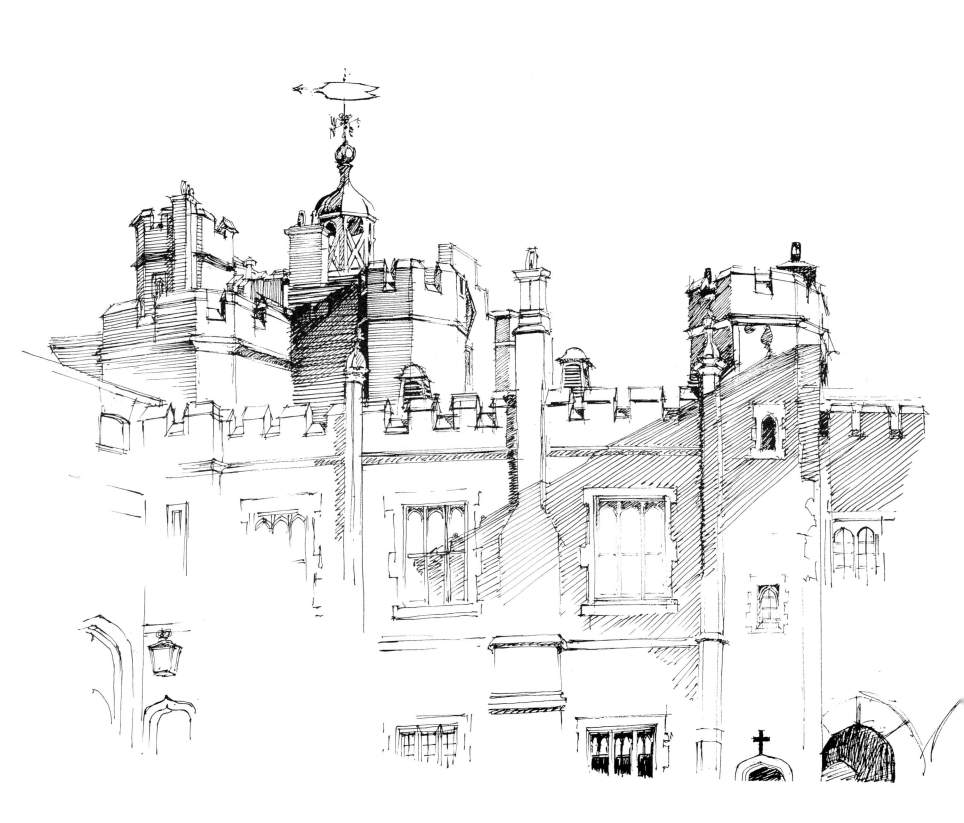

FOREWORD

I would like to express my sincere thanks to Her Majesty The Queen for her interest in this project and for graciously granting the permission for my access to these private precincts and to more public occasions. To have been granted this access was a privilege without which this book would not have been possible.

I would also like to thank those members of The Royal Household who were so helpful in furnishing me with information and pointing me in the right direction.

A very special note of thanks goes to those at The Chapel Royal whose friendship and help made working on this book so enjoyable.

My family and friends, who have encouraged me throughout the whole period of my work on the book, deserve my sincere thanks.

I would particularly like to thank the following who have made a substantial contribution to this book:

David Baldwin, BA, FRSA
Canon A.D. Caesar, CVO, MA, Mus.B, FRCO
Ghislain d'Hoop
Bryce Harland, QSO
Peter Hartley, MVO
Martin Lethbridge
Suzanne O'Rourke
Sir John Richards, KCB, KCVO
Sir Kenneth Scott, KCVO
Sgt. Maj. Tom Taylor, MVO, MBE
Michael Turk
Claude Wertheimer Sinnelier
Erik West, FRSA

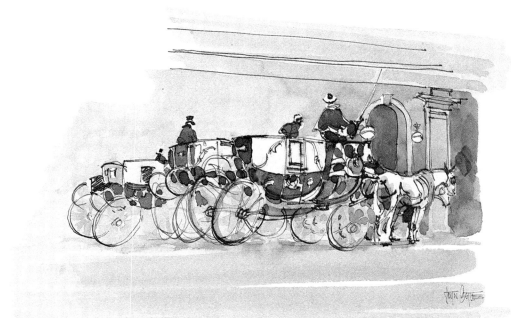

PROLOGUE

IT WAS A GREAT PRIVILEGE to have been allowed access to the private world of St James's Palace. It was the first time in living memory that such permission had been granted and it provided me with a unique opportunity of seeing from the inside the workings of twentieth-century monarchy.

The purpose of the book is to give through paintings and drawings an insight, without intrusion, into the daily world within the Palace's walls. It is not intended to be either a history book or a tourist brochure. Words are not my tools of trade: rather, paints and brushes. For the most part the paintings speak for themselves.

The book began accidentally in July 1989 when watching my nephew, then a chorister in the Chapel Royal choir, playing football. The scene captured my imagination: the boys of the Chapel Royal numbered only ten (my niece had to be called upon to make up the team) and the opposition, the choir of the Temple church, were much bigger and stronger. Most striking of all was the venue: the moat of the Tower of London (empty). The little boys seemed midget-sized against the giant stones that formed the moat which itself was dwarfed by the brooding Tower. Anxious parents cried encouragement to their offspring from the sidelines.

My sketches of the event were liked and it was suggested to me that paintings of the boys in uniform might be possible. Of necessity these had to be done in St James's Palace where, for several hundred years, the uniforms have been kept. Security arrangements were made for me and I became a regular visitor. Out of these visits grew *Royal Occasions*.

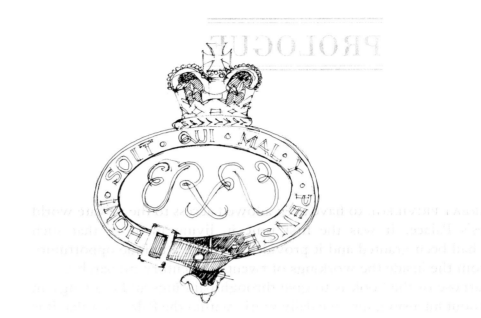

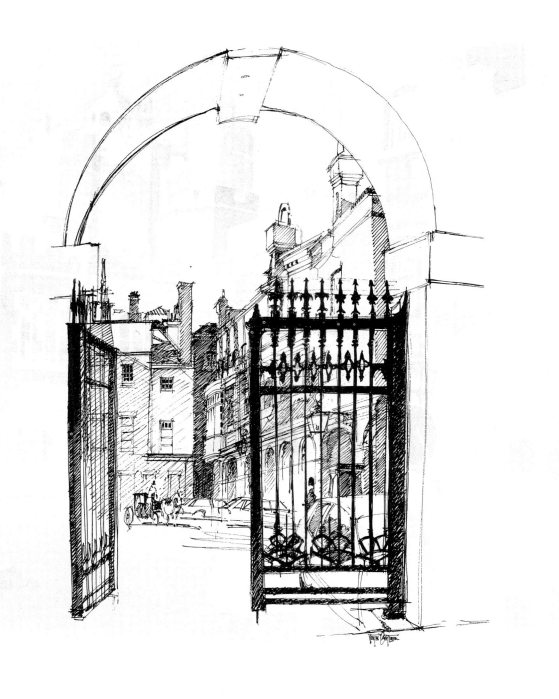

ST JAMES'S PALACE

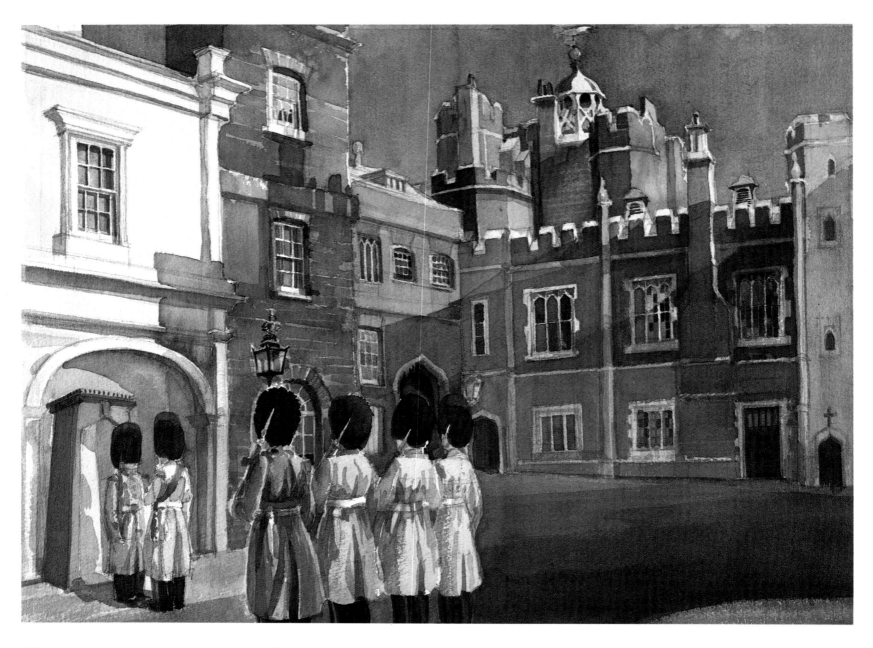

Changing the Guard,
Ambassadors' Court,
St James's Palace

ST JAMES'S PALACE is situated at the centre of London's West End where Pall Mall joins St James's Street. Two Guards posted at the Great Gates hint at its importance to the British Crown but few people realize that it is in fact the kingdom's senior palace. Although Buckingham Palace is where the Queen lives when she is in London and where much official entertaining takes place, St James's Palace is designated the Sovereign's official residence.

Nowadays, Buckingham Palace also contains administrative offices but it is St James's which is traditionally the hub of the whole 'business' of monarchy. Most royal ceremonies are organized from St James's and the colourful pomp of the British monarchy which tourists and Londoners so much enjoy emanates from here. St James's is much older than Buckingham

Palace. It was originally a leper hospital named in honour of St James the Less, whose work among lepers earned him beatification. The present building was begun in 1532 by Henry VIII but the royal connection goes back much further. A tile bearing the *fleur-de-lis* of Edward III (1327–77) who laid claim to the throne of France was unearthed in Colour Court.

Recently, a water filtration system was discovered, which may have had its source in Gray's Inn Fields, and dated back to medieval times when, as St James's Hospital by Westminster, it was officially under the King's protection. In 1450, King Henry VI granted the land to Eton shortly after the College's foundation but, less than a hundred years later, Henry VIII bought it back and its history as a royal palace properly began.

Most of the building for this new palace was carried out under King Henry's direction between 1532 and 1540. Carved in stone above the main entrance and also above the fireplace in the Great Hall are the King's initials lovingly entwined with those of his then wife and queen, Anne Boleyn.

Henry VIII was the first of a long line of monarchs to reside in St James's, finishing only when Queen Victoria preferred to live at Buckingham Palace. St James's became the official residence of the Sovereign when Queen Anne moved the entire Court there, after Whitehall Palace burned down in 1698. Even today, it is to the Court of St James that foreign diplomats are accredited rather than to the British Government.

The State Apartments, enlarged by Christopher Wren and redecorated by William Morris in the last century, are still used for official entertaining. They house a marvellous collection of royal portraits, tapestries reputedly commissioned by Charles I, and an impressive display of firearms.

The Queen's Life Guard, the Yeomen of the Guard, the Gentlemen-at-Arms, the Royal Watermen, the Chapels Royal – all have their headquarters in St James's Palace. The Prince and Princess of Wales and the Duke and Duchess of Kent both have their offices here while several senior members of

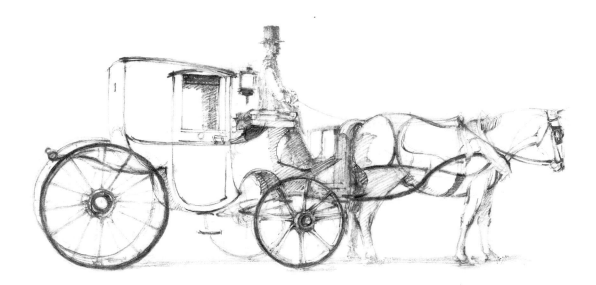

The brougham

the Royal Household such as the Marshal of the Diplomatic Corps and the Master of the Queen's Household have apartments in the Palace.

Outside the Great Gates the Guards stand seemingly unmoved by the tourists taking their photographs and the fumes from the traffic pounding up St James's Street. Beyond the gates is a different world – a maze of courtyards each with its own character but for the most part blessedly quiet.

The first court we come to through the Great Gates, walking on cobbles polished by centuries of wear and weather, is Colour Court. After the cacophony outside, the court is delightfully silent so that the delicate chimes of the clock in the tower can easily be heard. The red Tudor brick of the tower glows in the sunlight, the white struts of the bell-tower gleam and the Roman numerals, gold on black, glitter.

A white West Highland terrier, one of several dogs resident in St James's, comes up to me wagging its tail. It wants to call my attention to a curiously shaped pole in the centre of Colour Court. The pole has a hole in it in which the monarch's Colour or standard can be placed. For three hundred years the Colour was placed here when a foreign head of state visited but is now rarely used. The Colour is kept in the Guardroom.

OPPOSITE: The tower of St James's Palace viewed from Colour Court, every brick steeped in history. To the left of the tower is the original Chapel Royal. King Charles I received his last communion in the tower in which he had been imprisoned prior to his execution in Whitehall. The Great Gates these days are opened solely for visiting heads of state

York House. Sadly, restoration work here caused the demise of the Virginia creeper

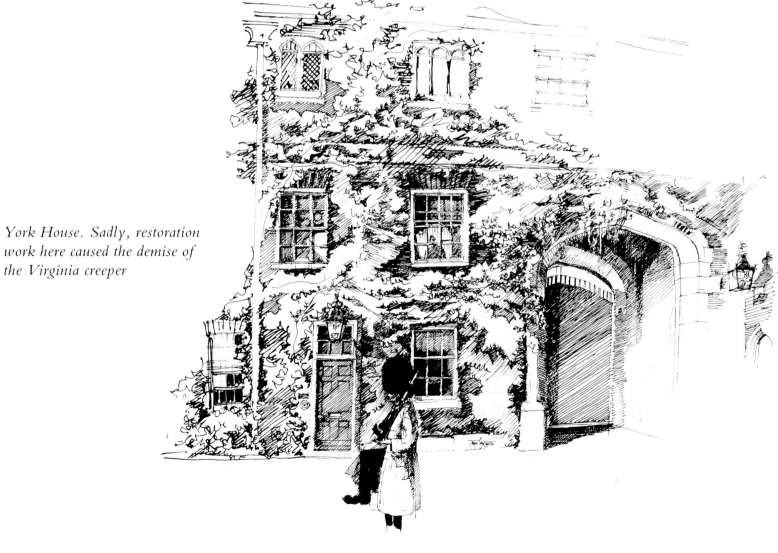

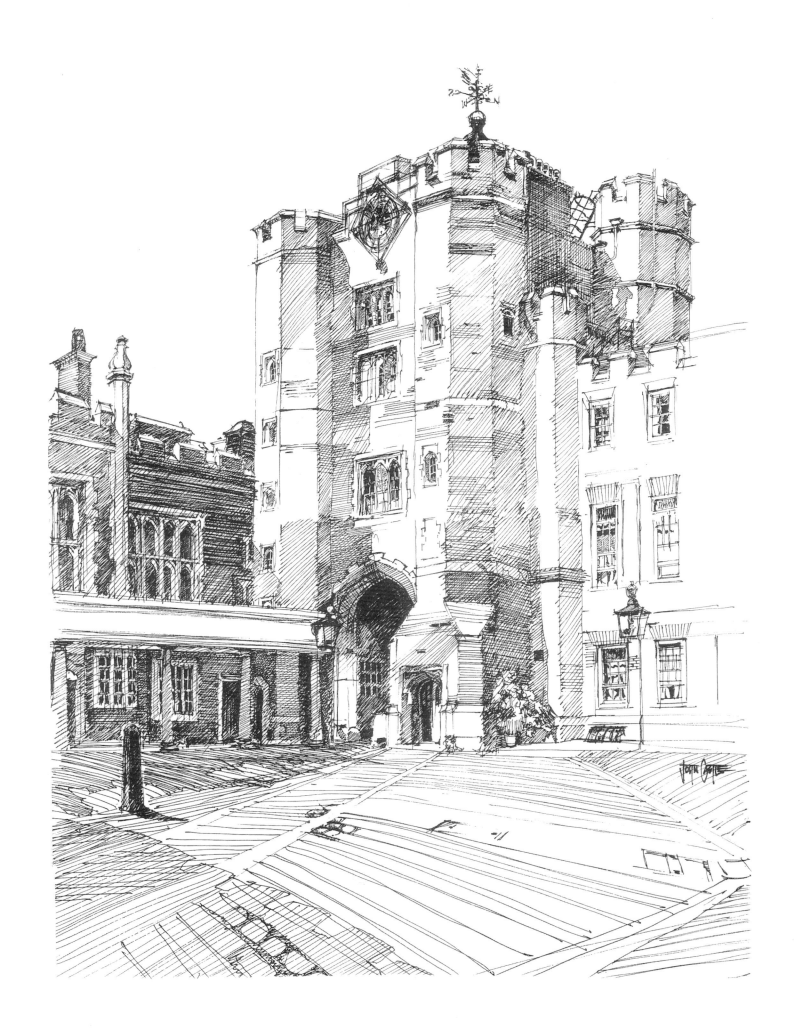

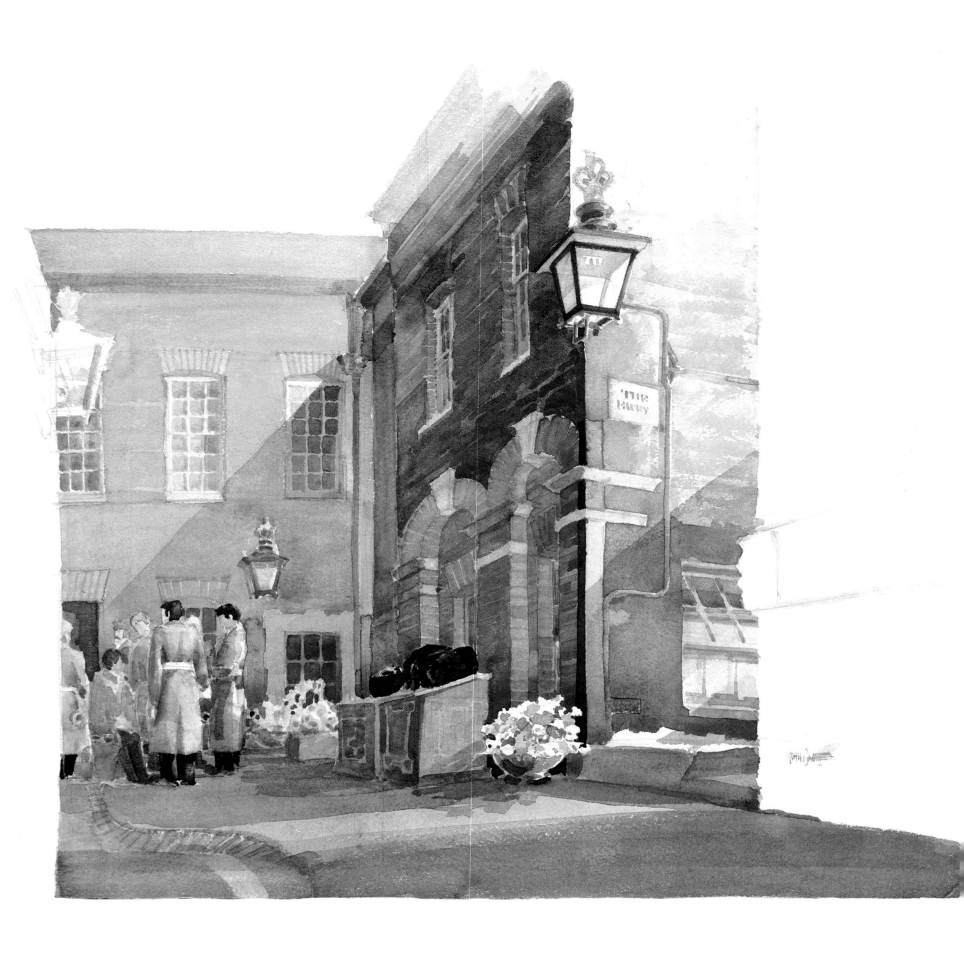

The pure sounds of a young chorister rehearsing a solo waft through an open door at the foot of the tower. The Sub-Dean walks through the colonnade and enters the vestry door of the Chapel Royal. The Marshal of the Diplomatic Corps, anonymous in his pinstripe suit, leaves his apartment in the tower accompanied by another white terrier to take a stroll in Green Park.

Green Park, it is said, was so named in the reign of Queen Anne. The Queen noticed a courtier picking flowers there one day. She waited in vain for him to present them to her and at last indignantly upbraided him. She ordered that all flowers be removed from the park so that she should never be so insulted again.

In Colour Court and throughout the Palace are lead boxes bearing the royal cypher and dating from the sixteenth and seventeenth centuries. Could these finely decorated boxes once have been used for storing powder for muskets or had they no practical use? My enquiries brought me down to earth. Then as now, they were litter bins.

From Colour Court one passes through finely wrought gates into Ambassadors' Court. Early one January morning, soon after permission had been granted to me to sketch in the Palace grounds and determined not to waste a moment, my well-travelled sketching stool stood waiting for me to begin work. It was almost too cold to draw so first one pair of gloves and then a second pair muffled my freezing fingers . . .

The brougham, delivering truly royal mail, appeared exactly on time as usual. A bowler-hatted gentleman handed over the letters and parcels to a liveryman in a black coat, resplendent in a scarlet waistcoat with gold buttons. The transaction over, the claret-coloured coach moved off, pausing briefly at Clarence House and two or three other ports of call before returning to the Royal Mews behind Buckingham Palace.

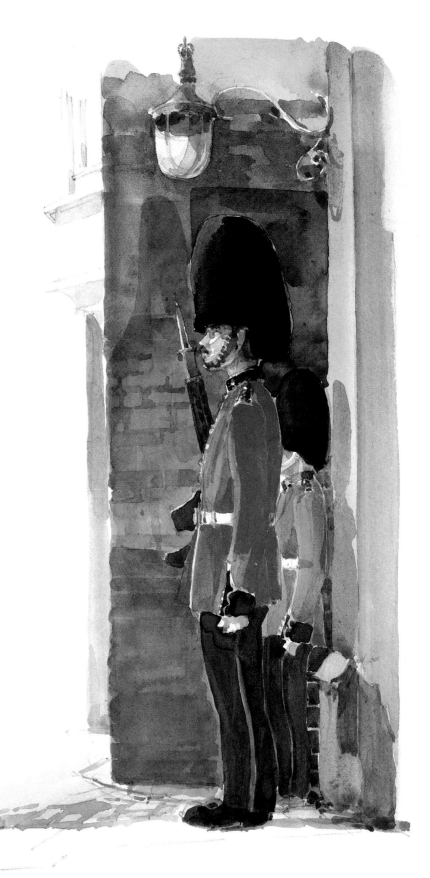

LEFT: *Guards at ease in Engine Court, St James's Palace.* RIGHT: *Sentries on guard outside the Great Gate*

The Colonnade, Colour Court. The original cobblestones have been recently replaced with a new concrete version but, after some negotiation, the glorious gas lamps have remained gas fuelled

Later still another small coach of quite a different model arrived with the groceries and departed, the horses' hooves slipping on the icy stone. Someone provided me with a life-saving cup of tea but when at last it became impossible to sketch, my stool would not close. It was frozen solid.

A few days later my stool finally gave up the ghost. It was the day that Prince Harry began school. There had been a few more cars than usual in Ambassadors' Court and the police were a little more in evidence. Just as the sentries were marching by and much to my embarrassment, the stool collapsed under me leaving me sprawling on the ground. A policeman helped me to my feet and provided me with a milk crate as a substitute perch. It touched me when the soldiers who had witnessed my discomfiture sent to find out if all was well. The observer was beginning to feel part of the scene he was observing.

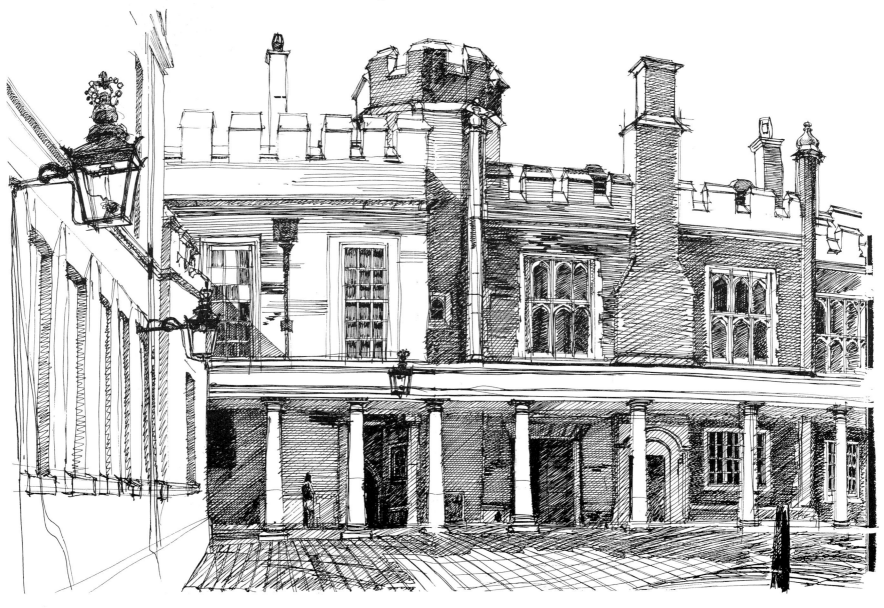

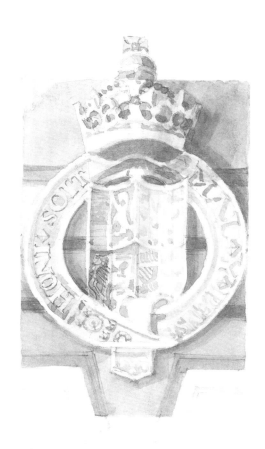

THE CHANGING OF THE GUARD

TRADITIONALLY, the life and the palaces of the Sovereign are guarded by the Household Troops. Until the Palace of Whitehall burnt down, this duty was performed by the Household Cavalry. When the Court shifted to St James's, the privilege was given to the Foot Guards, the Cavalry guarding the official entrance to the Palace and St James's Park – Horse Guards Arch.

The Queen's Guard is based at St James's Palace although, since the

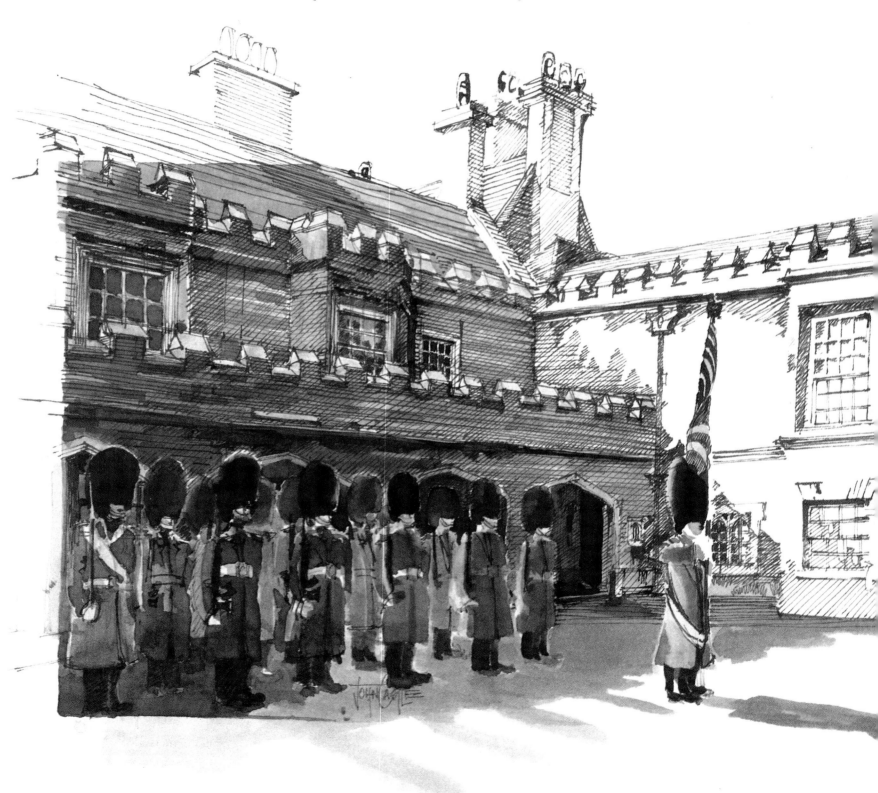

reign of Victoria, a detachment also guards Buckingham Palace. It is in the forecourt of Buckingham Palace that the Changing of the Guard or Guard Mounting takes place every day in summer and every other day in winter. Guard Mounting also takes place at Whitehall, Windsor Castle and the Tower of London, the latter having been a royal palace for nine centuries.

A visit to Swaine, Adeney, Brigg in Piccadilly had provided me with a sturdy stool much more suitable to supporting me in my task than my previous one and it was now possible to watch the world go by in safety. The first thing that is evident is how little life has changed over the centuries within the Palace precincts and yet how thin is the screen that separates it from the twentieth century.

Assembly of the Guard of the Colour, and the Fife and Drum Band, Friary Court, St James's

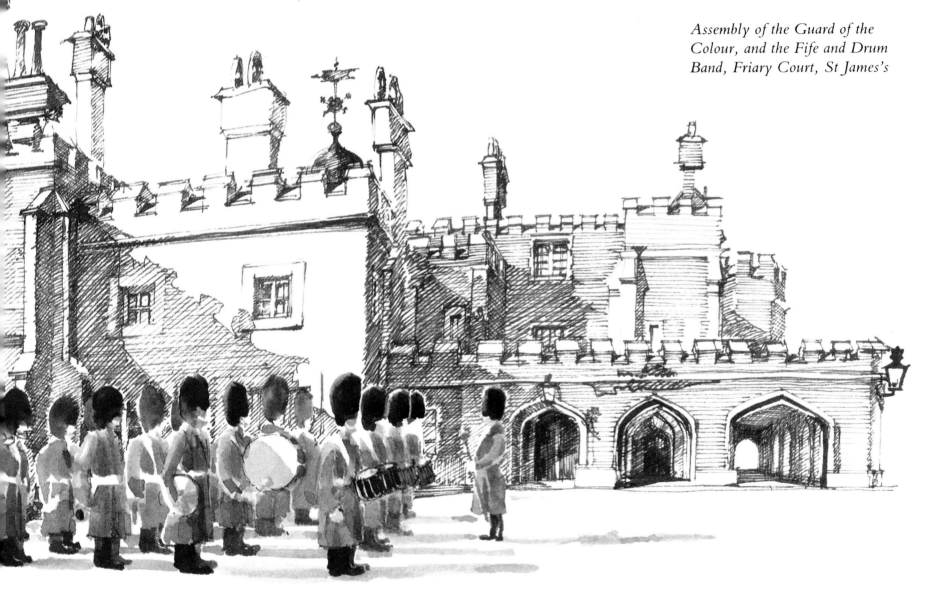

Every two hours, every day, there is a change of sentries at each of the four guard posts around St James's Palace – Buckingham Palace has a further four sentries. The weapons they carry are not antiques but modern, hi-tech arms. Listening to the shouted commands and to the noise of boots on the courtyard, it is easy to admire the precision with which each movement is performed. Eventually, Ambassadors' Court is silent again but not for long.

The ground shakes beneath my feet and then there comes the rumble of tyres on tarmac. Moments later, two enormous army trucks appear. These great vehicles, too large to go through the archway leading out of Ambassadors' Court, open at the back to disgorge soldiers with rucksacks, rifles and musical instruments.

These very modern soldiers are strangely out of place in this Tudor courtyard but they are soon to be transformed. After a short time behind a door marked 'Guardroom', they reappear in bearskins, tunics and the distinctive dark-blue trousers with a red stripe. It is exciting to be a privileged witness of the beginnings of that most famous of royal ceremonies – the Changing of the Guard.

The Queen's Foot Guards' uniform of bearskins and tunics dates from the reign of Queen Victoria. It replaced a variety of different uniforms, each regiment having its own. Today, there are only very small, though important, differences between the uniforms of different regiments of Guards.

The Guards, in their winter blue-grey overcoats, assemble in Engine Court. Bearskins and musical instruments are balanced on the lead litter-bins. The winter sunlight reflects off gold buckles and buttons and on brass instruments. They talk among themselves and notice the man in the blue suit sketching them.

The Old Guard,
Buckingham Palace

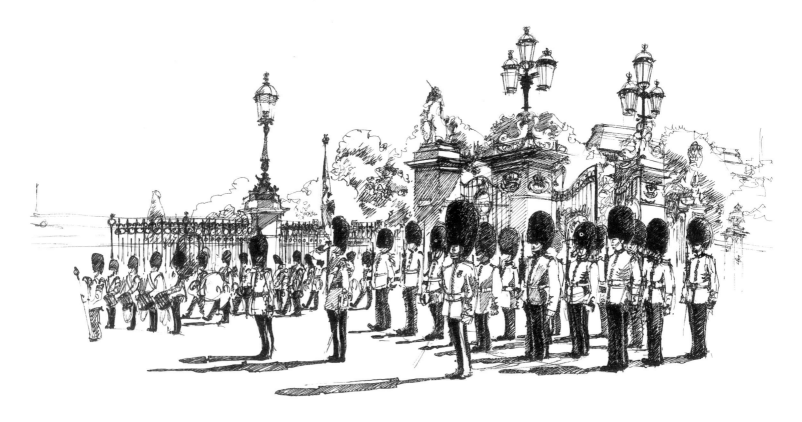

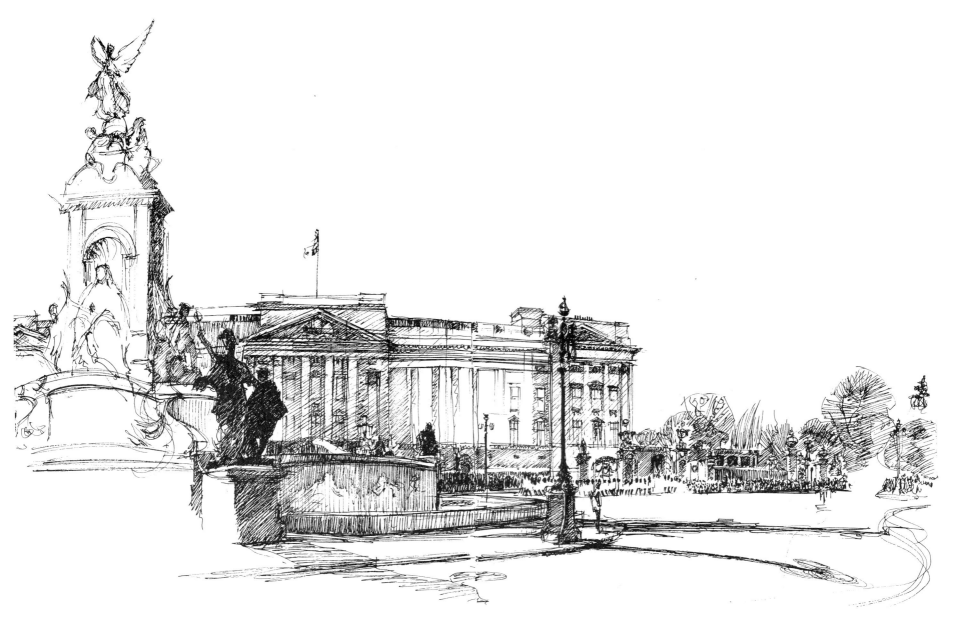

Through an archway across Engine Court, can be seen a closed iron gate. A crowd of tourists mill around a bronze statue of Queen Alexandra. Mounted police are also there seen against the imposing backdrop of Marlborough House.

Finally, everything is ready. In single file, the bandsmen first, the Old Guard march through the gate which opens before them. The Guard of Colour, as it is properly called, forms up beneath the famous balcony in Friary Court from which is proclaimed the death of the Monarch and the accession of the new Sovereign.

The Guard is brought to attention, the fife and drum band strikes up and, on the command, the Old Guard moves off down Marlborough Road and into the Mall. It enters the forecourt of Buckingham Palace through the left-hand gate. There it joins the Buckingham Palace detachment and awaits the arrival of the New Guard. The New Guard's arrival is heralded by a regimental brass band which leads it through the Privy Purse (the right-hand) gate.

Entry of the New Guard into the forecourt of Buckingham Palace

OVER: . . . and the band played Billy Joel

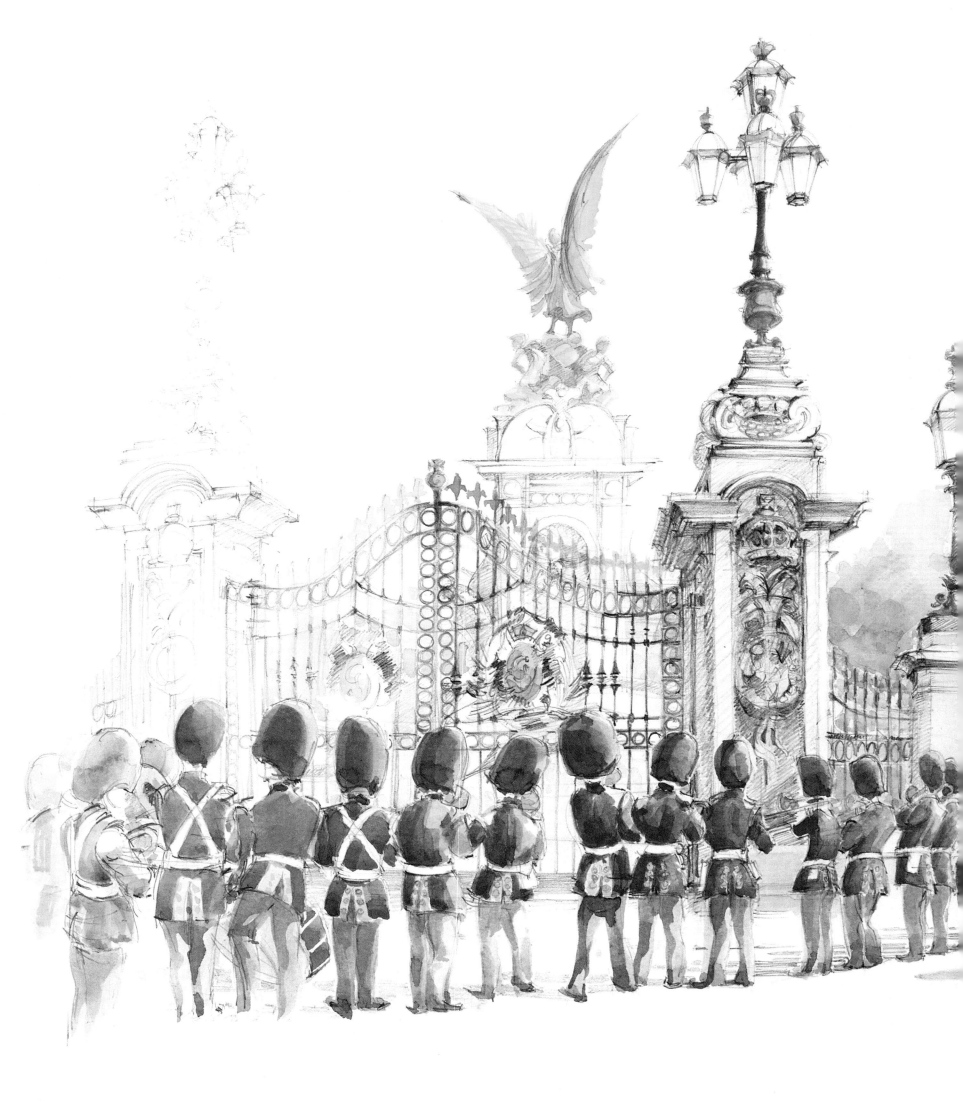

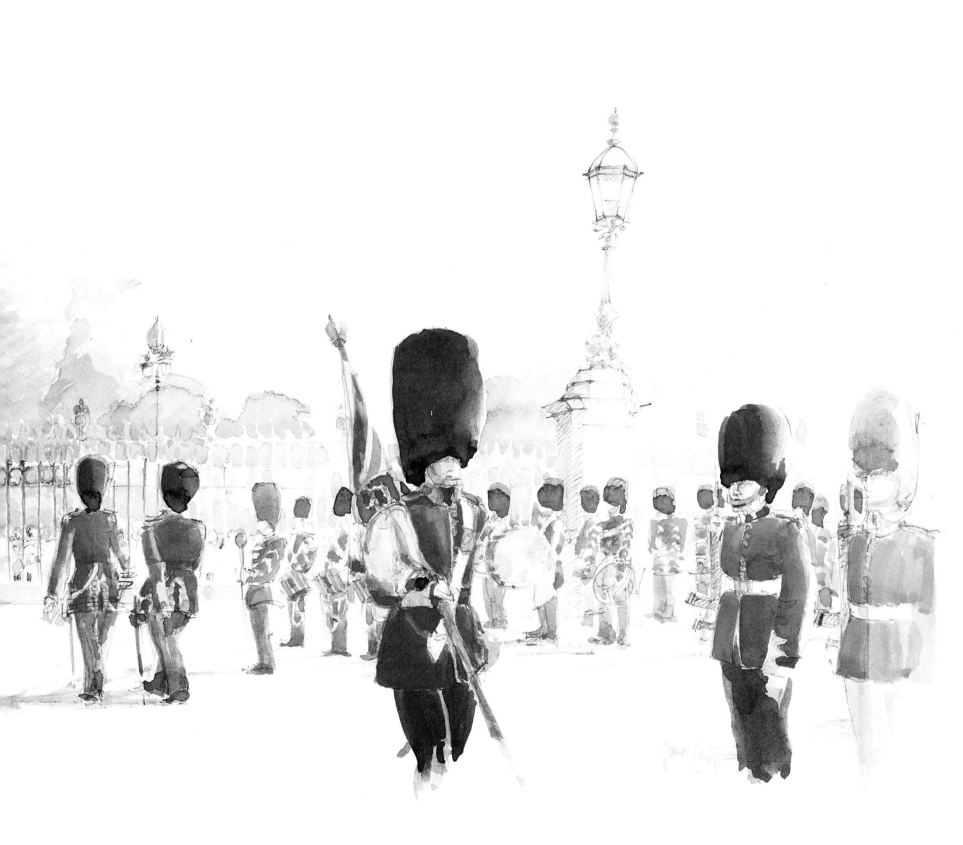

Aftermath of the Changing of the Guard

As the Guard is changed the band plays. Each regiment has its own signature march and a wide repertoire of well-known tunes. The Grenadiers have 'The Grenadier Guards'; the Scots Guards play 'And the band played Annie Laurie'. On one occasion, the Queen not being in residence and it being the last day prior to the Scots Guards taking up a posting in Northern Ireland, I was entertained to hear the band suddenly swing into a pop number by Billy Joel.

The ceremony of Changing the Guard over, the New Guard, with its corps of drums, marches back to St James's Palace while the Old Guard with the band returns to Wellington Barracks.

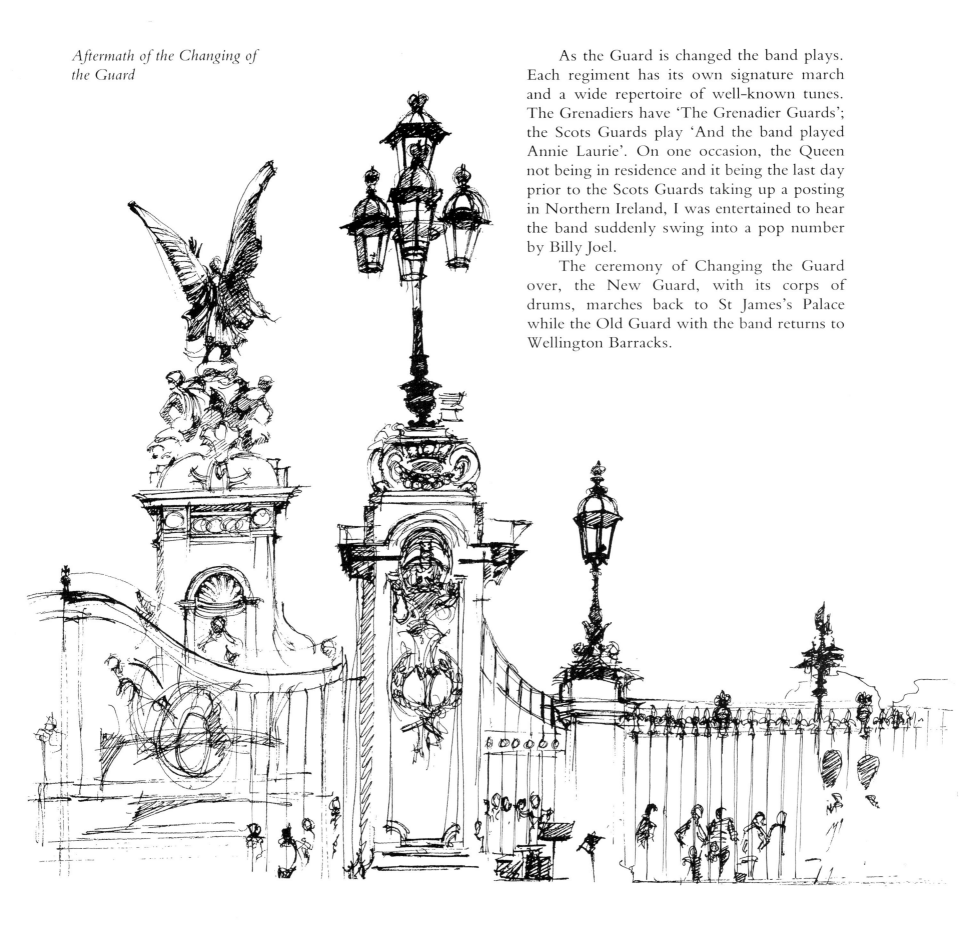

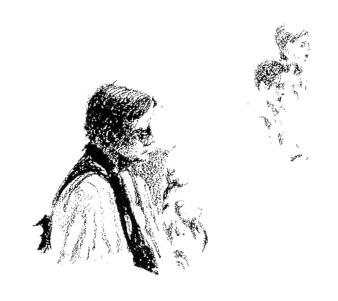

THE CHAPEL ROYAL

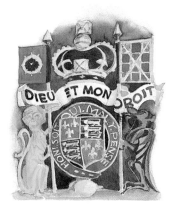

*The Arms of Queen
Elizabeth I*

*The choir and clergy
of the Chapel Royal
in procession*

THE CHAPEL ROYAL is an institution defined as 'the priests and singers who together serve the spiritual needs of the Sovereign'. Henry VIII had royal chapels in many palaces including Hampton Court, Greenwich, Whitehall and St James's. Among the oldest are those of the Tower of London and the Palace of Westminster.

As early as the eleventh century there are records mentioning a keeper of the Chapel, who, before the establishment of permanent chapels, accompanied the king on his travels. He is described as a clerk or cleric who travelled with four serjeants and two packhorses on which were loaded vestments, books and all things necessary to his office. As the institution grew, the whole body of priests, singers and servants travelled with the king. For example, the Chapel Royal went with Henry V to the French war and in 1415 sang mass before the Battle of Agincourt.

The Chapel Royal, St James's, was built for Henry VIII and, since 1702, has been the home of the Royal Choir. It is an integral part of St James's Palace and accessible only from its precincts. From at least the beginning of the fourteenth century there has been an office of Dean of the Chapels Royal.

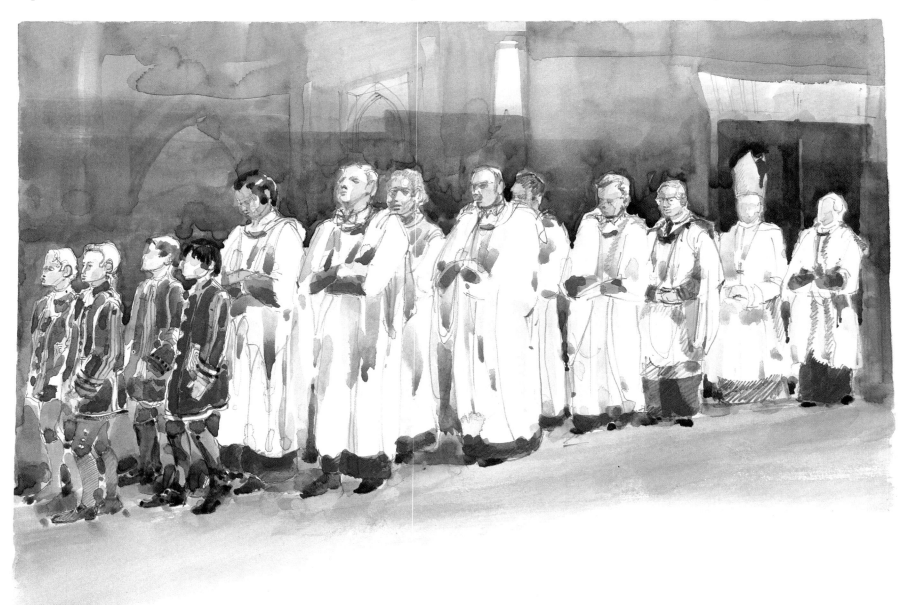

The Dean had no spiritual superior except the Archbishop of Canterbury and he had the authority previously vested in the king's chancellor. His jurisdiction extended over all members of the king's household 'of whatever dignity'. In the late fifteenth century an office of Sub-Dean was created and since 1603 the Dean has been a bishop but retaining all his former powers.

At the entrance to the Chapel Royal is a notice which reads:

The Chapel Royal, Saint James.
This Chapel formed part of Henry VIII's
Palace. The ceiling traditionally
attributed to Holbein bears the date 1540.
The Chapel was enlarged in 1837.
Here, Charles I received the sacrament of
Holy Communion on the morning of his
execution, 1649. Queen Victoria was
married here in 1840 and King George V
in 1893 when Duke of York.

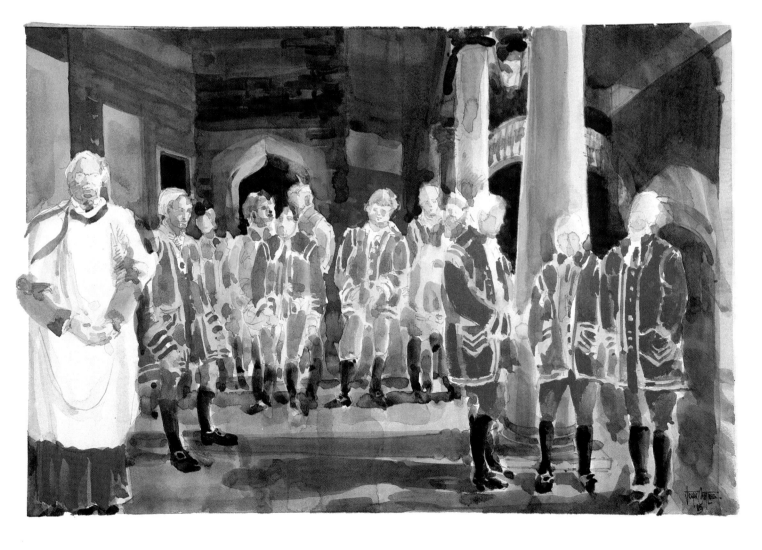

The 'Organist, Choirmaster and Composer' of the Chapel Royal with choirboys off duty

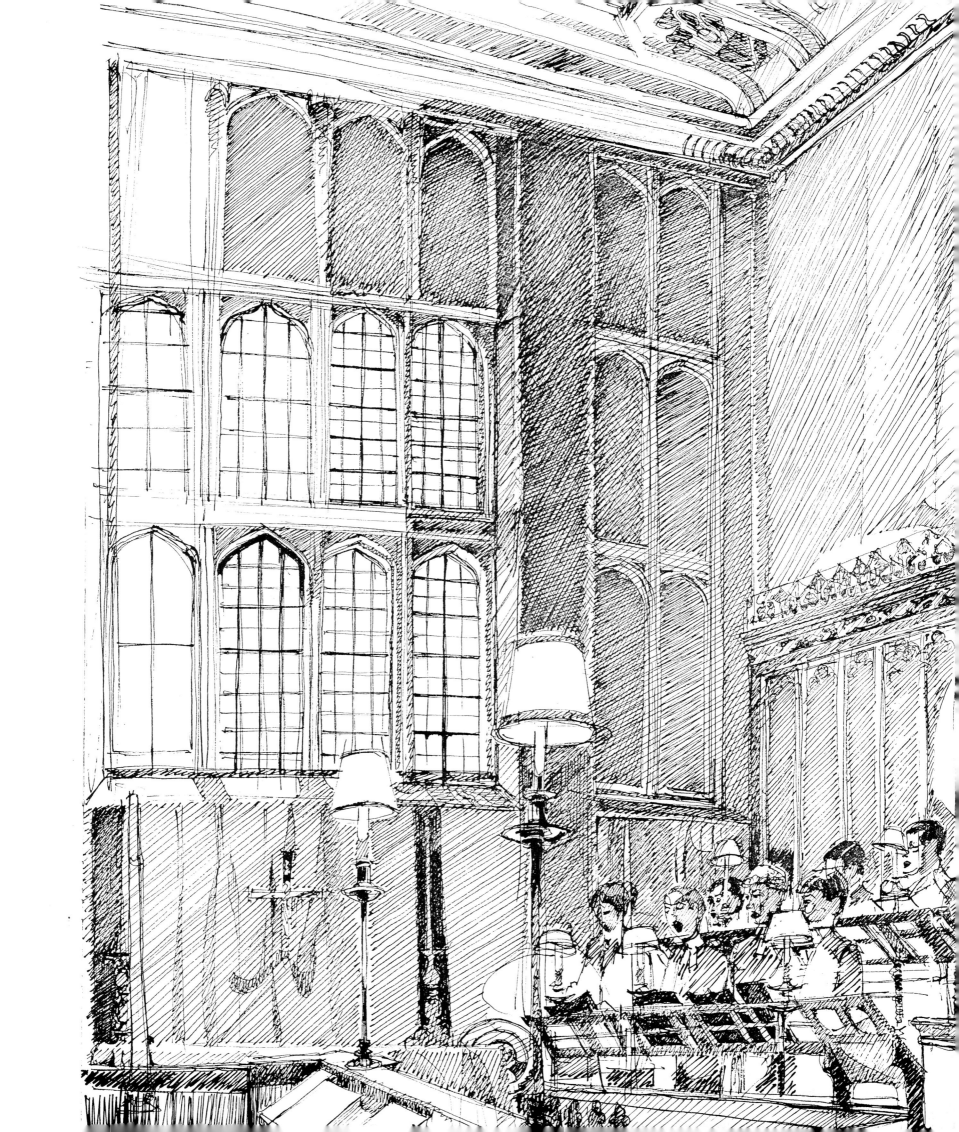

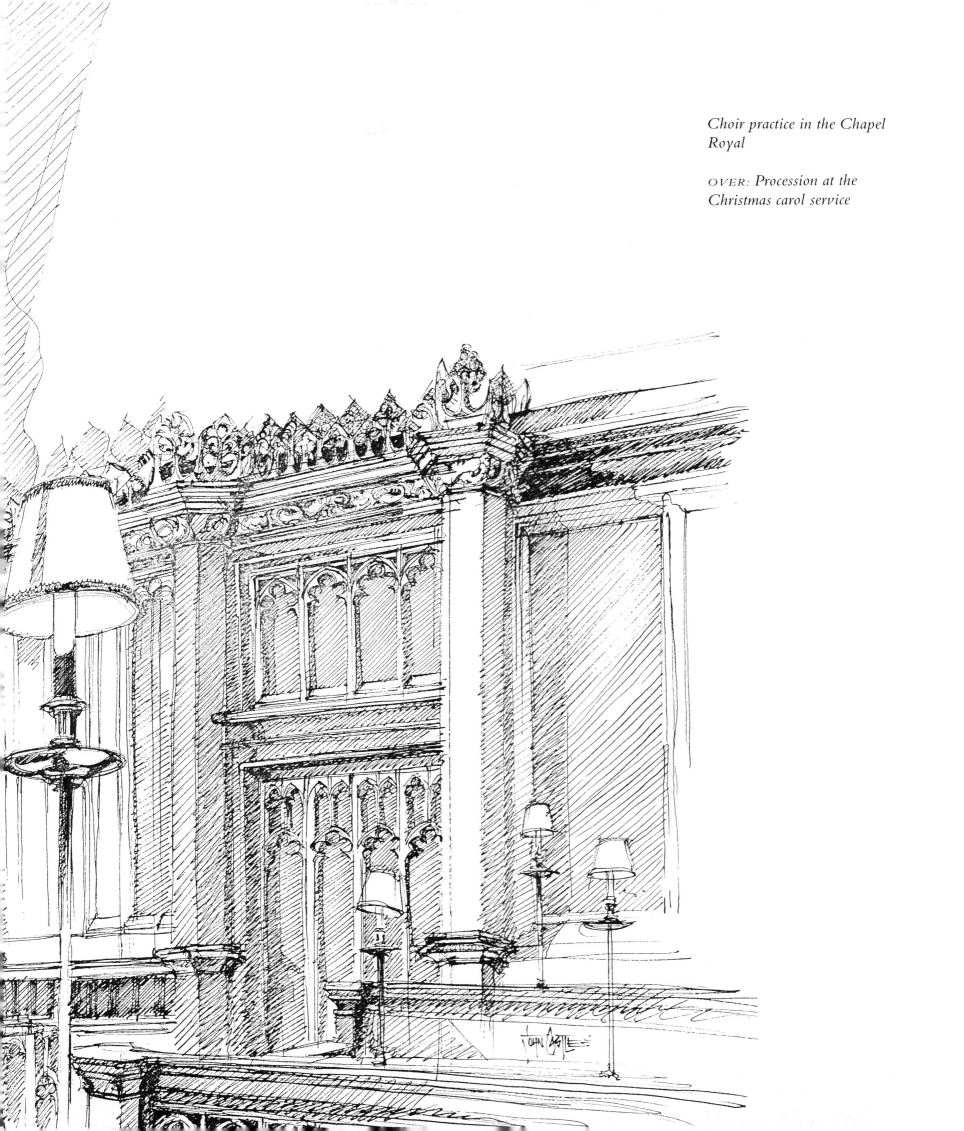

Choir practice in the Chapel Royal

OVER: *Procession at the Christmas carol service*

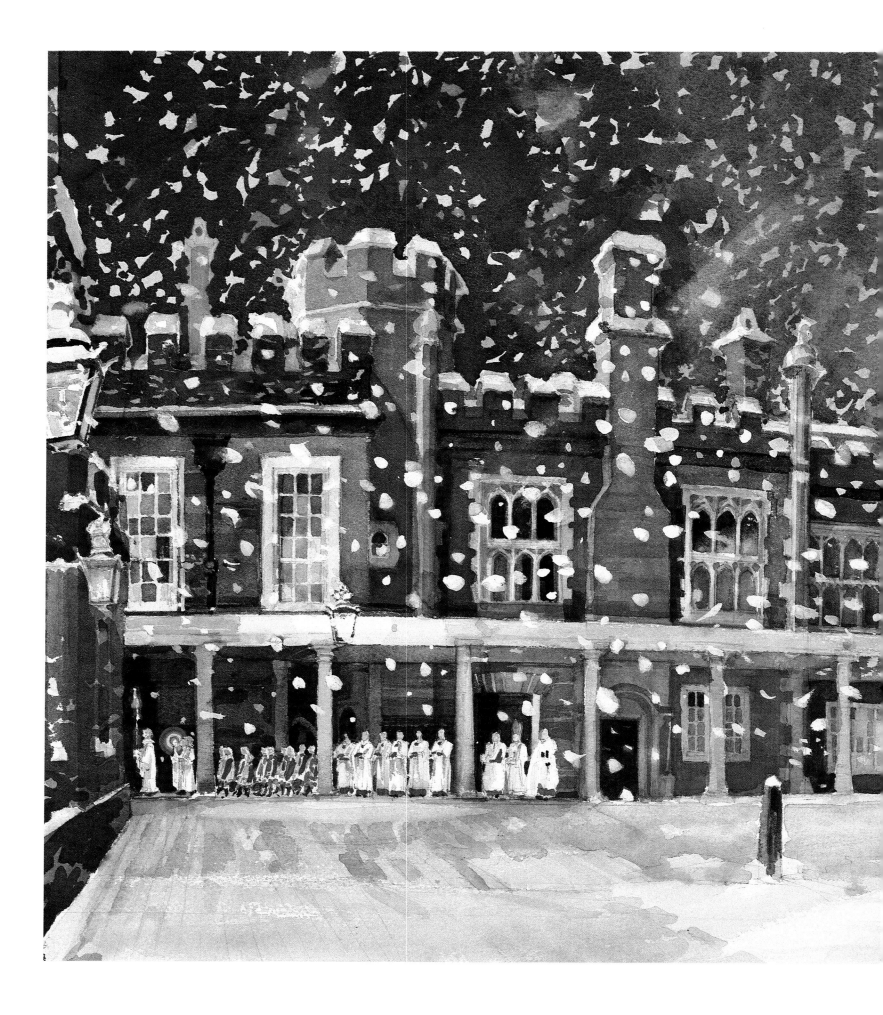

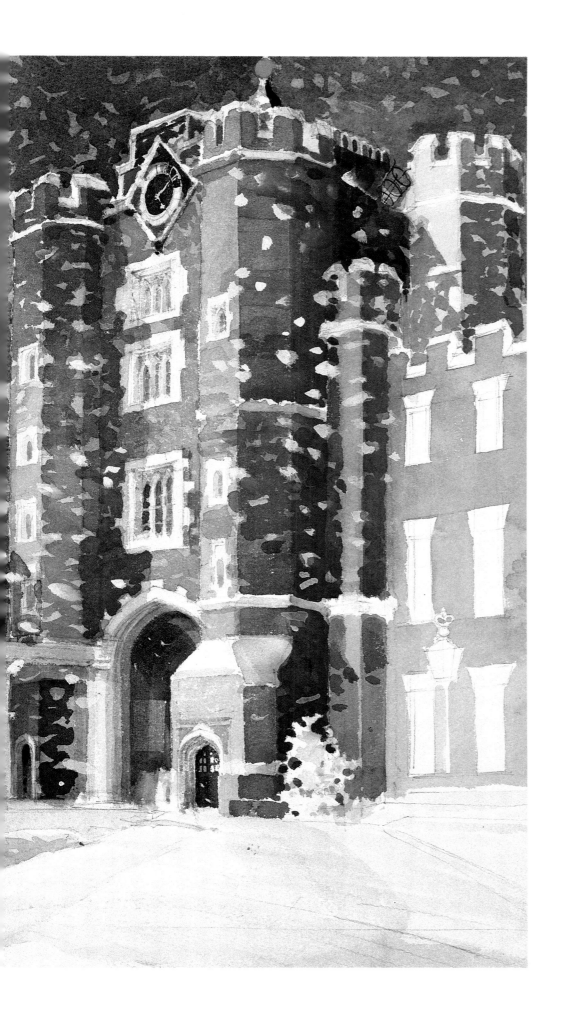

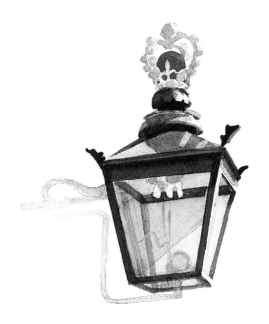

The choir arrives for practice – perhaps for a special occasion but probably just for Sunday service. In their City of London School uniforms, these ten Queen's Scholars look like any normal schoolboys although because of their surroundings they may be a little less boisterous.

They change into the uniform of the Chapel Royal – scarlet with gold – as designed for Charles II in 1661. In the vestry, alongside a sculpture, the gift of a recent Pope, hangs an eighteenth-century watercolour. It depicts the ten Chapel Royal choirboys of the time in a pastoral setting, possibly Green Park. Aside from their hats, which are no longer worn, the uniforms are identical to those worn by their successors today.

It is not surprising given the long history of the Chapel Royal that many famous names feature as past organist, choirmaster and composer. Now combined as one post, it originated as three distinct offices. The post of organist was originally filled by the Gentlemen-in-Ordinary of the choir who were originally required to play the organ as well as sing. The first person to be given the title of 'Organist' was Dr John Bull who is credited with composing the National Anthem in about 1615 (though the version we recognize is as arranged by Thomas Arne).

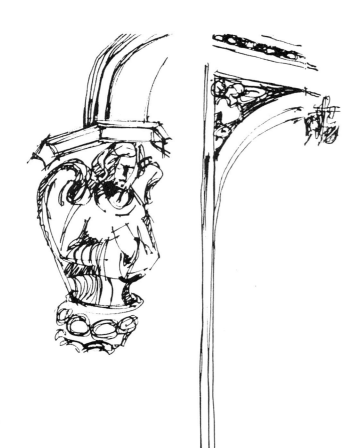

The office of composer was held by, among others, Henry Purcell, William Boyce, John Blow and George Frederick Handel. One name one might not expect to find is that of Sir Francis Drake who held the position of Serjeant of the Vestry. The offices of organist and composer were amalgamated in 1872, and combined with the office of master of the children when the Chapel Royal School was abolished in 1923. Today, there are six Gentlemen and ten choirboys who are trained by the Organist Choirmaster and Composer of the Chapel Royal Choir.

Within the Chapel Royal St James's there is much of artistic interest. The ornate ceiling is painted with royal cyphers, those in the original part of the Chapel commemorating the short marriage between Henry VIII and Anne of Cleves. In the central section are entwined the initials of William IV and Queen Adelaide. Over the main entrance is Queen Elizabeth I's cypher including an unusual lion and the Cadwallader dragon.

Many royal weddings and christenings have been held in the Chapel Royal but perhaps even more memorable are two annual services: the Christmas carol service, and the sung Eucharist to celebrate Epiphany when gold, frankincense and myrrh are offered on behalf of the Queen.

A sketch of the Christmas carol service,
Queen's Chapel

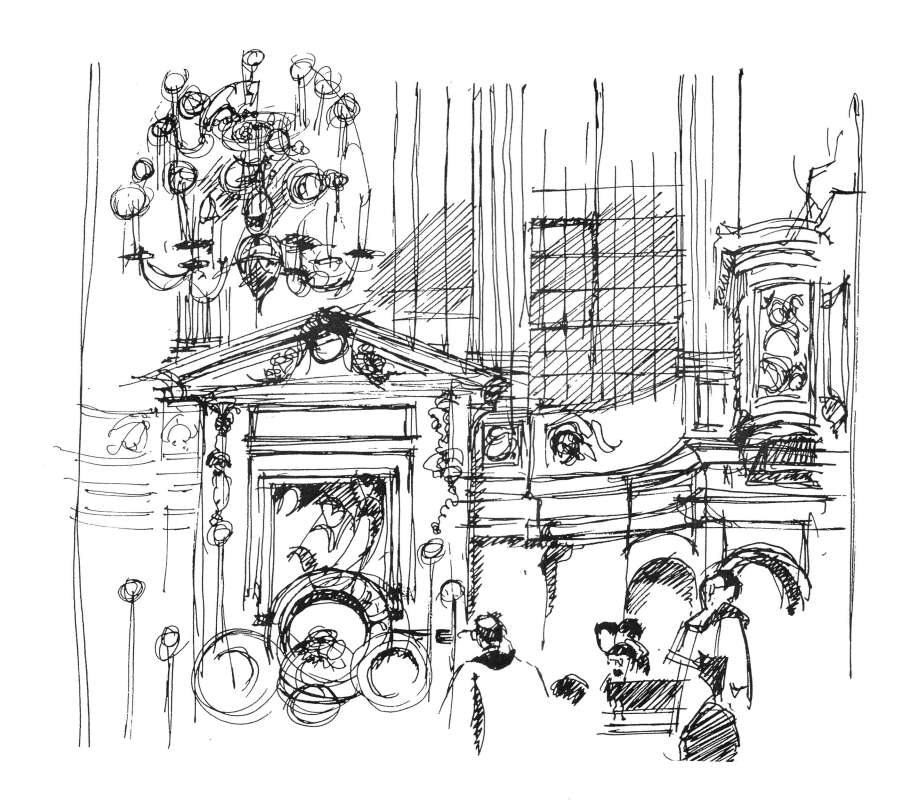

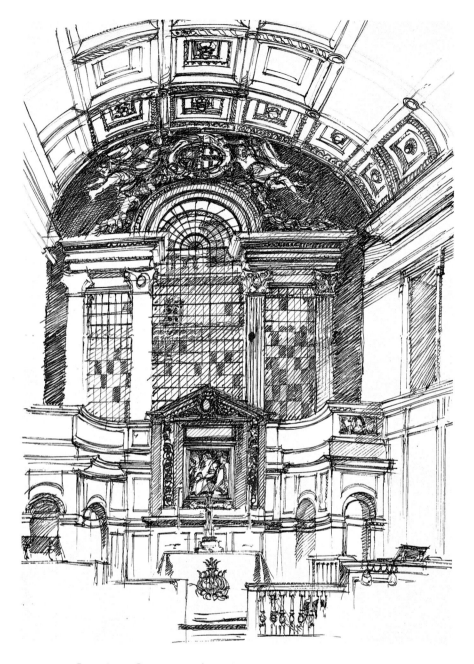

It is at this Epiphany service that the ceremony of Spur Money takes place. In a tract of 1598 there is a reference to the Children of the Chapel 'hunting after Spur Money, whereon they set their whole mindes'. King James I in 1622 set down that 'Noe man whatsoever presume to wayte upon us to the Chappell in bootes and spurs'. The Dean further decreed 'that if anie Knight or other persone entituled to wear spurs, enter the Chappell in that guise he shall pay to ye quoristers the accustomed fine but if he command the youngest quorister to repeat his gamut, and he fails in ye doing, the said Knight or other shall not pay ye fine'.

The ceremony these days (restored in 1977 after it was pointed out that the sovereign's representative at this service usually wear boots and spurs) involves the Queen's representative being informed by the Sub-Dean that a Child of the Chapel Royal desires the honour of addressing them. The child makes the claim and repeats the 'gamut' – a brief solo. The chorister is then paid and congratulated.

ABOVE: Interior, Queen's Chapel

RIGHT: Entrance of the choir and clergy into Queen's Chapel as seen from the Royal Balcony

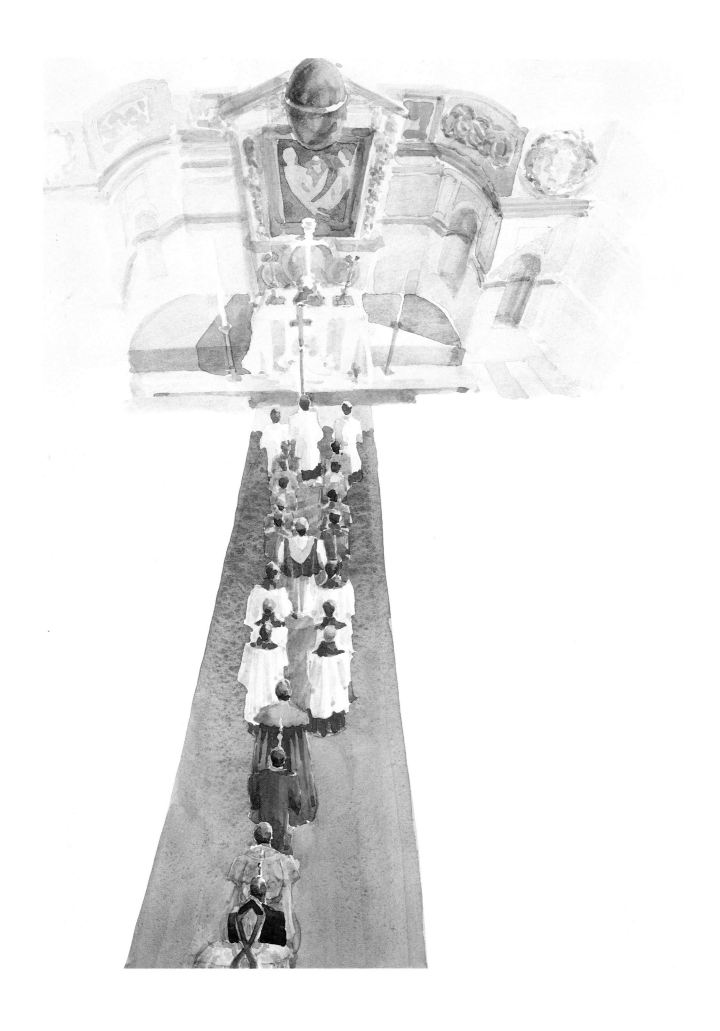

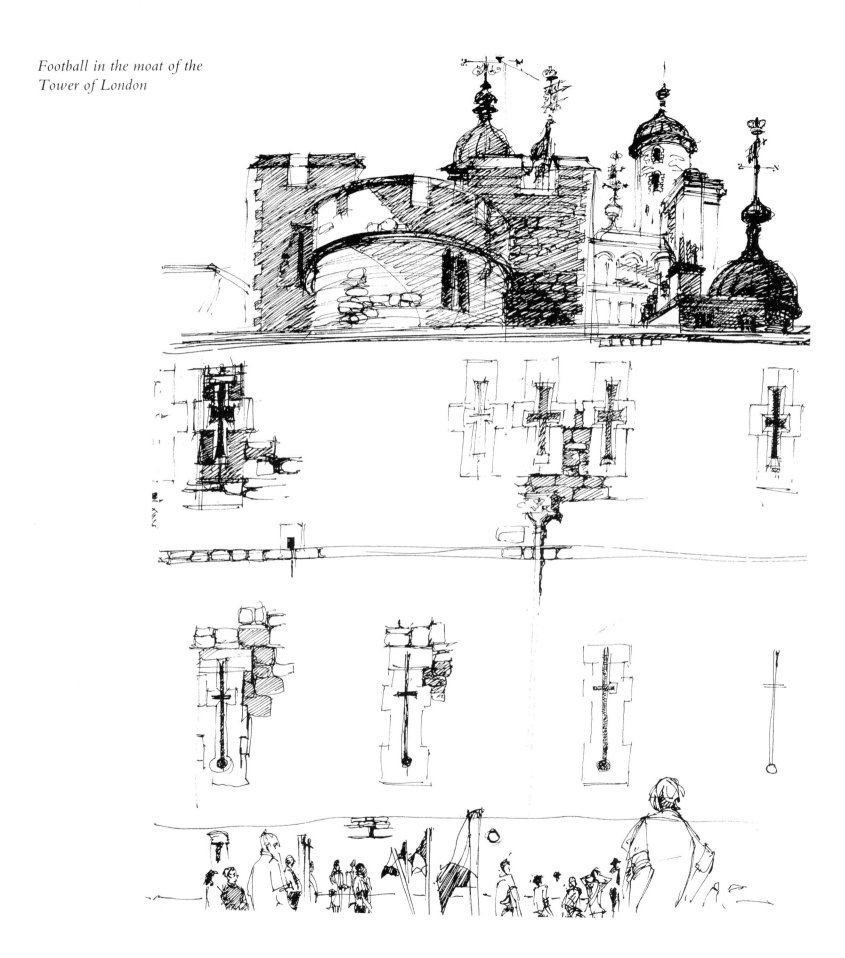

Football in the moat of the Tower of London

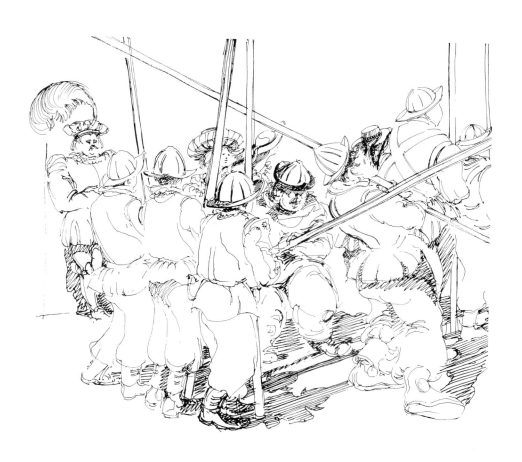

THE PARADE OF
THE KING'S ARMY

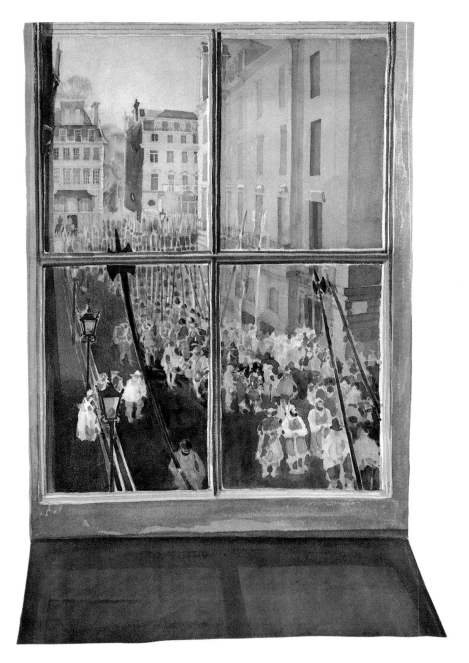

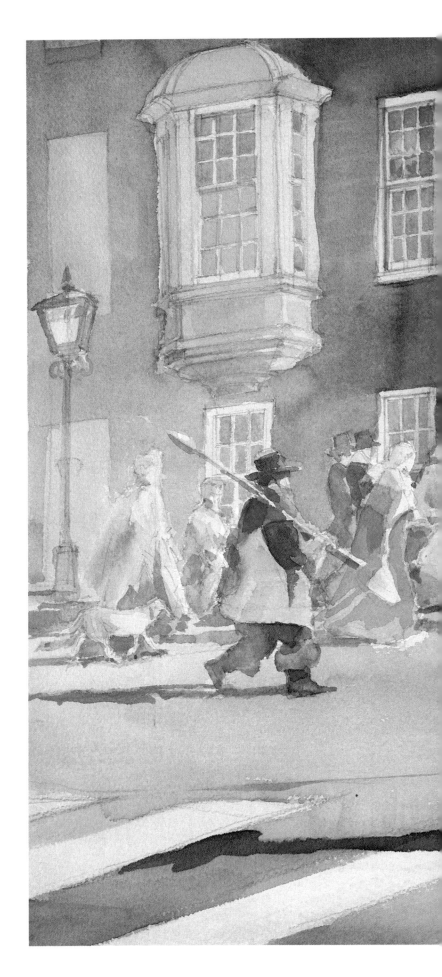

ABOVE: *The assembling of the 'King's Army' seen from the very room in which King Charles I spent his last days*

RIGHT: *Return of the 'King's Army' down Cleveland Row, St James's, after the ceremony at Whitehall*

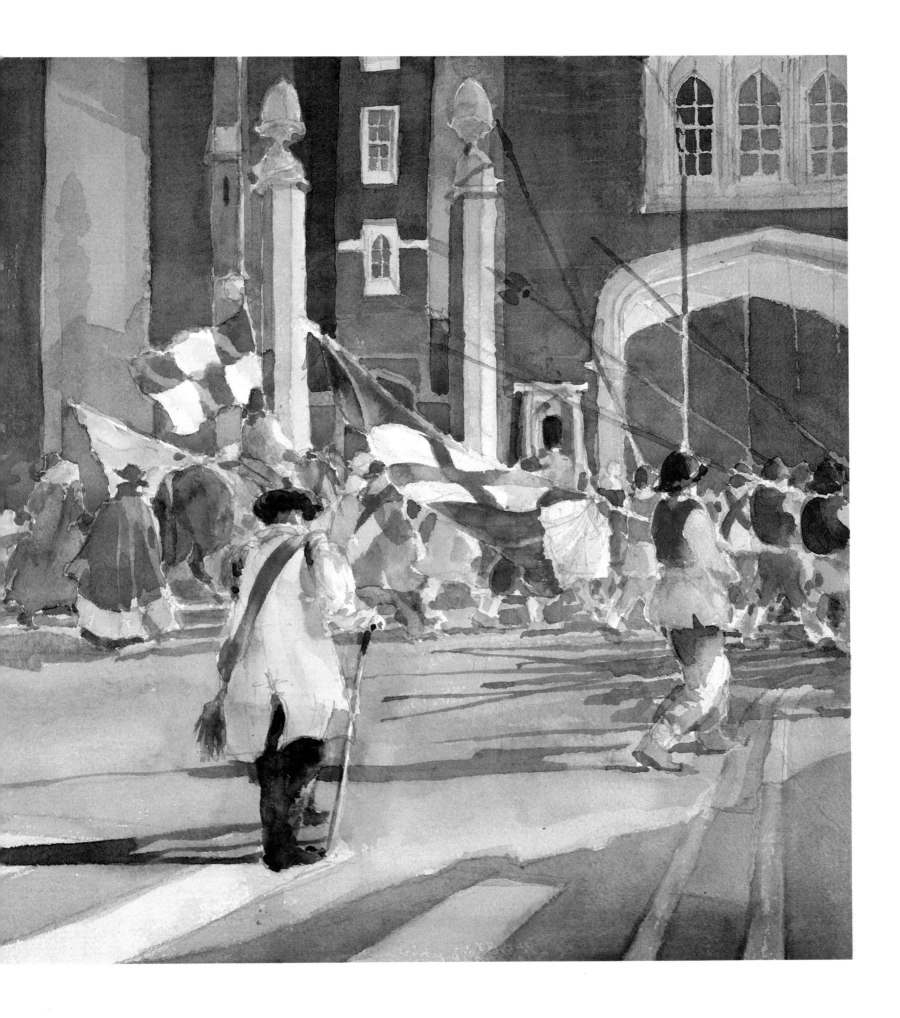

One of the more unusual royal ceremonies is the annual Parade of the King's Army. It takes place on the Sunday nearest to January 30 and is, in fact, not so much a royal occasion as the re-enactment of an historical event with royal connections.

The Parade recalls the Cavaliers' march in support of King Charles I on the day he was executed: January 30 1649. The King had been imprisoned in Hampton Court Palace before being taken to the tower of St James's Palace (now used by the Chapel Royal Choir) where he took his final Holy Communion. He was then taken down The Mall, through Horseguards to the Banqueting Hall of the Palace of Whitehall, where he was executed.

The King's Army must not be confused with the King's Troop, a body of professional soldiers which used to be known as the Riding Troop. The King's Army comprises five hundred or so ordinary citizens who enjoy dressing-up and pretending to be Cavaliers.

They assemble outside St James's Palace in Cleveland Row dressed in appropriate uniforms and brandishing more-or-less authentic weapons. They are supported by women, children and dogs, all but the last in seventeenth-century dress and all intent on having a good time.

After a brief practice walking with pikes and other ancient and awkward weapons of war, the King's Army prepares to march. Bugles sound, drums beat and supporters bang pots and pans. The wagons bearing cannon rumble. A service is being held in the Chapel Royal and the choir and organist valiantly compete with the noise outside.

The Guard is being changed at Buckingham Palace and St James's and, in delightful contrast, the King's Army straggles rather than marches down The Mall behind the smartly stepping Old Guard. As the latter turns right into Buckingham Palace, the Kings's Army turns left towards Whitehall. A short service is held at the statue of Charles I which stands near the place of his execution. Then the parade breaks up where it began, in Cleveland Row, and the King's Army disperses for refreshment into nearby watering holes.

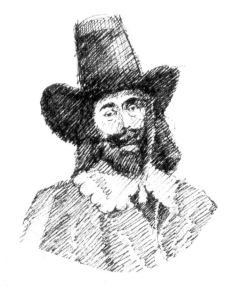

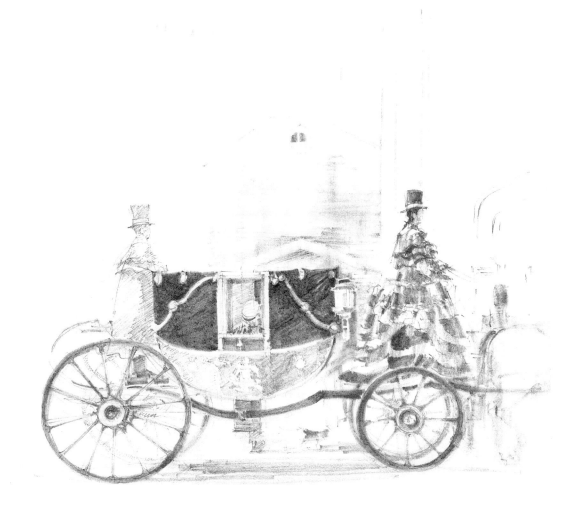

THE PRESENTATION OF CREDENTIALS

Before ambassadors to the United Kingdom can formally take up their office as the official representative of their head of state, they are required to present a 'letter of credence', less formally called simply 'credentials'. By handing this letter over to the Queen as head of state along with his or her predecessor's letter of recall, the ambassador becomes 'accredited' to the Court of St James.

In days gone by, it was the custom for a new ambassador to make a formal state entry into the capital but nowadays this does not happen. The ambassador is met by a senior official from the Foreign and Commonwealth Office who liaises with the Royal Household on arrangements for the presentation of credentials.

The ceremony is the same for all ambassadors of non-Commonwealth countries and for high commissioners of Commonwealth countries with their own head of state, who have to present their letters of commission to the Queen. For most Commonwealth countries the procedure is different. Letters are exchanged, Prime Minister to Prime Minister, and the new high commissioner pays the Queen a formal visit.

The Presentation of Credentials takes place during a private meeting between the ambassador and the Queen. The ambassador is collected from his or her residence by the Marshal of the Diplomatic Corps and taken to Buckingham Palace in the State Landau carriage. His staff travel in two Semi-state carriages.

PREVIOUS PAGE: The Diplomatic Marshal departs from St James's Palace

RIGHT: Kensington Palace Gardens – liverymen, postillions and their carriages await the Ambassadorial staff

EXTREME RIGHT: The carriages passing the Queen Victoria memorial en route to Buckingham Palace

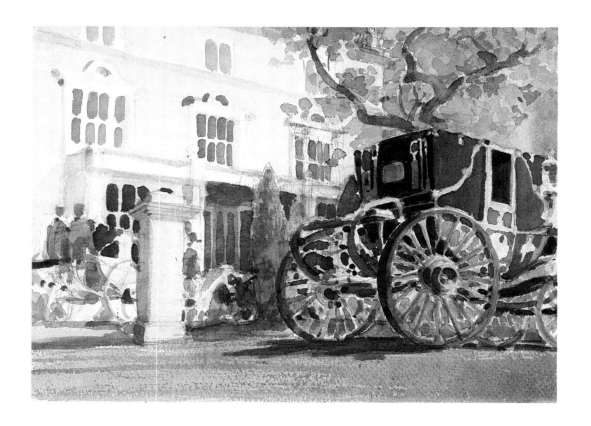

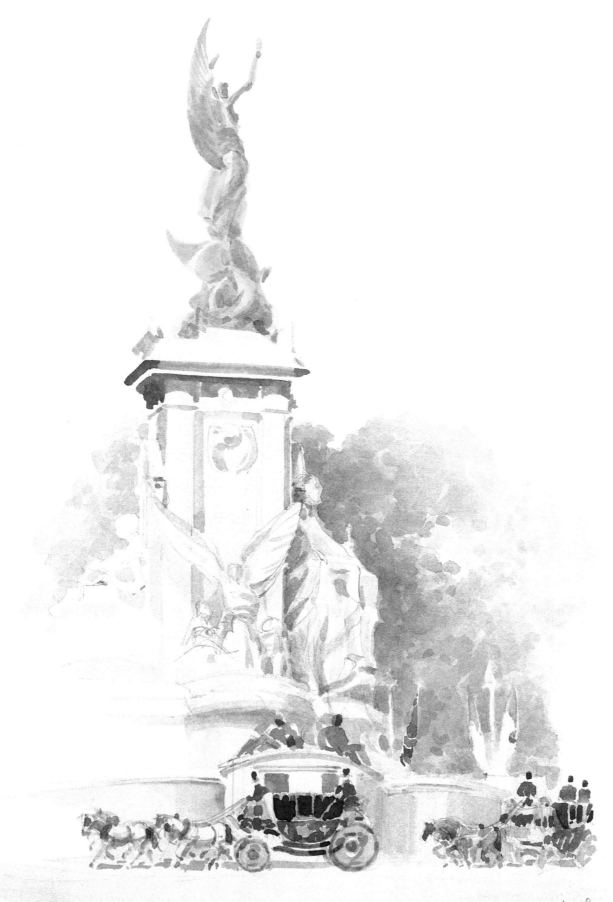

Very early on a weekday morning the horses are harnessed to exercise brakes and taken from the Royal Mews to Hyde Park. There they are exercised not only to warm them up but also to tire them so that they will be less high-spirited in the traffic. On their return to the Mews, they are harnessed to the ceremonial carriages. The elegant harnesses are black leather with highly polished brass and carry the royal cypher, as do their blinkers.

The 'claret' Landaus, the beautifully groomed horses and the liverymen with their scarlet capes and black top hats with gold bands, make a splendid sight. Preceded by mounted police, the cortège clops up Buckingham Palace Road, round 'the Wedding Cake' (the Victoria Memorial) and on to St James's Palace. Liverymen lower the window covers by their cords, lower the steps and open the carriage door. The door of the gatehouse tower opens

The Ambassador alights,
Buckingham Palace

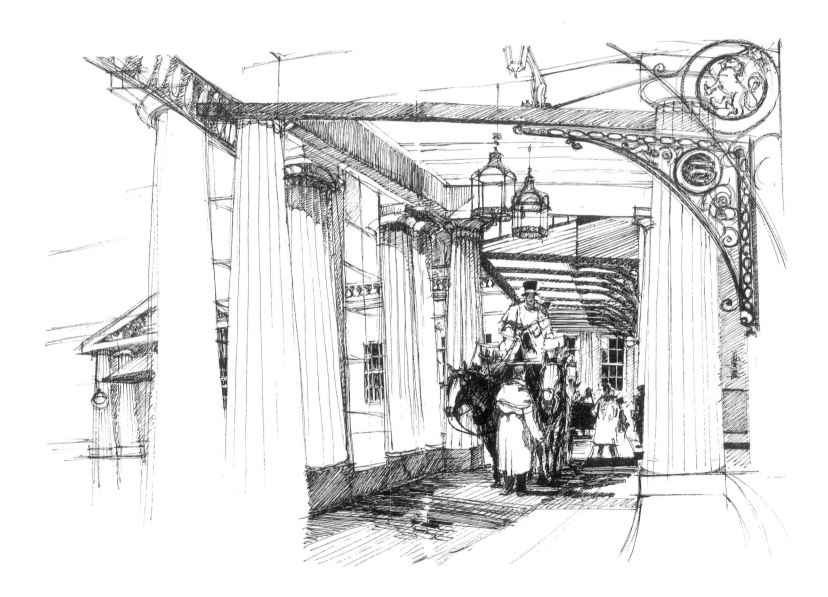

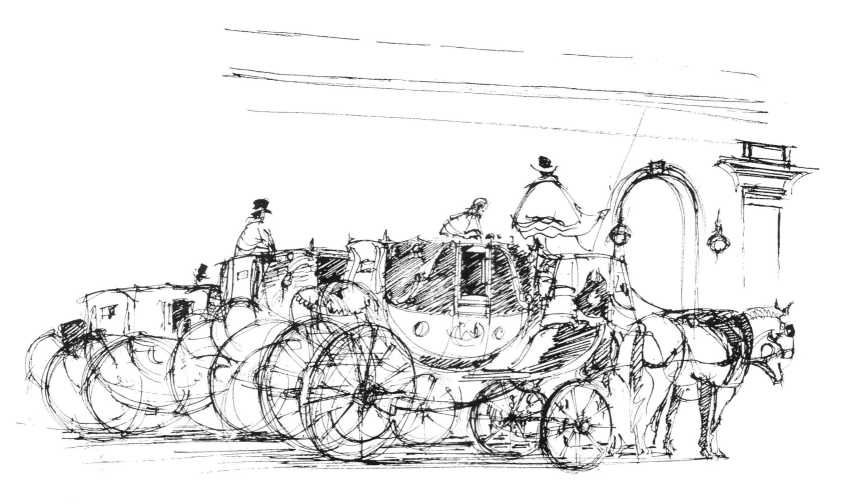

Landau carriages: sketches

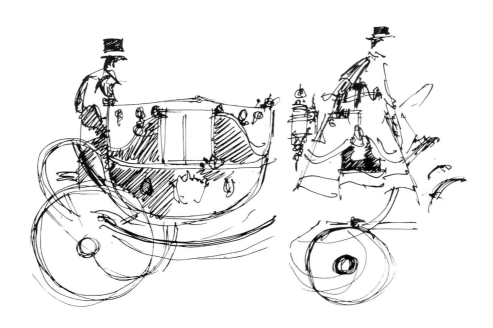

Return to an Ambassadorial residence, Mount Street in Mayfair

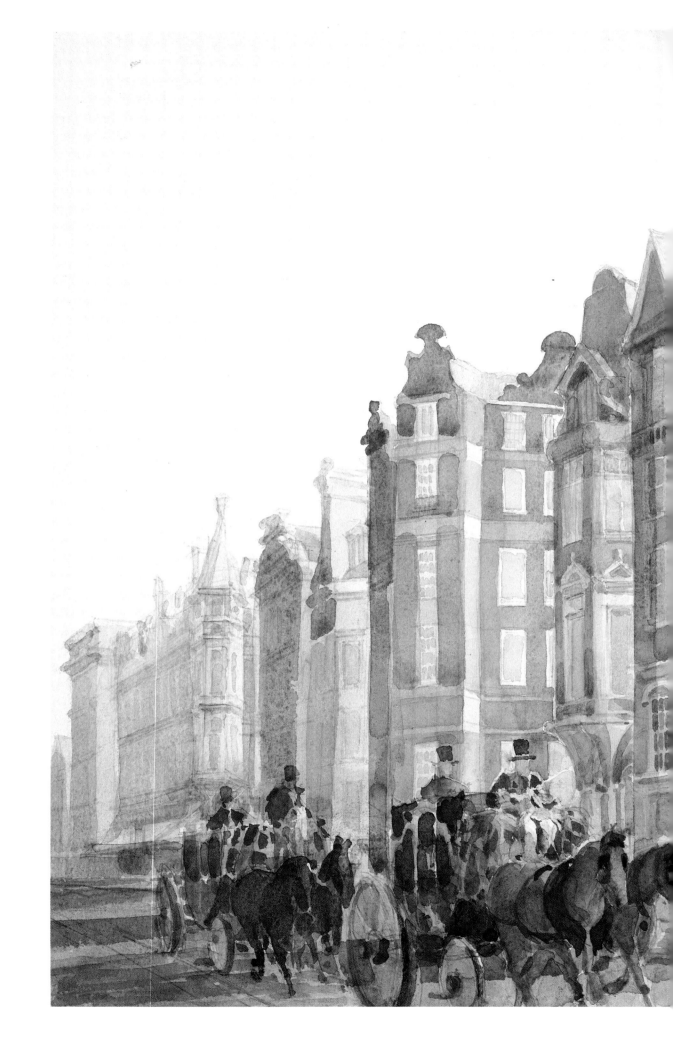

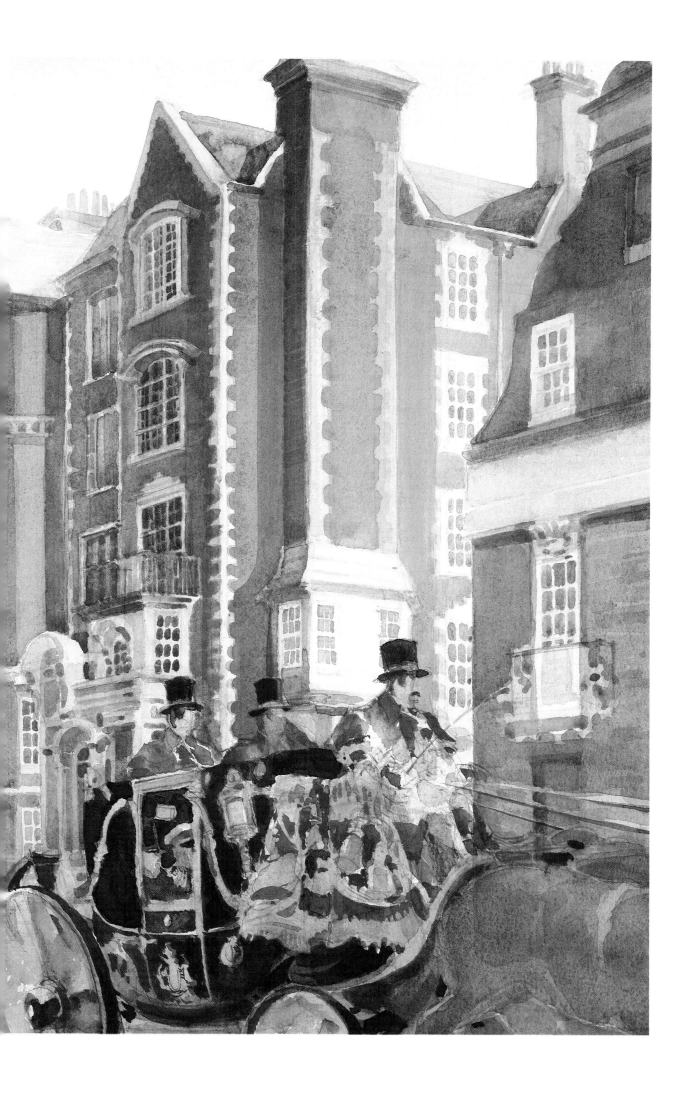

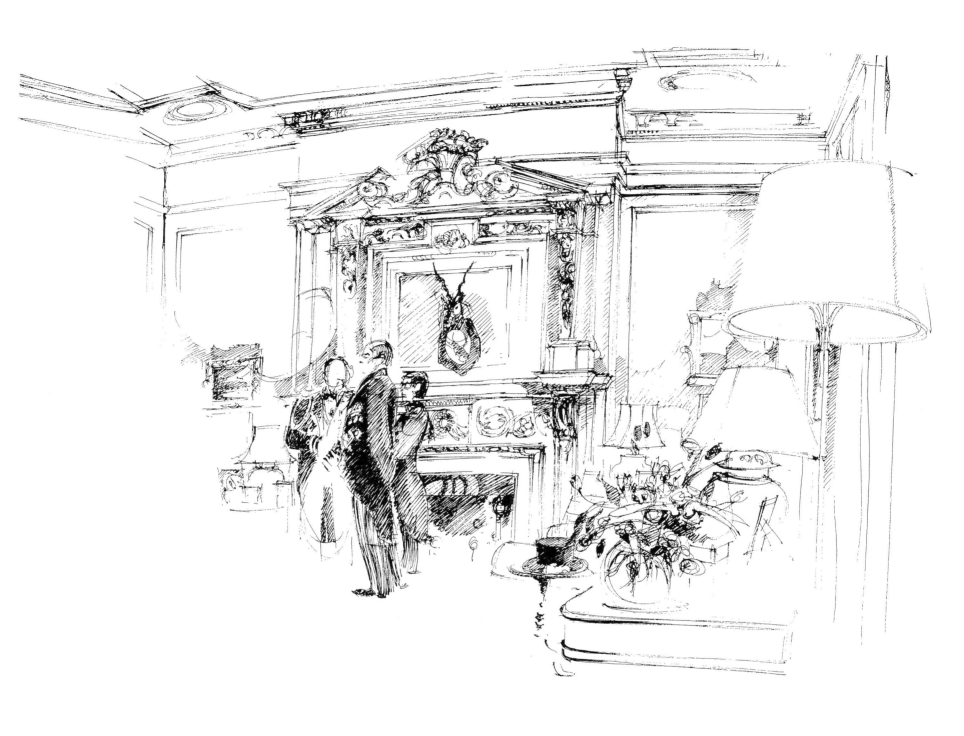

Vin d'Honneur:
the Ambassador and staff await
the guests

and the Marshal of the Diplomatic Corps appears resplendent in his uniform and soon the carriages depart for the ambassador's residence.

The ambassador, with no more than eight staff and dressed in white tie and decorations or in national costume, is already in the care of the Vice-Marshal of the Diplomatic Corps. The ambassador's wife, if such there is, is looked after by the lady ceremonial officer and travels to the Palace by car.

At the Palace, the cortège is greeted by the Vice-Marshal and the

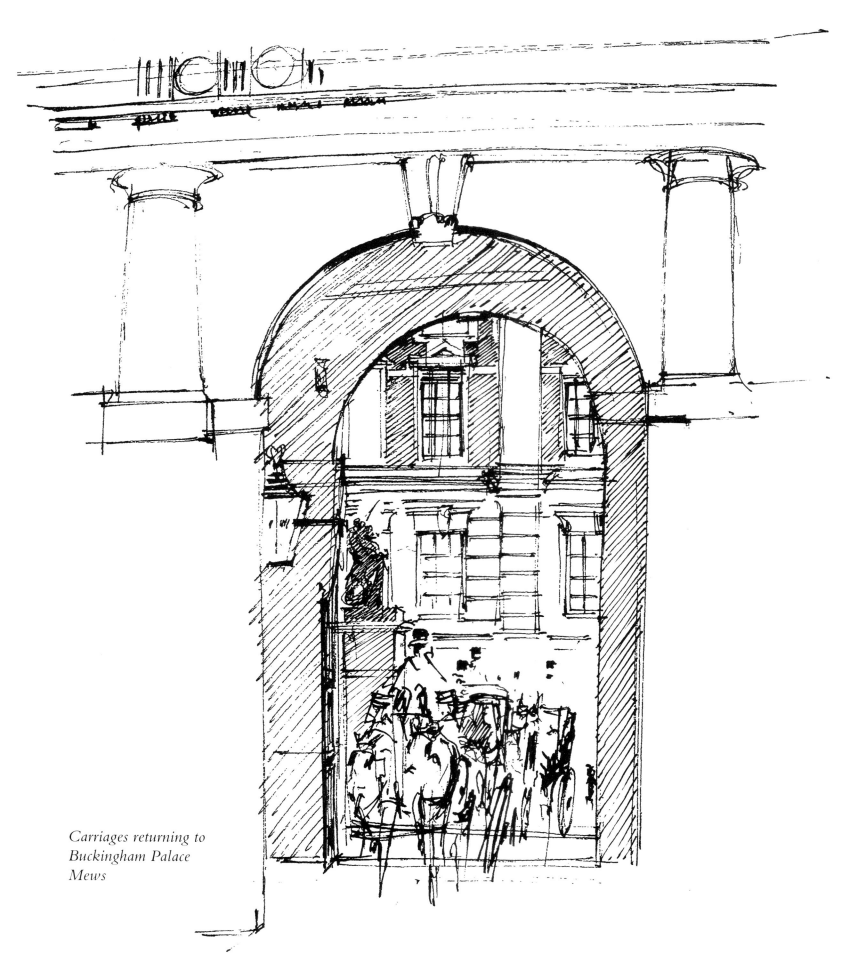

Carriages returning to Buckingham Palace Mews

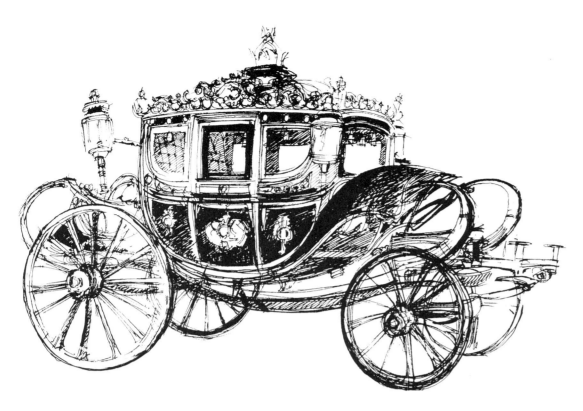

The Irish State Coach

THE ROYAL FAMILY'S cars, carriages and carriage horses and the staff who look after them are mostly to be found in the Royal Mews. Situated behind Buckingham Palace, the entrance to the Royal Mews is in Buckingham Palace Road, alongside the Queen's Gallery. The department is headed by the Crown Equerry who has a staff of about fifty. This includes the Head Coachman who is responsible for the horses and the day-to-day running of the Mews. Under him are coachmen, postillions, grooms, liverymen and farriers. The carriage restorers, whose work is admired the world over, are rather strangely, and no doubt only theoretically, under the control of the Daily Ladies of London and Windsor who in turn are under the Storemen who are answerable to the Comptroller of Stores.

The word 'mews' originally described the place where hawks were kept under cover during moulting or 'mewing'. The royal hawk houses were situated at Charing Cross until George III bought Buckingham House and converted the stables for their use. George IV selected a new site in adjoining gardens. John Nash undertook the building which was completed in 1825. The mews building in Stable Yard in St James's Palace is now offices.

The Royal Mews is like a village. Below the clocktower, which sports a weather vane, is an archway supported by doric pillars leading to the main quadrangle. Off this are those areas open to the public – the harness room, stables and coach-houses. On display here are some of the finest historic coaches in the world as well as beautifully designed harnesses.

However, the Mews is by no means just a museum. There are some thirty carriage horses and over a hundred carriages in working order besides sleighs and even a goat cart. The superb Rolls-Royce Phantoms are garaged in the rear of the Mews.

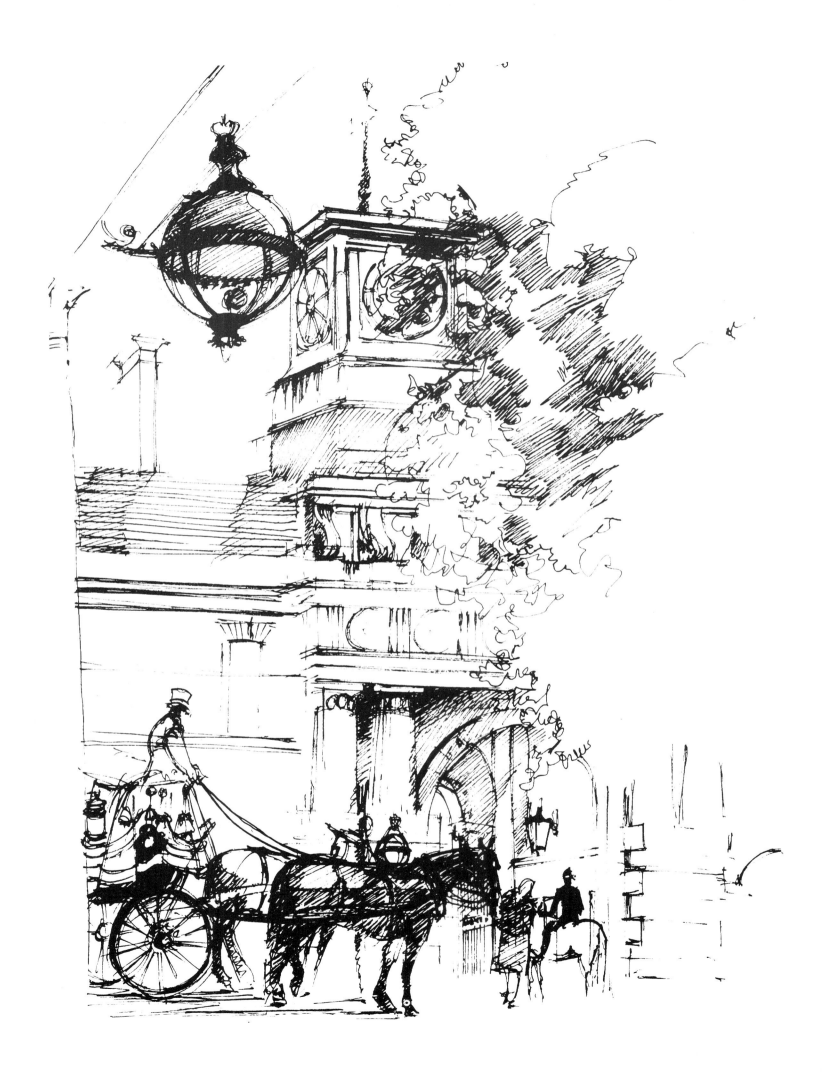

Among the coaches is the magnificent Gold State Coach covered in more than a thousand books of gold leaf. There is the graceful barouche used to take the Queen Mother and the Princess of Wales to Trooping the Colour and the ivory-mounted phaeton. The phaeton was restored for the Queen's use at the Trooping in 1987, the year her horse Burmese retired.

One of the most impressive and interesting carriages in the Mews is the recently restored Irish State Coach. It was built in 1851 by Mr Hutton who was Lord Mayor of Dublin and a coachbuilder by trade. An earlier version was exhibited in Dublin where it was seen by Queen Victoria on her visit to Ireland in 1849.

A similar coach had been exhibited in London a year earlier and the Master of Horse had asked for an estimate. Though nothing further had been heard from him, the coachbuilder had gone ahead and made the carriage. Now, on the Queen's command the order was made but it was two years before the Royal Mews took delivery since alterations were required. Despite this, the price was kept to that given in the original estimate.

Edward VII did not use it and it was loaned to his son Prince George, the future George V. In 1911, he had it completely refurbished for use at his coronation. Unfortunately, no sooner was the work completed than the coach was all but destroyed in a fire. By herculean efforts it was rebuilt in time for his coronation.

After the Second World War it was used by George VI for the State Opening of Parliament. In 1988 it was decided that it was showing its age and the Mews carriage restorer was given the task of stripping it down and completely renovating it.

Layer by layer, the many coats of varnish it had received over the years were removed, revealing the original colour to have been claret. The embellishments ordered by Queen Victoria boasted ordinary gold leaf except the crown which was 24 carat. The wheels had a broad gold leaf line outlined in black. Two door panels had to be replaced, the filigree work having to be identical to the original nineteenth-century pattern. The work took eighteen months and the Irish State Coach was ready for the Opening of Parliament in November 1989.

RIGHT: 'Warming up' in the Mews

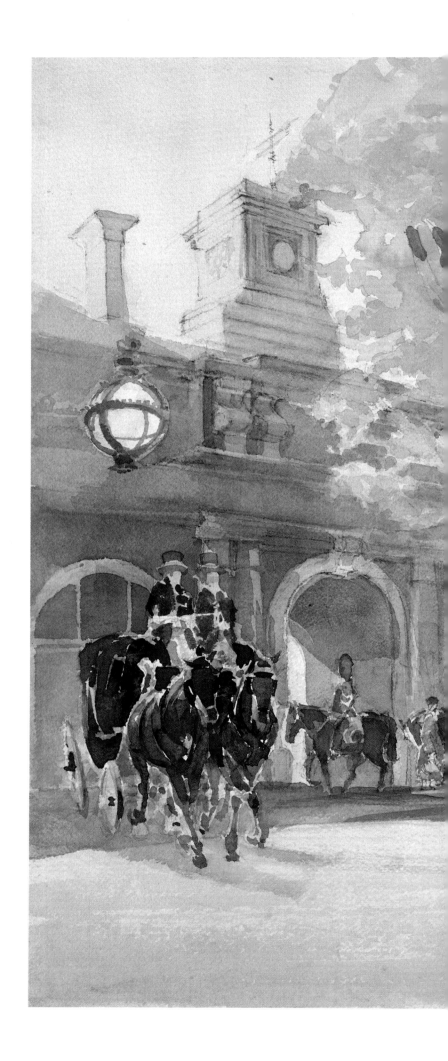

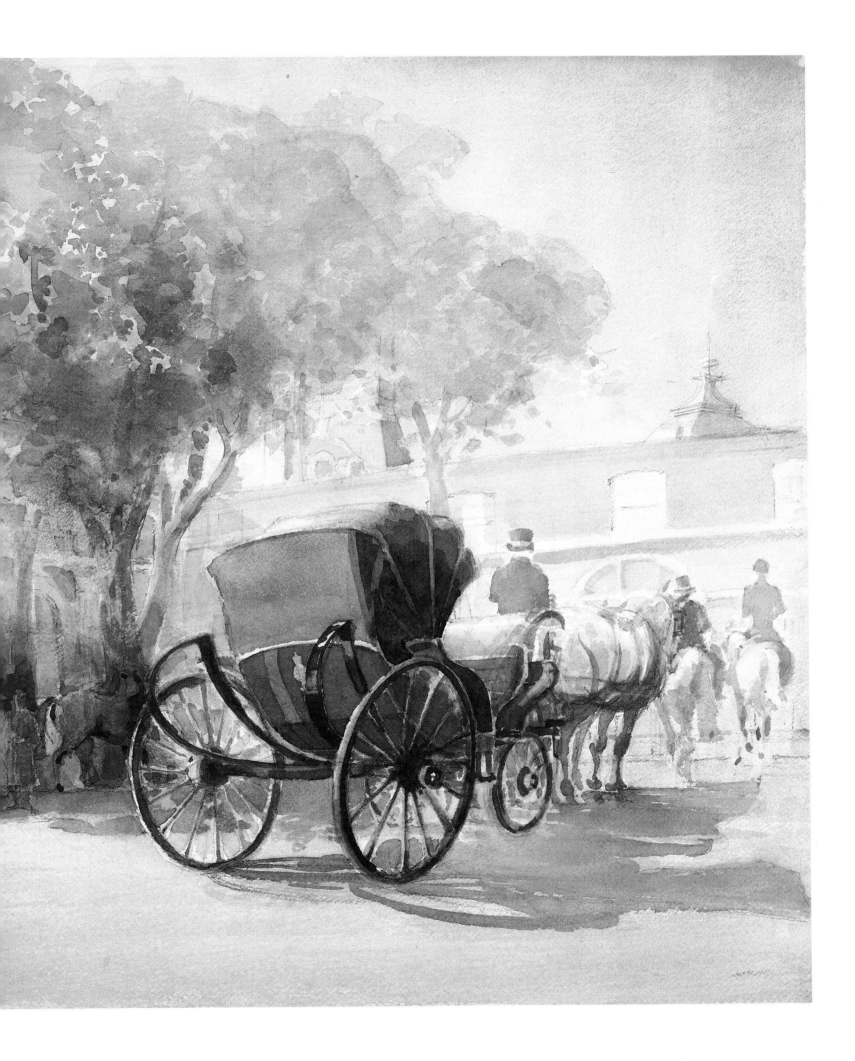

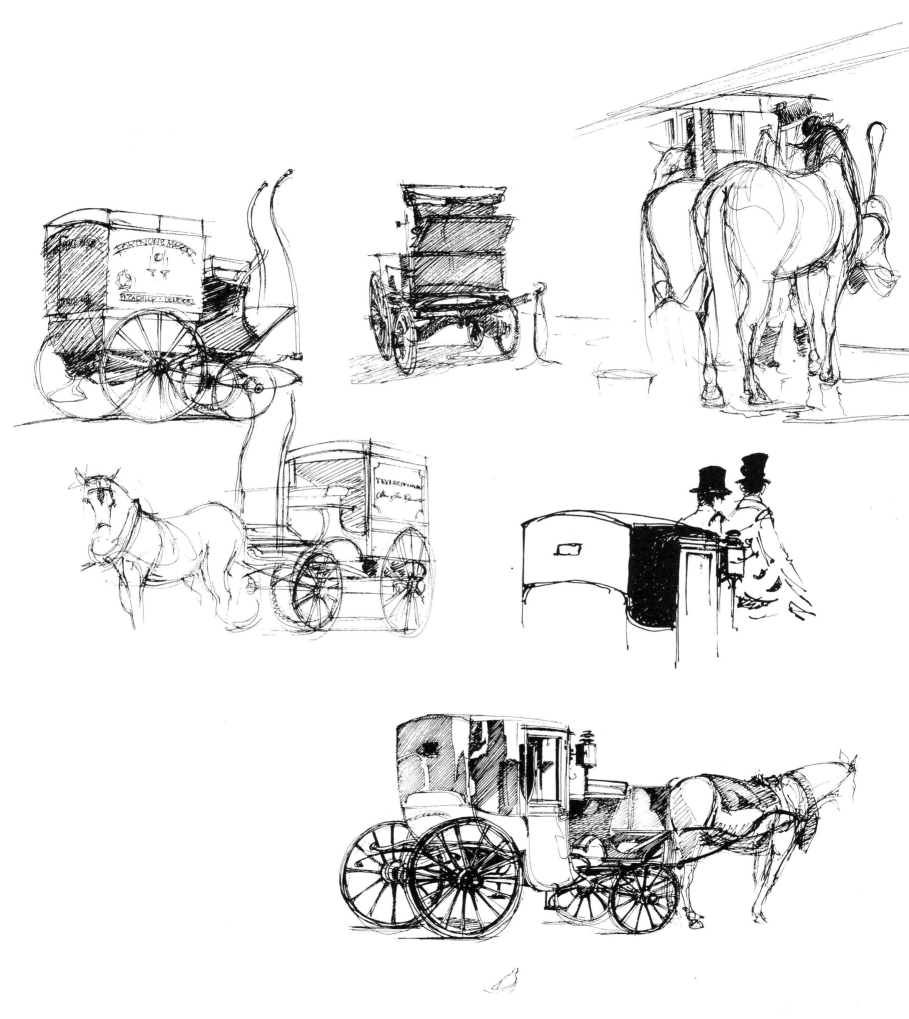

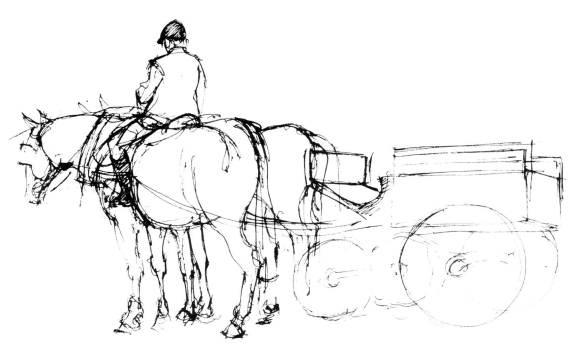

One special 'royal' occasion stands out in my memory. While drawing the hive of activity in the Royal Mews, an invitation to don a top hat and travel through London traffic in an exercise brake gave me an enviable opportunity of seeing London from a privileged position. On this particular day we were rehearsing for a state visit. We were drawn smartly out of the Royal Mews, past Buckingham Palace and the Victoria Memorial, up Constitution Hill to Hyde Park. Had this been a Landau with its excellent

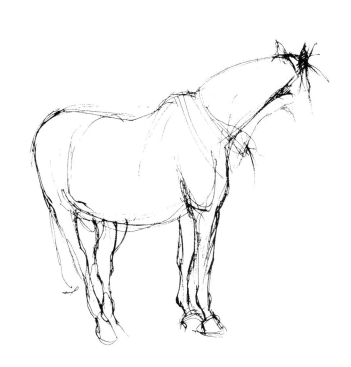

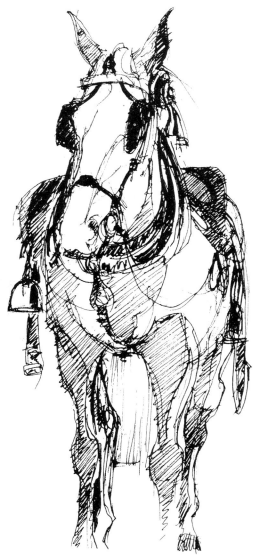

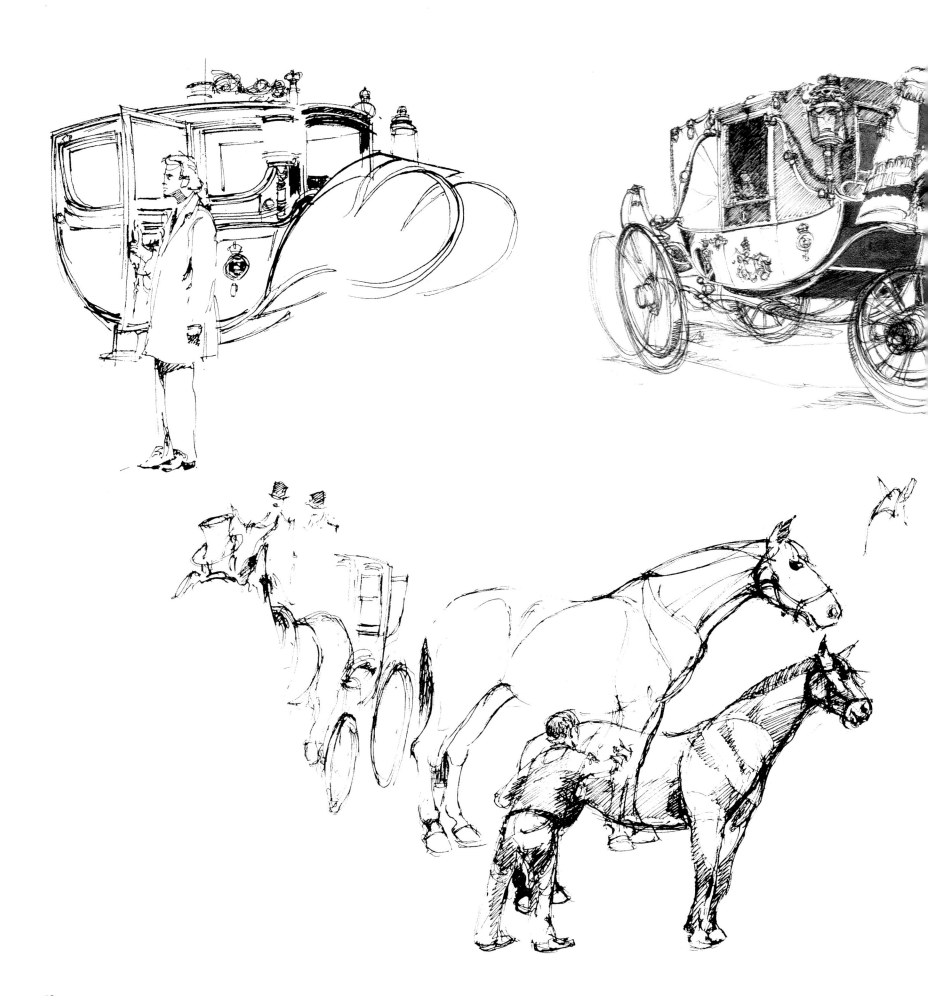

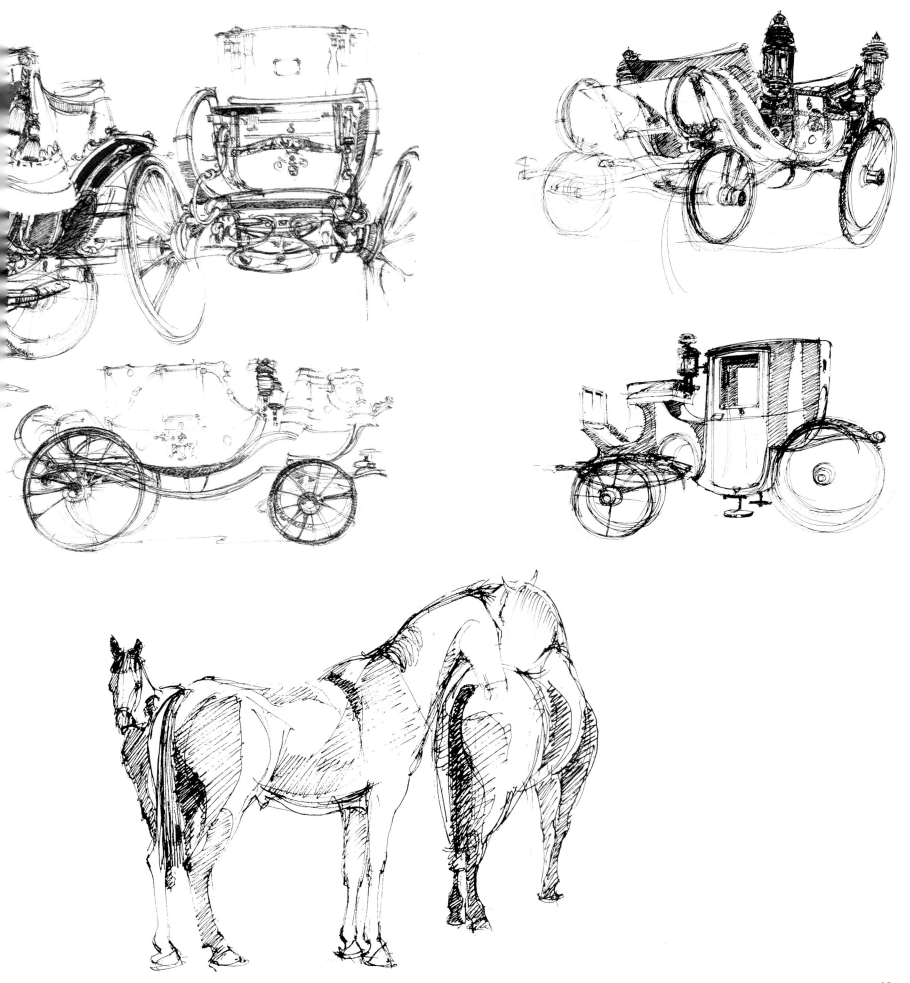

suspension rather than a brake, Rotten Row might not have felt so hard beneath me. As the horses broke into a trot each bump registered as though my sketch pad was a seismograph.

Rotten Row may have been so called as a corruption of *route de roi* but one legend has it that it was named in tribute to Dick Turpin. The highwayman planned his exploits in the Spaniard's Inn in Hampstead but carried them out on this stretch of road. True or not, the Crown Equerry arranged a celebration of old coaches to mark the tercentenary of his death.

As we slowed to walking pace, we were able to take pleasure in the blossom showering us with pink and white confetti as we passed. It was early and there was mist in which trees still bare of leaves tried to conceal themselves. In Carriage Road, a Long Guard of the Household Cavalry *en route* to Whitehall made me think for a moment of medieval knights. This memorable jaunt was too soon over.

BELOW: Kensington Palace Gardens

RIGHT: Exercising in Hyde Park

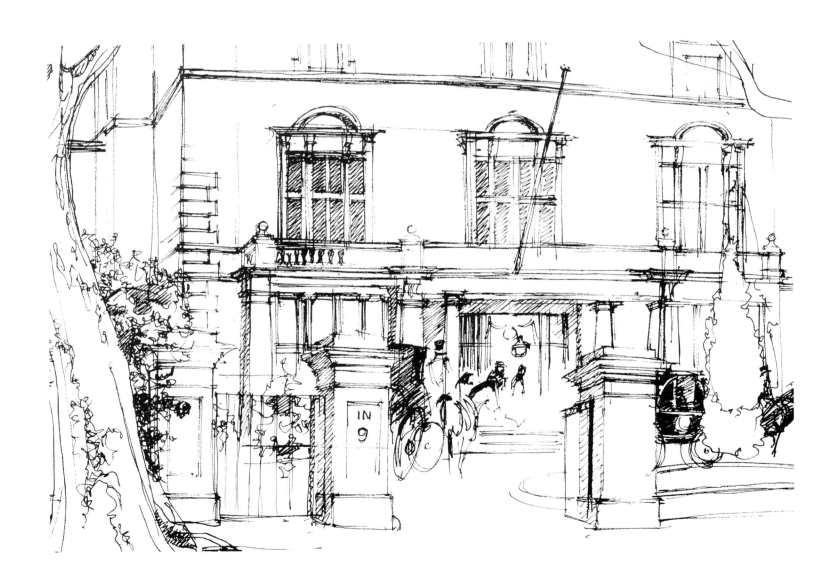

64

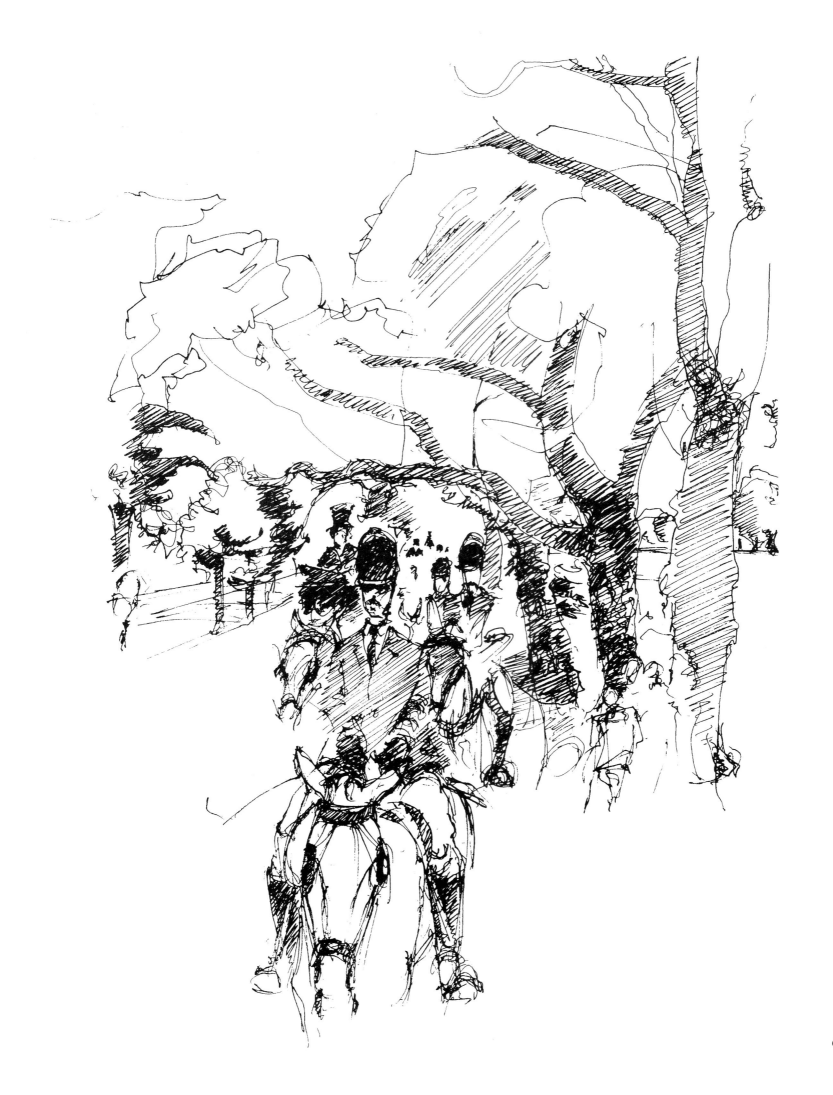

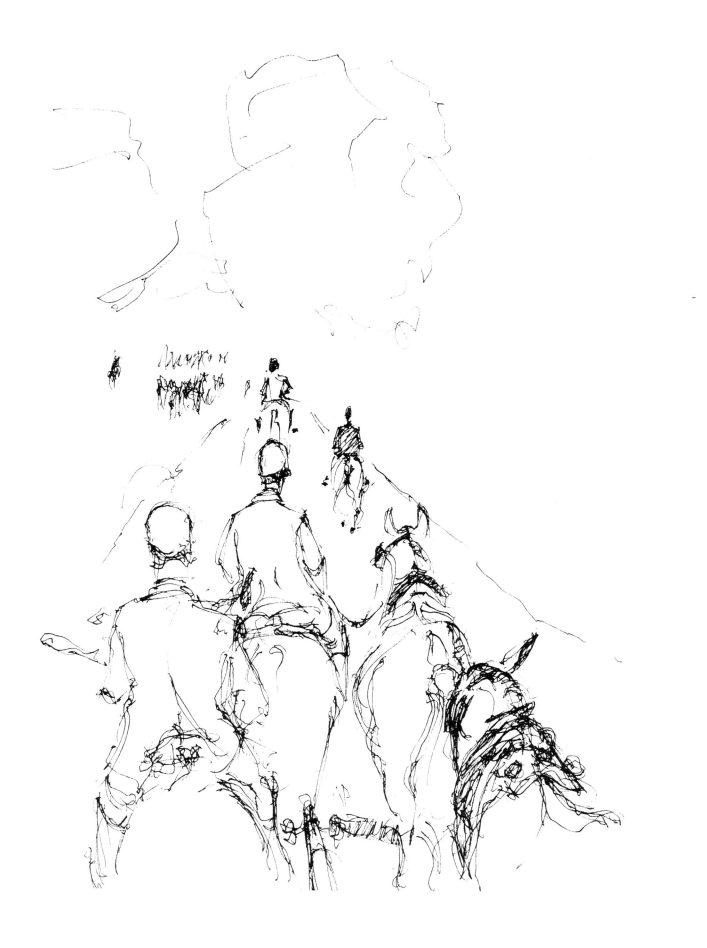

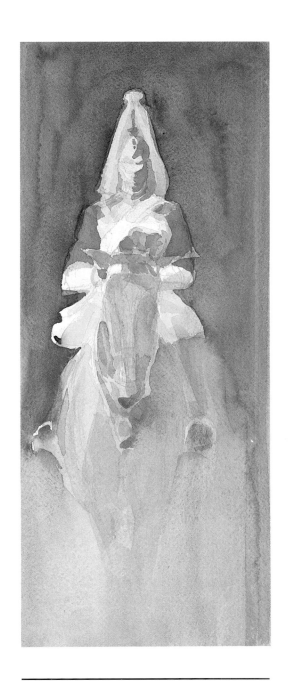

HORSE GUARDS

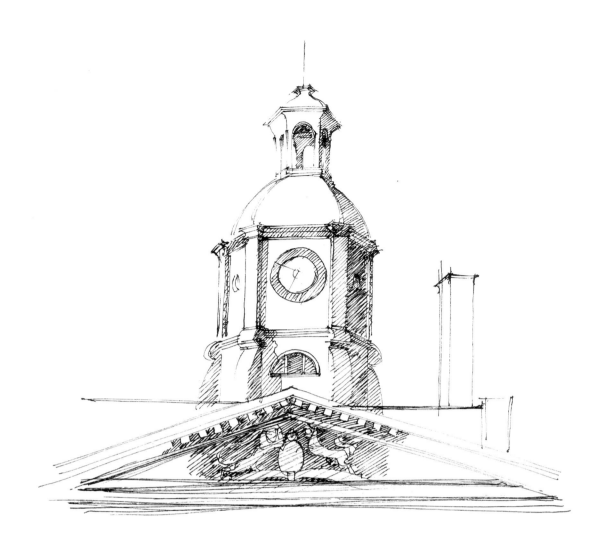

THERE WERE TWO previous buildings on the site of the present Horse Guards. The original building was a small guardhouse erected in about 1650 in the tilt yard of Whitehall Palace. This was replaced in 1663 by a larger building for the use of both Horse Guards and some Foot Guards and it became the headquarters of the General Staff. The present Horse Guards was built between 1750 and 1758 to a design of William Kent, executed after the latter's death by John Vardy. It now houses the headquarters of London District and the Household Division.

The Queen's Life Guard is mounted daily on Horse Guards Arch in Whitehall at 11am in a ceremony which lasts thirty minutes. This is the oldest Royal Guard dating back to 1660. The Guard is mounted by two regiments of the Household Cavalry – the Life Guards and the Royal Horse Guards known as the Blues. In 1969, the Blues became the Blues and Royals when the First Royal Dragoons were merged with the Royal Horse Guards. Together they constitute the mounted Household Troops, now called the Household Division, of the Sovereign. (Sadly, tradition is soon to be broken as the Household Cavalry is to be merged with other regiments.) At present, they are under the command of the Major-General of the Household

Sketches. LEFT: *The tower at Horse Guards, Whitehall*
BELOW: *At Clarence Gate*

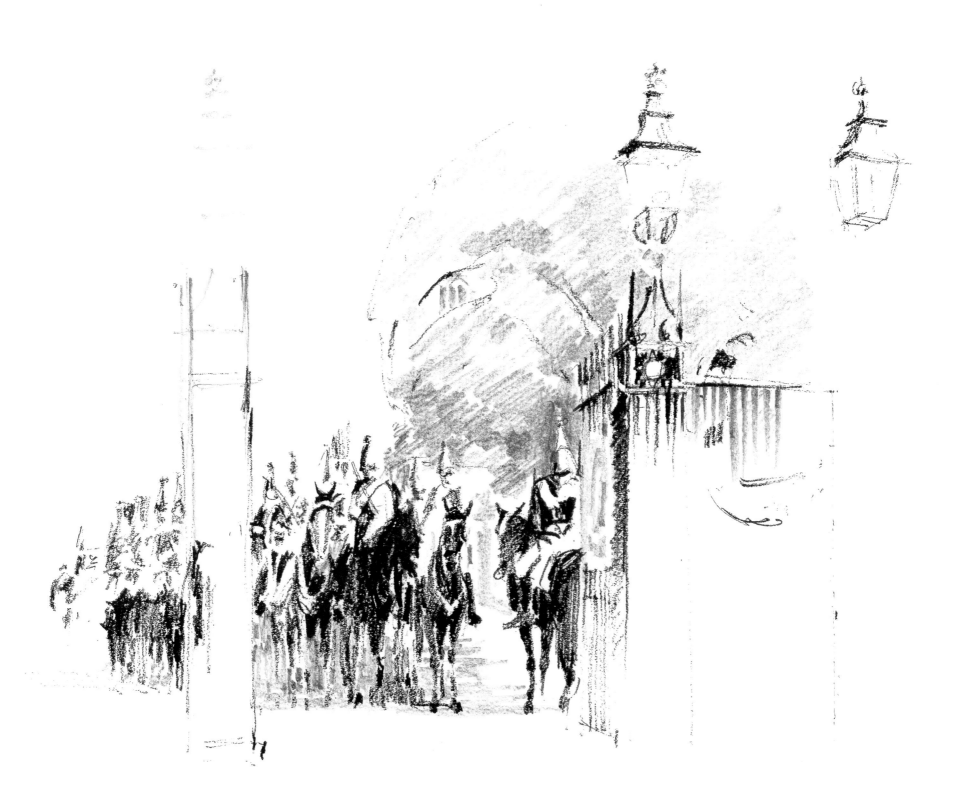

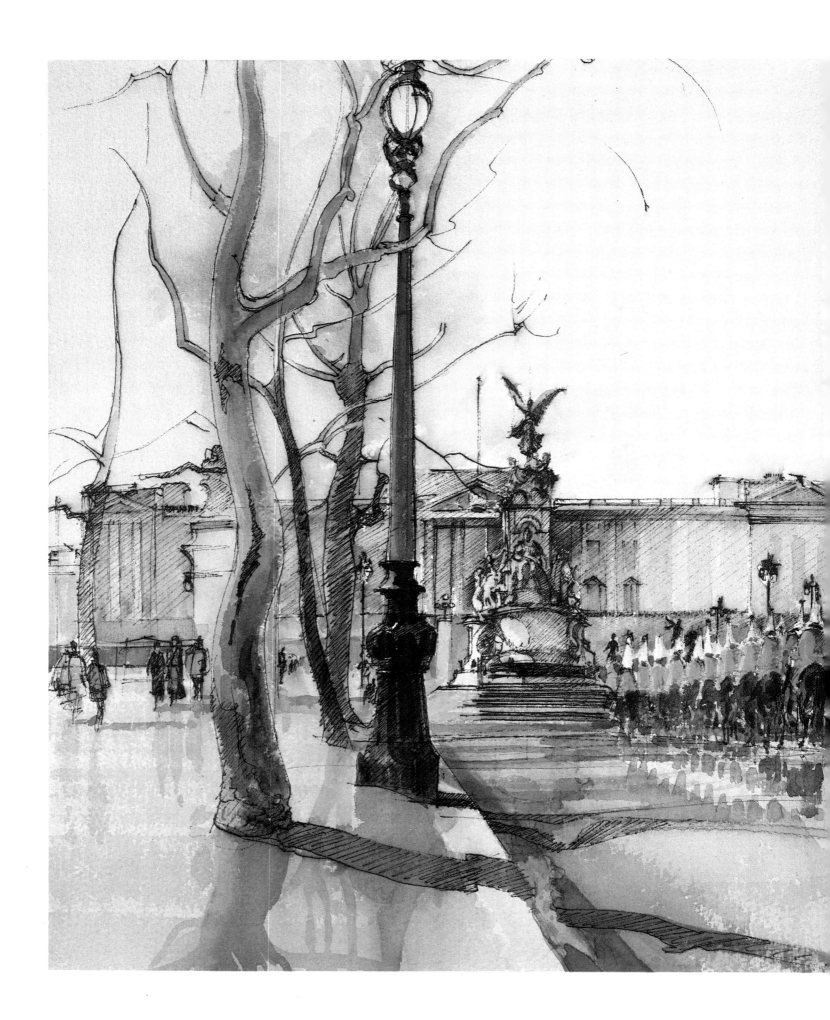

After a guard change in Horse Guards Parade, the Queen's Life Guards ride down the Mall passing Buckingham Palace en route to Hyde Park barracks

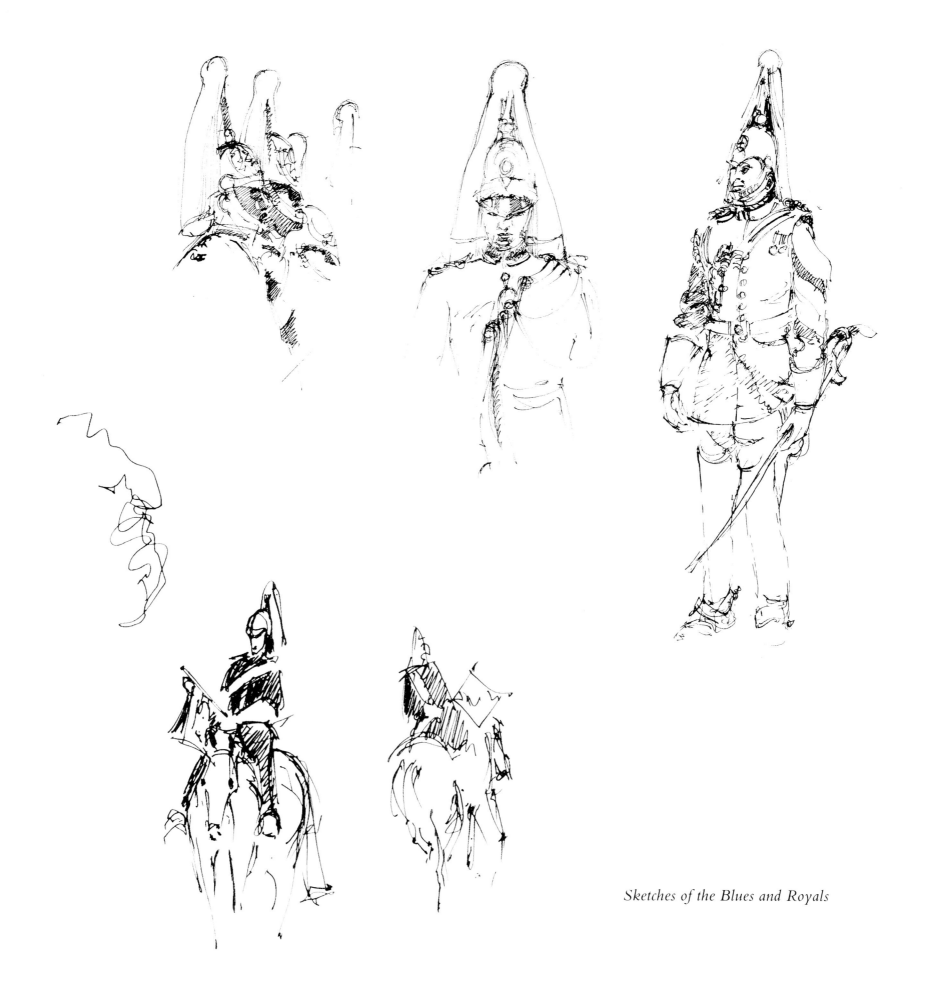

Sketches of the Blues and Royals

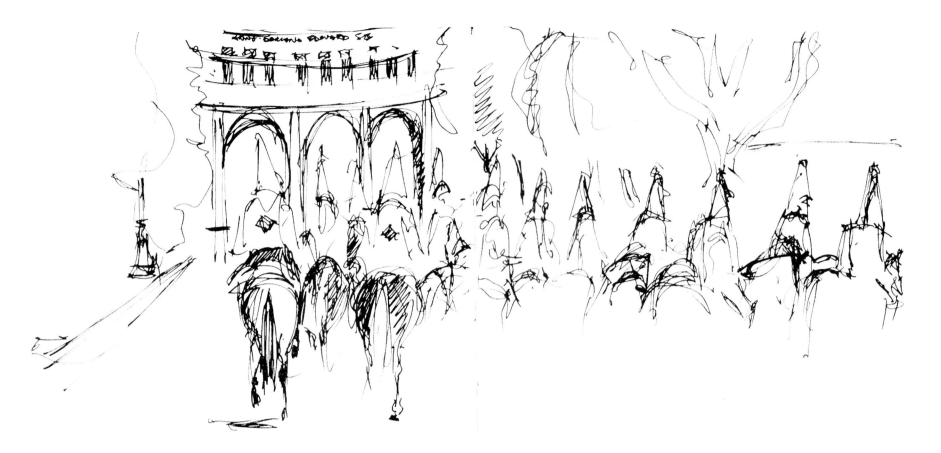

Division who is himself always a Guard. His headquarters are in the Horse Guards building.

Passing through Admiralty Arch

Horse Guards Arch is the official entrance to both St James's and Buckingham Palaces. Apart from the Royal Family, no one can drive through the arch, even on a bicycle, without an Ivory Pass. The Guard change, with its mounted march, a colourful and glittering procession from Hyde Park Barracks to Horse Guards, is one of London's most memorable sights. The tourists' cameras click, the harnesses jangle and the hooves clatter on the stone. The noisy, impatient traffic has to slow and give precedence to a more ancient transport. Serene and infinitely superior, the Guard carries out its duty today as it did yesterday and will do again tomorrow – to protect their Sovereign.

When the Sovereign is in residence at Buckingham Palace, a Long Guard is mounted comprising an officer and fifteen men and horses. When the Sovereign is away from home there is a Short Guard of two non-commissioned officers and ten troopers.

My subject is the Wedding Cake – the Victoria Memorial. The Life Guards in their scarlet tunics and proud, white plumes on silvergilt helmets add a splash of brilliant colour to my painting. The Blues and Royals boast red plumes and dark blue tunics but both wear silvergilt vests, white cross-belts, gloves and breeches, black boots and brass spurs.

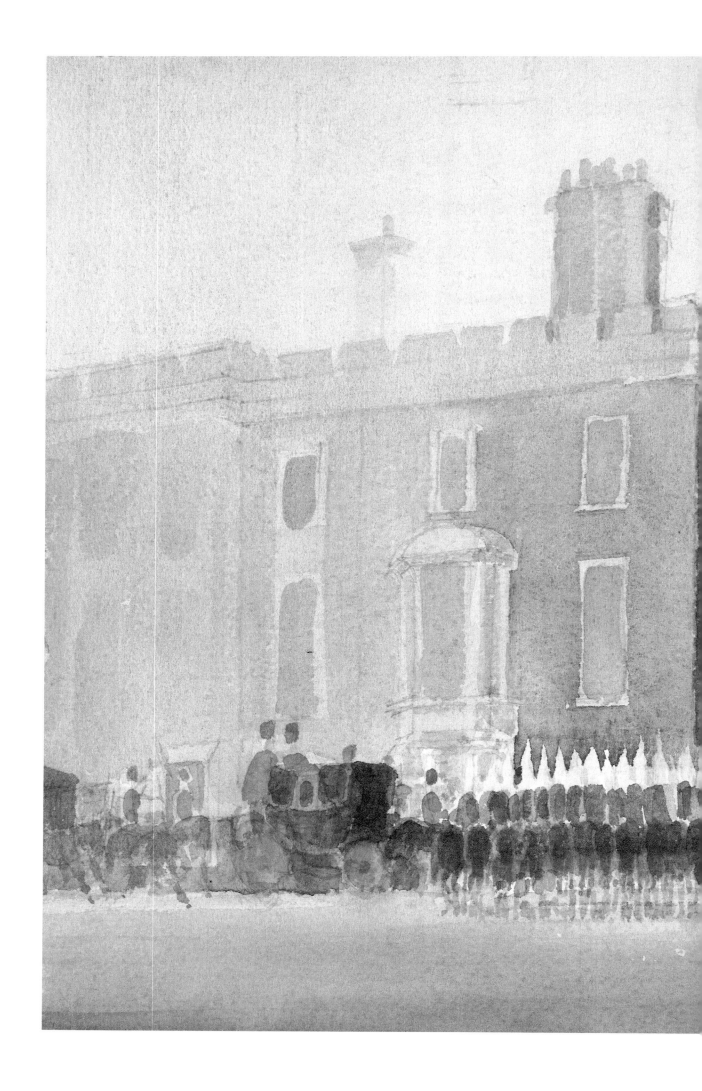

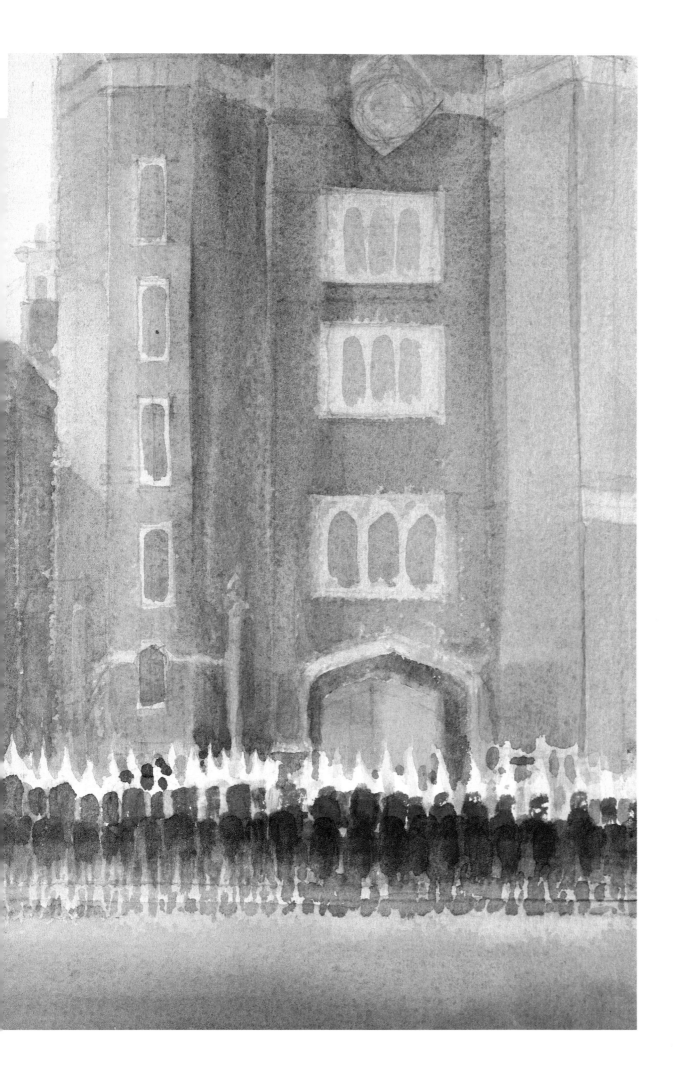

Arrival of a visiting head of state at the Great Gates, St James's Palace

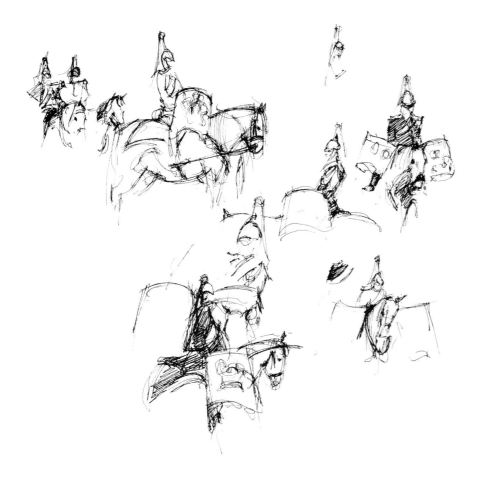

Sketches at Horse Guards

The brass band of the Household Cavalry, whose members are all trained medical assistants, is led by drummers astride magnificent Shire horses. The sound of the drums which rallied and inspired the troops in battle do not disturb the measured pace of the great horses. The trumpet calls, different for each regiment, were often the clearest way of conveying orders in battle. Today the band's duties are ceremonial providing an essential ingredient on many great occasions.

No portrait of royal ceremony would be complete without paying tribute to the Household Cavalry, the most senior of the Sovereign's Guards and by no means 'toy' soldiers. After two or three years posted to the Mounted Regiment for these ceremonial duties they return to fully operational armoured units. Of all the ceremonies in which the Household Division play a leading role, perhaps the best known is the Queen's Birthday Parade, otherwise known as Trooping the Colour.

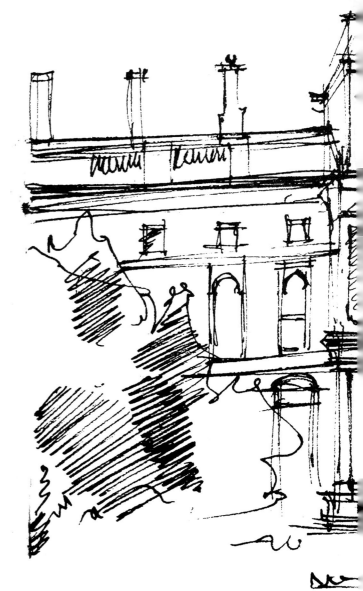

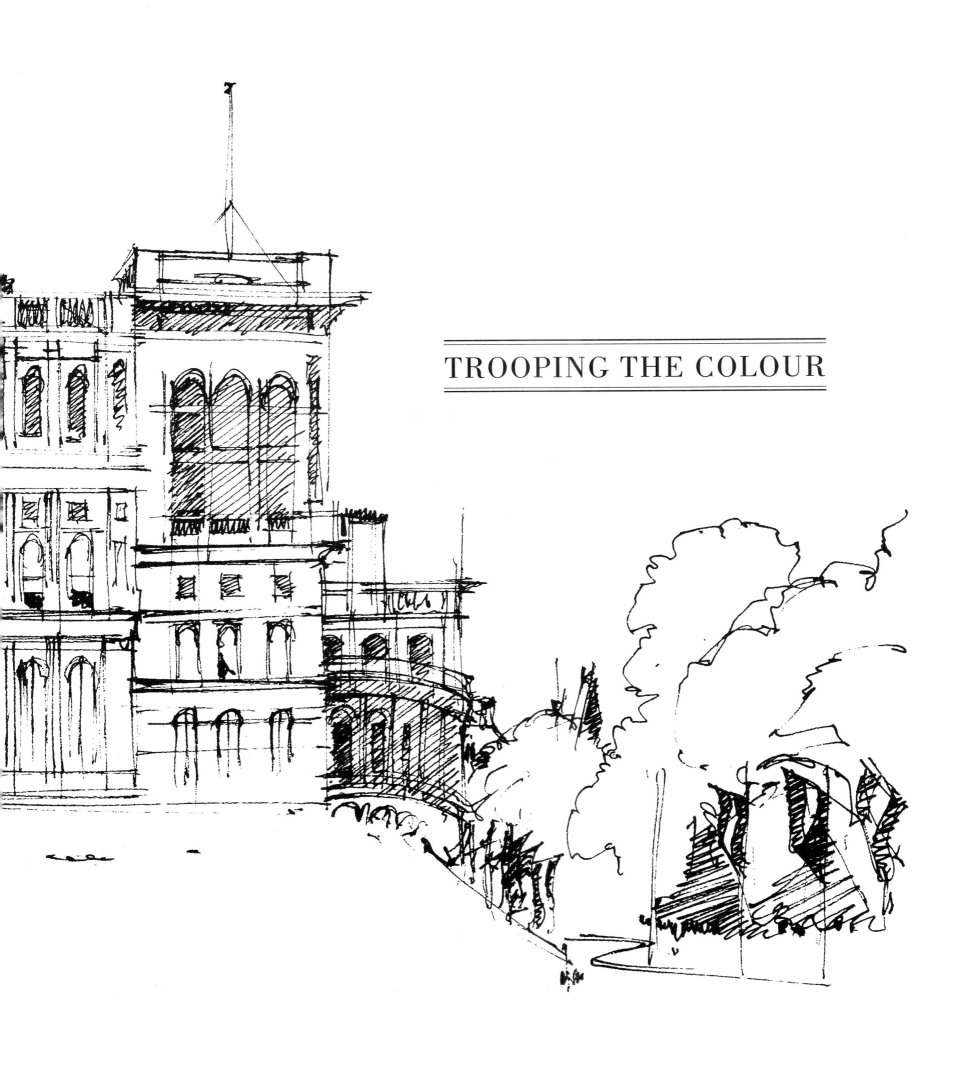

TROOPING THE COLOUR

Each year in June, to mark the Sovereign's official birthday, a battalion of Foot Guards parades or 'troops' the Queen's Colour on Horse Guards Parade in a display of marching and military music which is nowadays a great attraction for tourists and Londoners alike.

Trooping the Colour dates back to the eighteenth century when sentries paraded every day next to the Horse Guards building in Whitehall. One of the features of these parades was the flag or 'colour' which was used in battle as a rallying point. The flag was trooped; in other words, it was carried slowly up and down the ranks in order that it should be easily recognized by every soldier in the confusion of battle. The flags became a symbol of honour.

After 1748, trooping the Colour marked the Sovereign's birthday. However, it is only since the reign of Edward VII that the reigning monarch has taken the salute. On his accession Edward VII became Colonel-in-Chief of all the Household regiments and regularly attended the Birthday Parade.

BELOW: Salute, the Colonel's review

RIGHT: At the Trooping

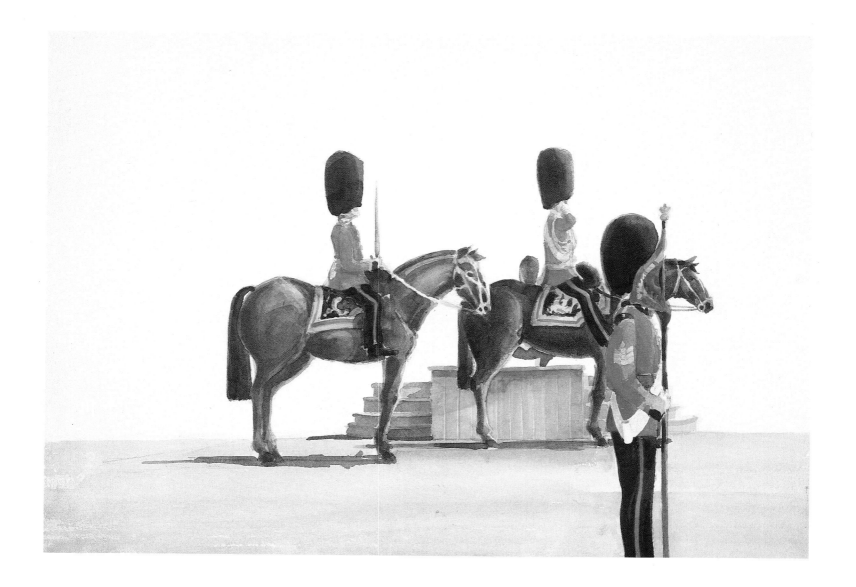

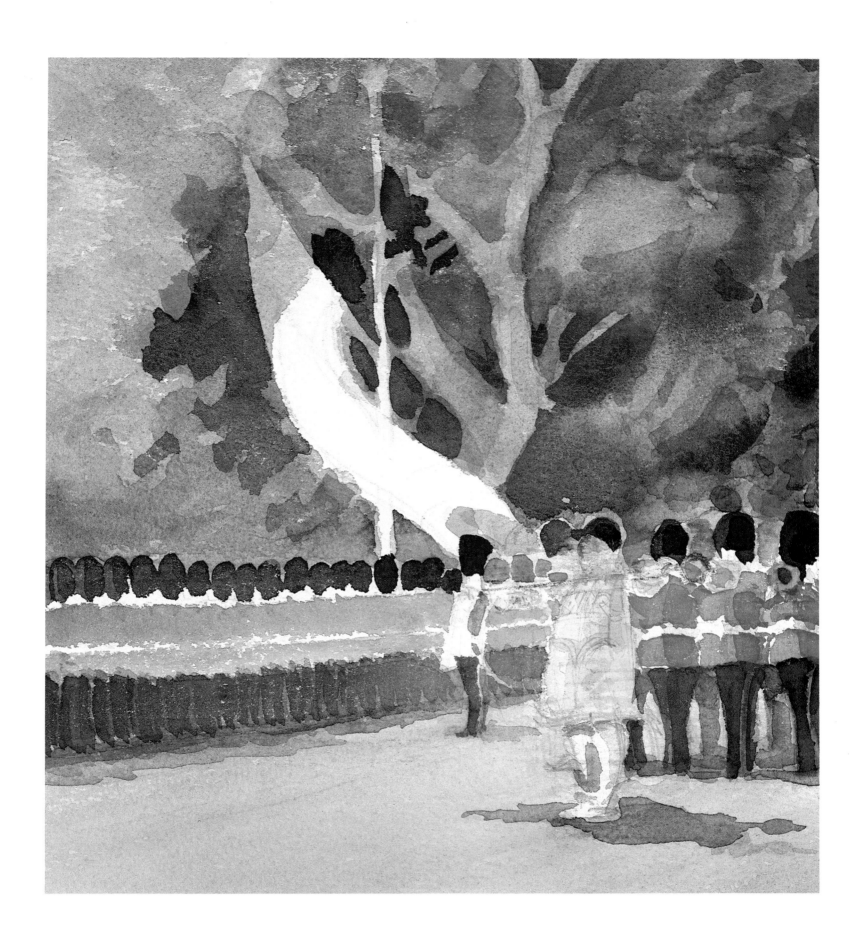

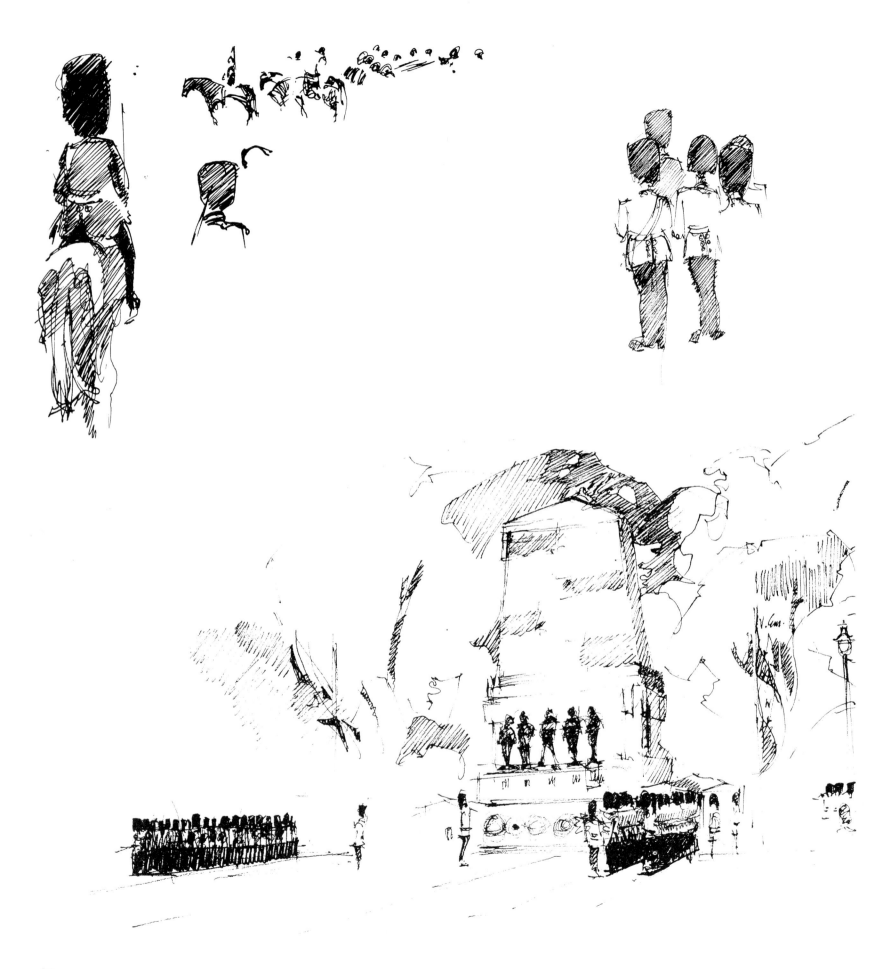

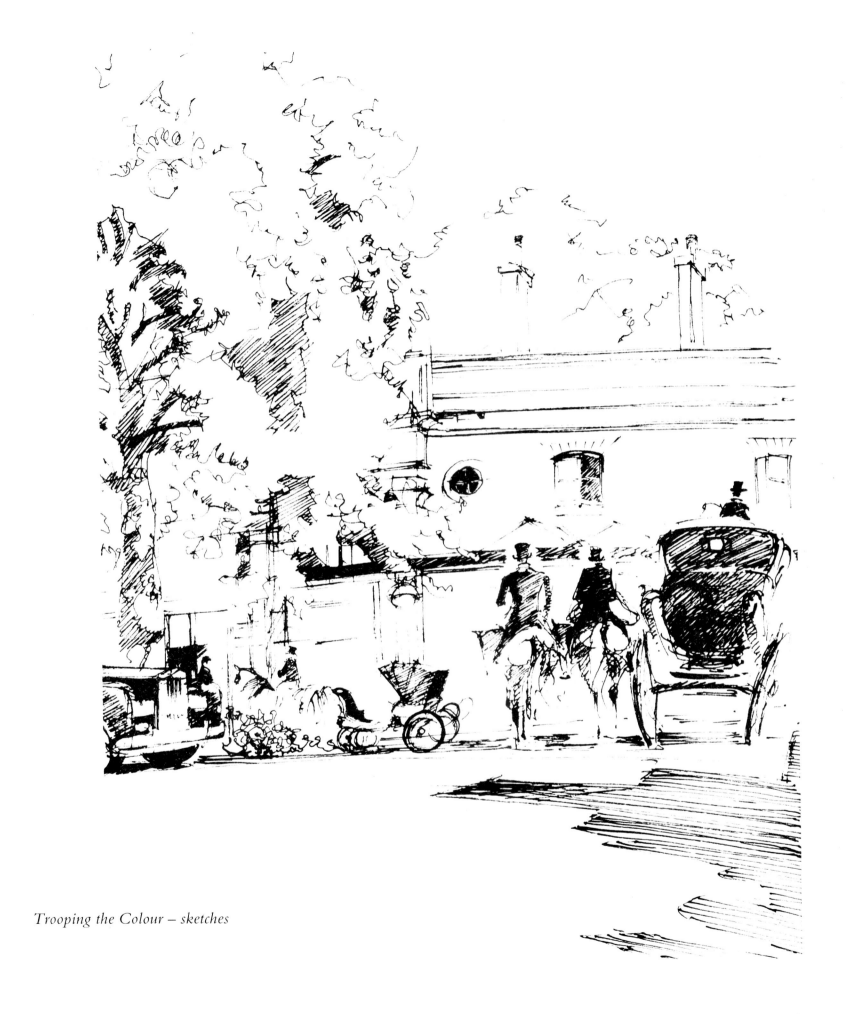

Trooping the Colour – sketches

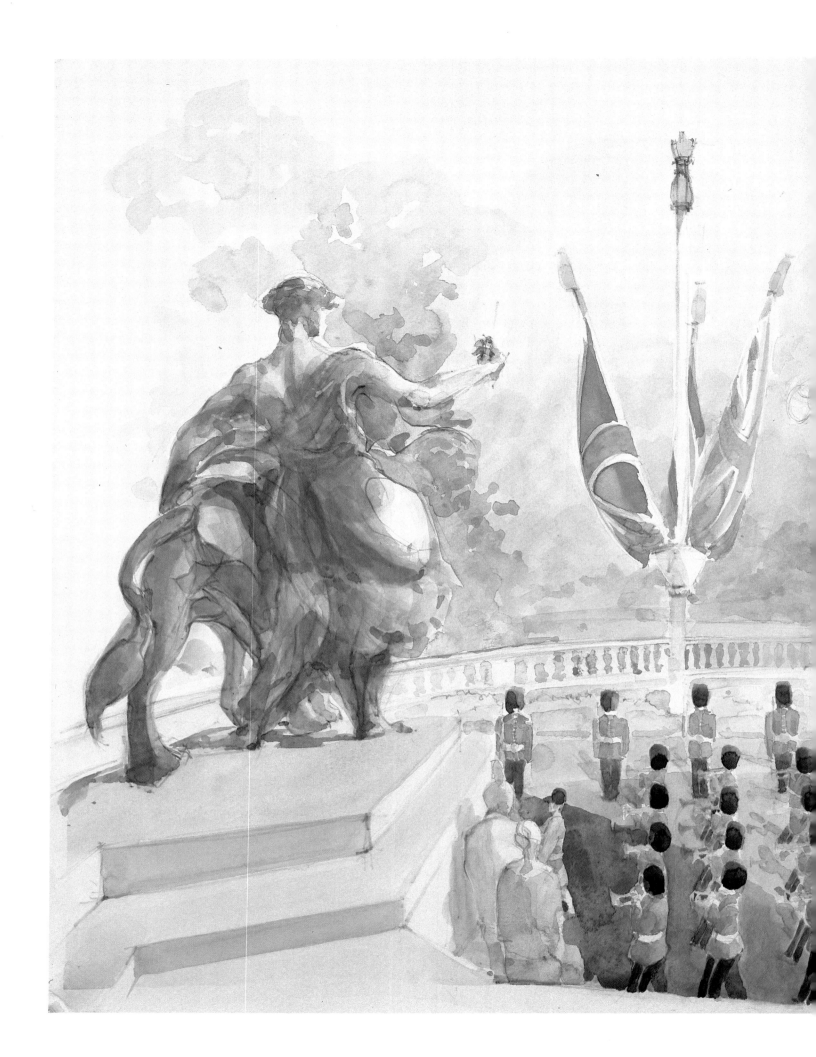

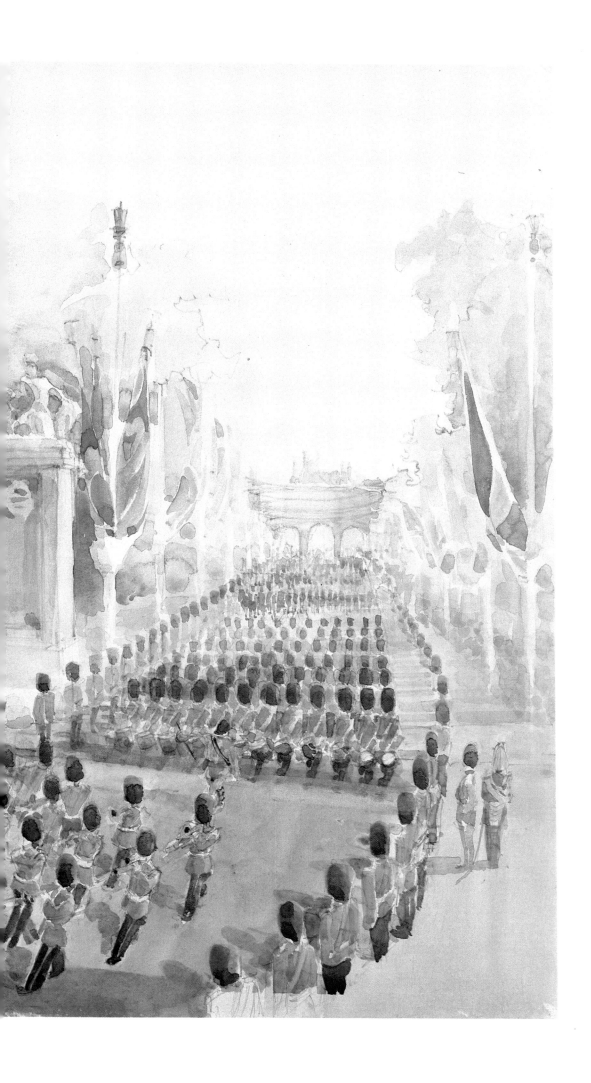

Massed bands in the Mall

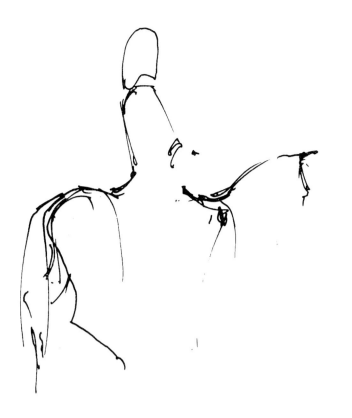

It was still a relatively private affair in that it was watched only by the King, princes of the blood royal and any visiting foreign royals. The Army Council, senior officers, military attachés and members of the royal households also attended. On one occasion, King Edward brought with him an entourage of over fifty royal highnesses, imperial highnesses, and mere highnesses. By this time, in addition to the traditional slow march past of the King's Colour, other marches to music had been added.

After the accession of King George V,

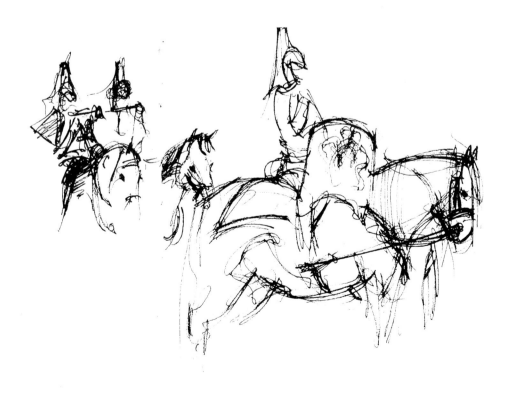

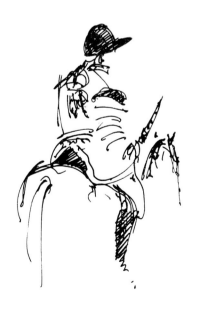

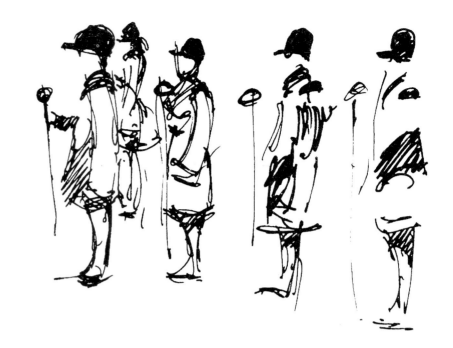

the Birthday Parade became a much more grandiose display designed to impress the ever-growing number of spectators. At the conclusion of the ceremony the King, preceded by massed bands, rode down the Mall at the head of his troops. On reaching Buckingham Palace, the King's Guard marched into the forecourt in readiness for Changing the Guard. The King, at the centre gates, took the salute before the old Guard returned to barracks. This impressive spectacle is what happens today with just a few modifications.

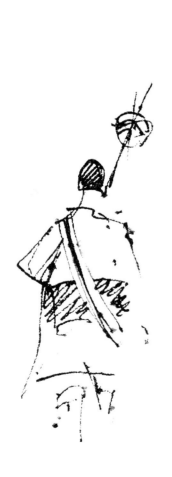

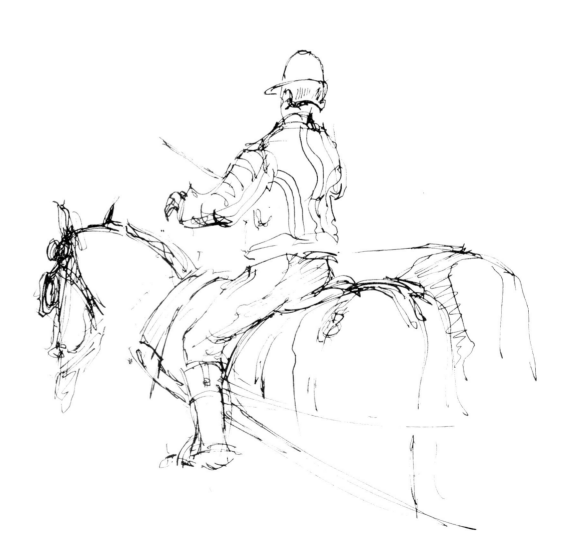

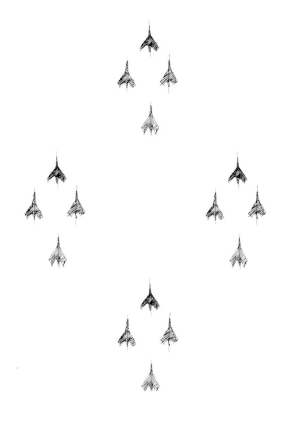

When King George VI made the Household Cavalry, until then an independent body, part of the Household Division, he gave the mounted regiment a much more important role in the Birthday Parade. Instead of just escorting the Sovereign to the parade and returning to barracks, the Lifeguards and the Blues and Royals with their mounted bands now walk or trot past the Sovereign preceding or following the Foot Guards.

At one time the Royal Horse Artillery (the King's Troop) fired a gun salute but now they simply join the march-past at Buckingham Palace after the ceremony. The present Queen has taken the salute every year of her reign. Until 1986, the Queen rode side-saddle on her much-loved charger, Burmese. Since Burmese's retirement she has inspected the troops from a carriage and takes the salute from a dais.

The Trooping is London's most colourful military event and every year it attracts thousands of spectators who revel in the splendour of Britain's military heritage.

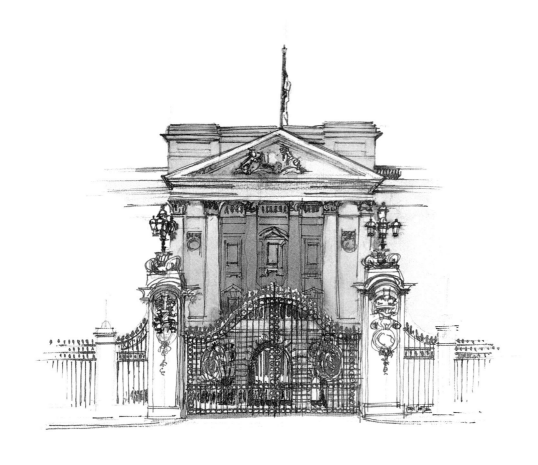

THE QUEEN'S GARDEN PARTIES

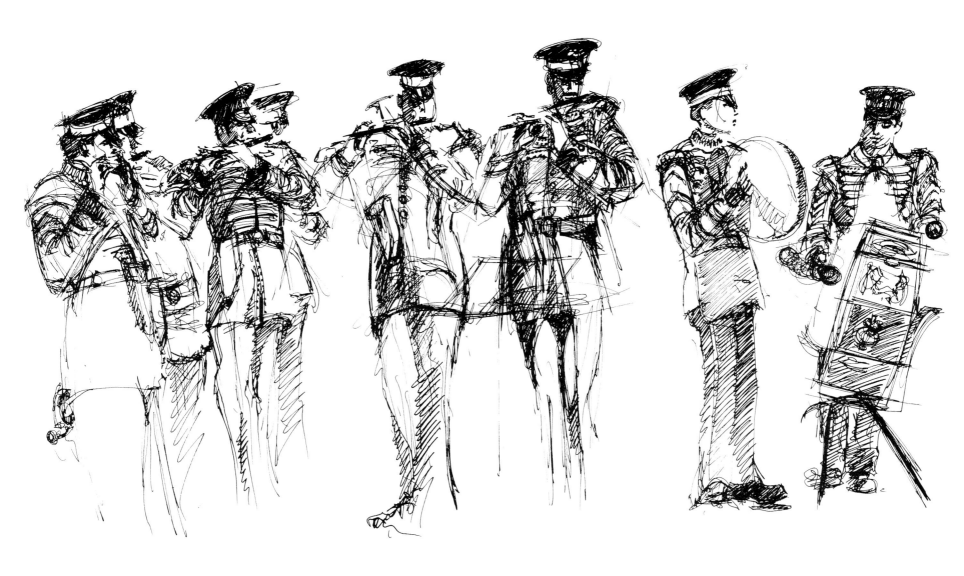

The Fife and Drum Band of the Grenadier Guards in rehearsal

ONE OF THE most effective ways in which the Queen gets to meet her subjects is the Garden Party. In fact there are four of these – three at Buckingham Palace in July and one in Edinburgh at the Palace of Holyroodhouse either in late June or early July.

On the Sovereign's command, the Lord Chamberlain invites several thousand people from all walks of life to put on their finery and come and meet the Queen. Diplomats, civil servants, judges, politicians, social workers, members of the armed forces and many others who are thought to have served their country well jostle with each other for tea and cakes in well-tended gardens.

The traffic in the Mall is blocked solid and as my little car did battle with

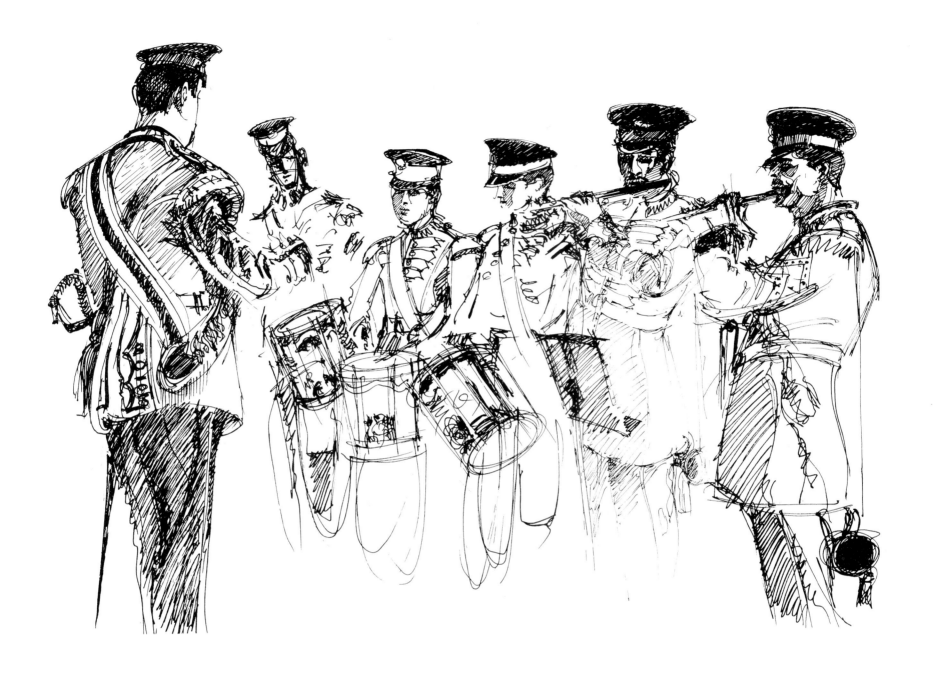

the chauffeur-driven limousines, pennants fluttering, it seemed to wilt visibly. The once-gold stripe might have been acceptable at a distance, the navy blue was respectable, but the rust was only too obvious. A smile to a lady built like a battleship – either a dowager duchess or a Labour councillor was returned with withering disdain.

The intention was to park in an allotted space in front of Lancaster House but it was not to be. Unable to circumnavigate the Victoria Memorial, we found ourselves entering the gates of Buckingham Palace. As we did so, our gallant steed backfired, loudly, not once but twice, in clear disparagement of its grand neighbours. The policemen smiled gently and we blushed.

Security is now a priority and security men dressed in morning suits,

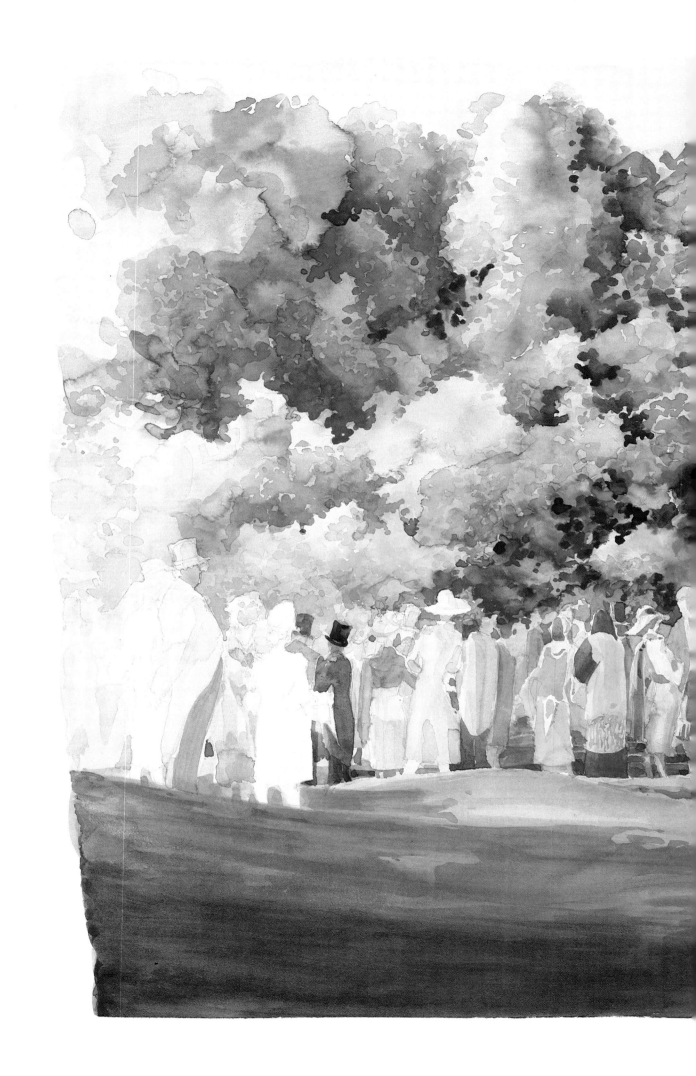

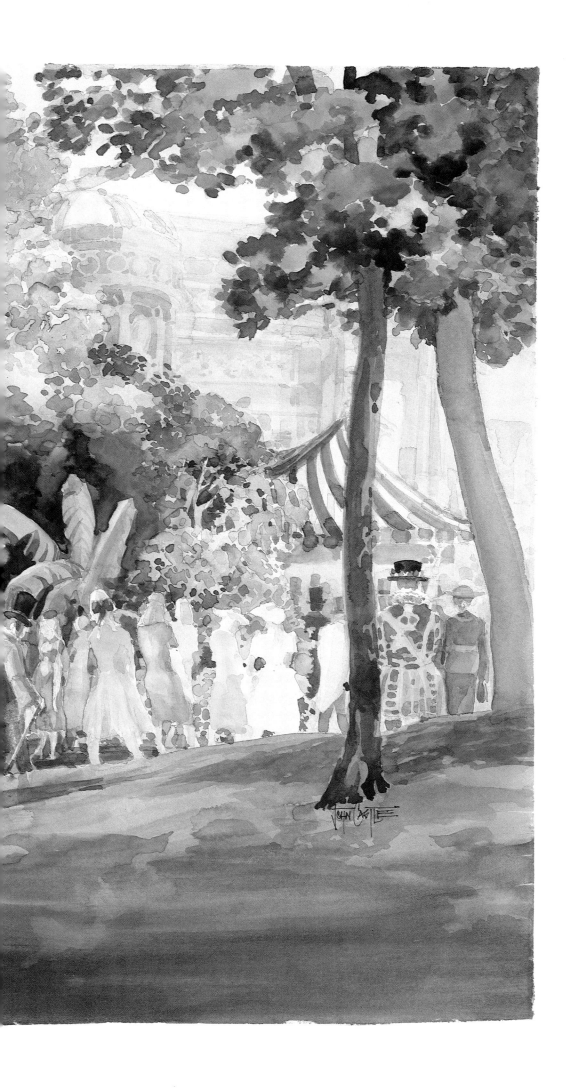

Buckingham Palace garden party. A walk around the garden

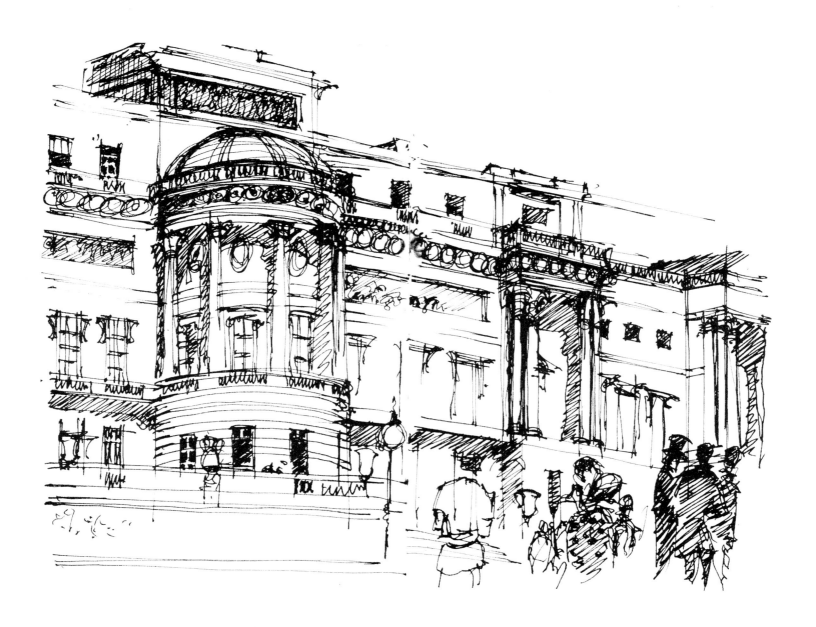

Sketches of a garden party

indistinguishable from the guests wander sharp–eyed amongst the crowd. One such sees me sketching and checks my credentials, telling me not to worry as he 'believes the Tower to be quite comfortable nowadays'. Given the distance the press are kept from the festivities, this freedom to sketch within the gardens gives me a pleasant feeling of superiority.

Unlike the security men, the Yeomen of the Guard cannot be missed. Their uniform of red and gold delight the eye but their menacing-looking partizans or halberds seem not altogether decorative. Two military bands play at different ends of the garden, the one nearest to me urging me to consider myself at home, consider myself one of the famil*ee . . .* Dream on.

At the far end of the garden is a lake in which one can admire the upside-down image of Nash's architecture. The 'back' of Buckingham Palace, so reflected, is in fact the front of the building and should always be referred to as such. For my especial pleasure, perhaps, New Zealand plants flourish nearby in a walled garden – the micro-climate of central London being suitably antipodean. A banana palm, azaleas and a profusion of chrysanthemums seem to mimic the ladies' colourful hats and dresses bobbing and dancing in the sunshine.

The lawn is now a riot of colour. Guests are drifting towards the yellow ochre stone of the palace where Yeomen are forming a guard of honour. Behind them the guests crowd hoping for a good view of the Queen who now appears at the main doorway of the Palace with, in this instance, the Princess of Wales. They stand at the top of the steps leading down to the lawn and the crowd is hushed. Gentlemen remove their top hats and the two bands play the national anthem.

The royal party, escorted by a Gentleman Usher in uniform and a Gentleman-at-Arms resplendent in his plumed hat, descends onto the lawn.

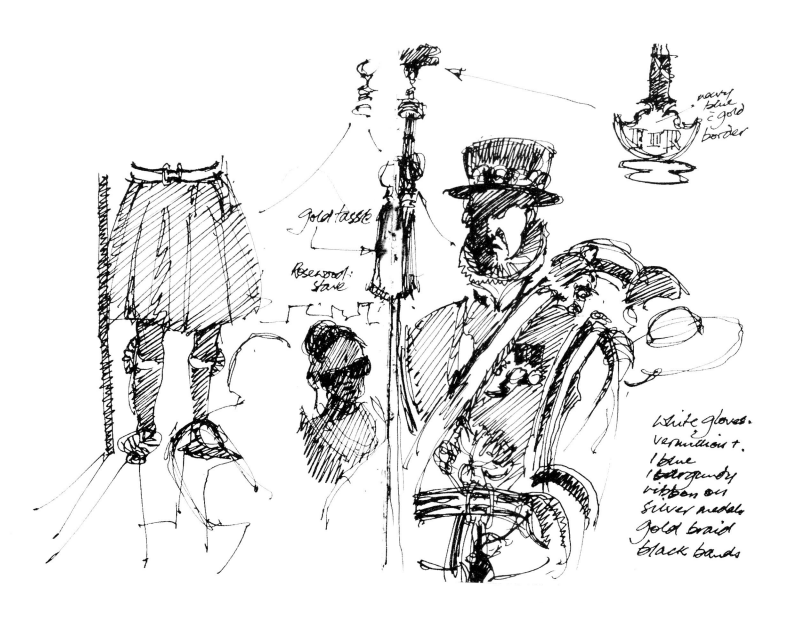

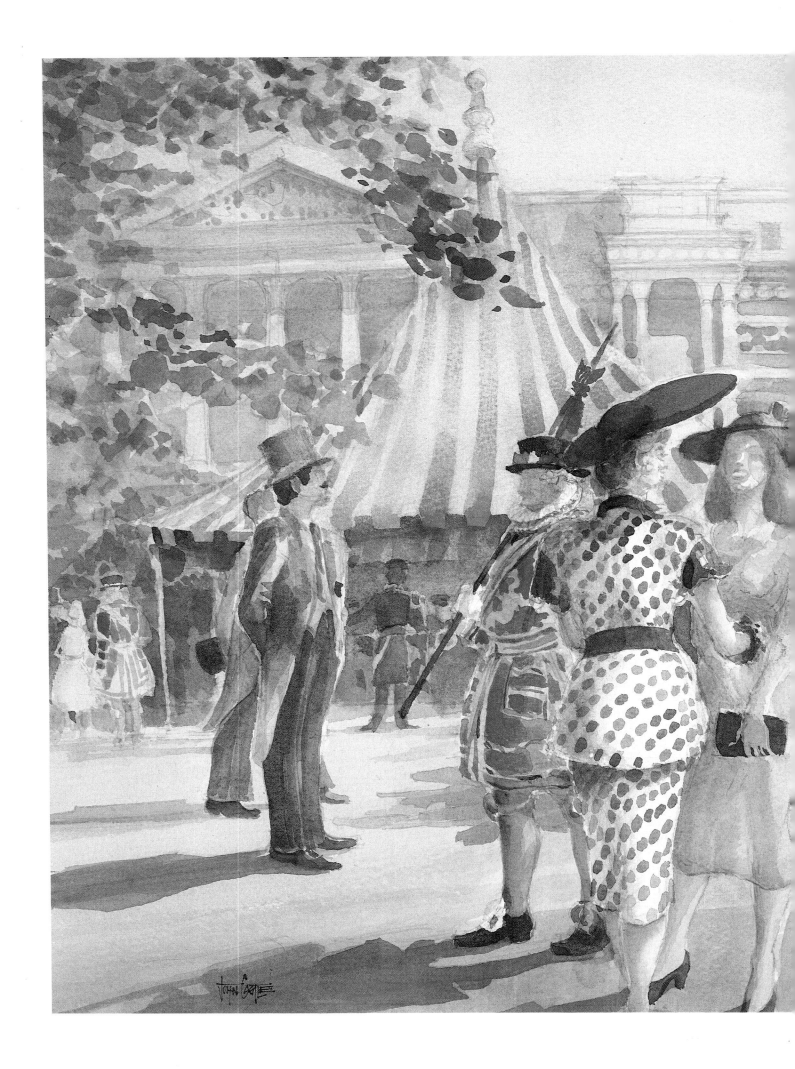

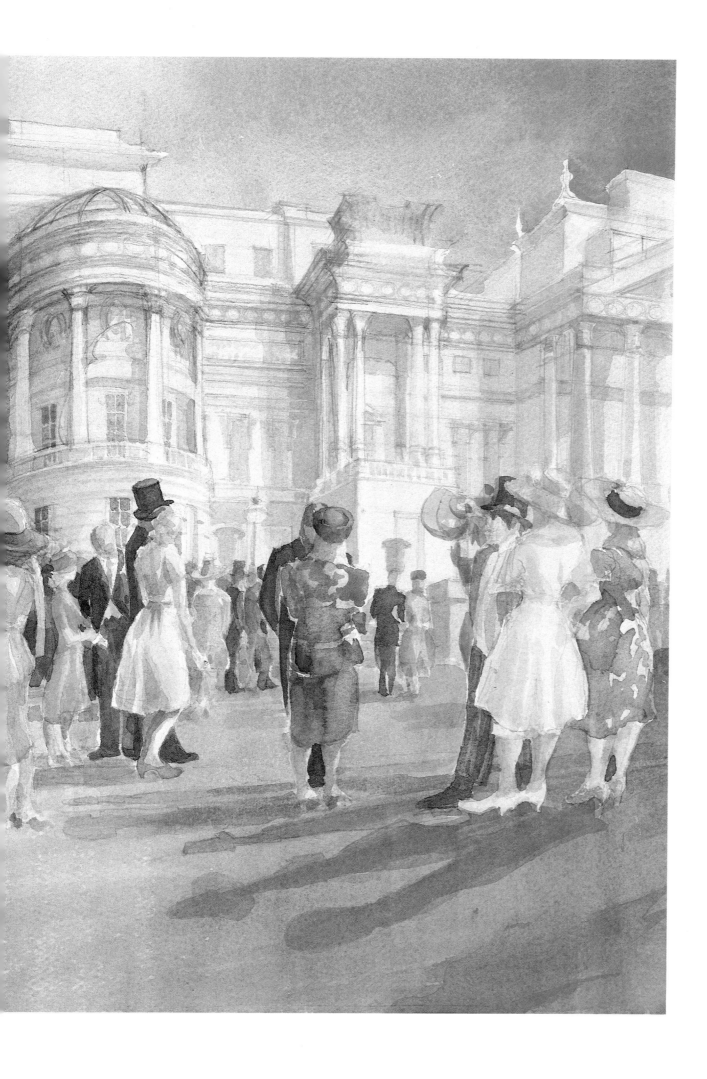

On the lawn

Each member of the royal party takes a different route in order that as many people as is possible can see or be introduced to them. The Princess of Wales makes a particular point of talking to those in wheelchairs or with an obvious disability.

At last they reach the Diplomatic tent where the royal party takes tea or lemonade (made to a special recipe) surrounded by guests in many different national costumes. After a further perambulation, the Queen and the Princess depart and the Garden Party is over. It has once again proved itself to be a most effective way of saying thank you to many worthy people who work in the community for the good of others, often without much recognition, and of making people in very different areas of public service feel part of and proud of a great tradition.

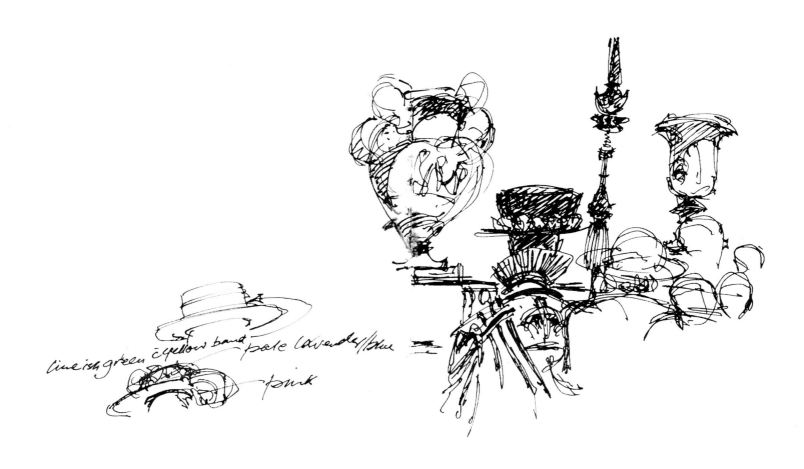

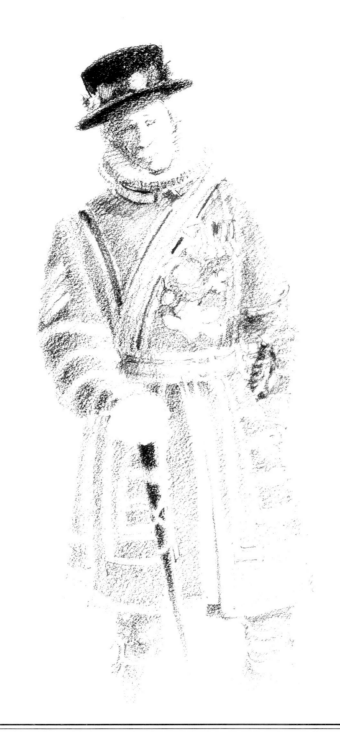

THE ROYAL BODY GUARD OF
THE YEOMEN OF THE GUARD

THE ROYAL BODY GUARD of the Yeomen of the Guard, created by Henry VII after the battle of Bosworth Field in 1485, is the oldest military corps in the United Kingdom and the oldest of the royal bodyguards. Originally yeomen were 'gentlemen just below the rank of esquire' and the Yeomen of the Guard was created in recognition of their exceptional valour. They were made responsible for the personal safety of the Sovereign and numbered six hundred. Queen Elizabeth I reduced their number to around two hundred and after the Restoration of Charles II their number was reduced again to about eighty which is what it is today.

Nowadays of course, their role is purely ceremonial and the Yeomen are all retired warrant or non-commissioned officers. The Yeomen of the Guard are often confused in the public mind with Yeomen Warders of the Tower of London and both are sometimes erroneously called Beefeaters. However, although their uniforms are similar, their history is very different.

There have been guards at the Tower of London since the days of William the Conqueror. Their efficiency so impressed the Duke of Somerset, Edward VI's Protector, when he was imprisoned in the Tower in 1549 that he promised to grant them a favour if he were ever released. When this happy day arrived, they held him to his promise and asked to be made Yeomen of the Body Guard. They were therefore sworn in as extraordinary members and their full title is Yeomen Warders of Her Majesty's Royal Palace and Fortress of the Tower of London, Members of the Yeomen of the Guard Extraordinary.

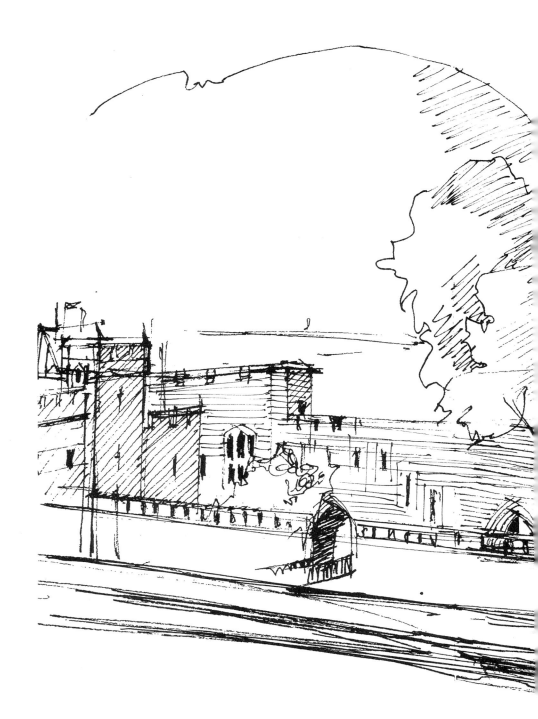

The Tower of London

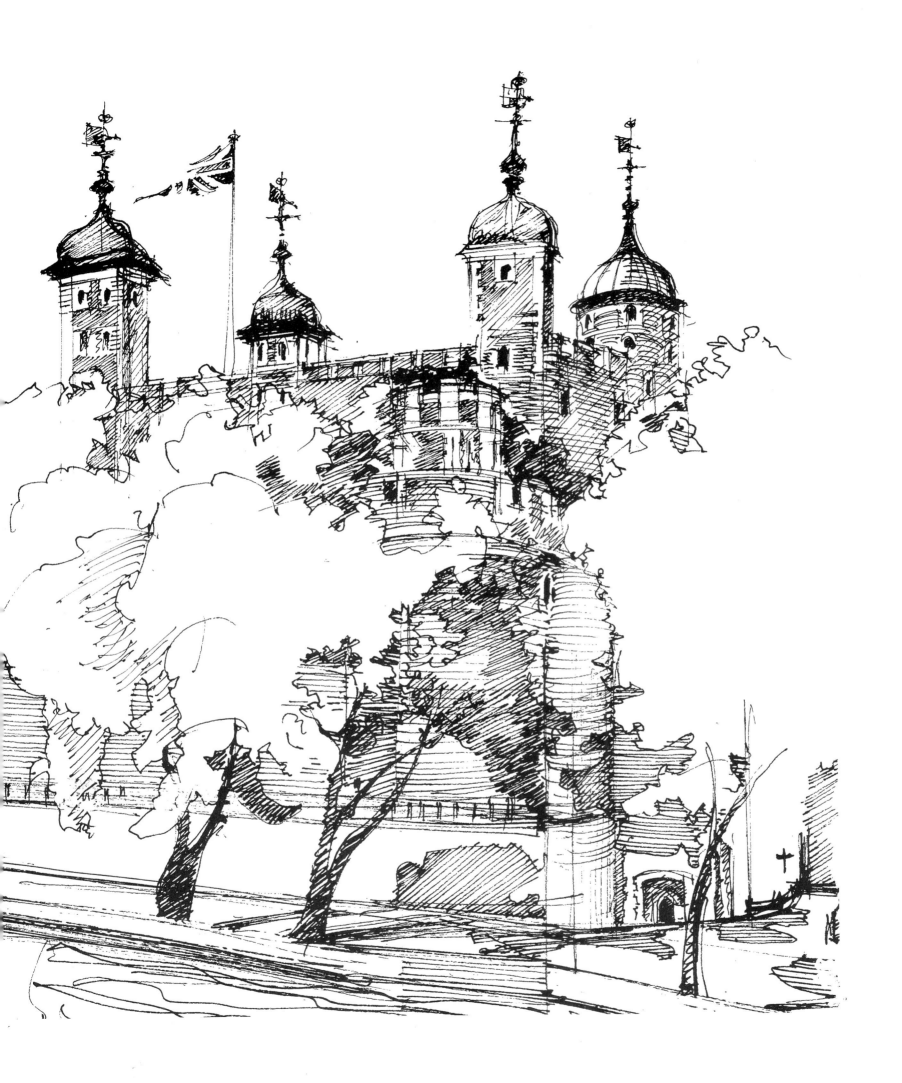

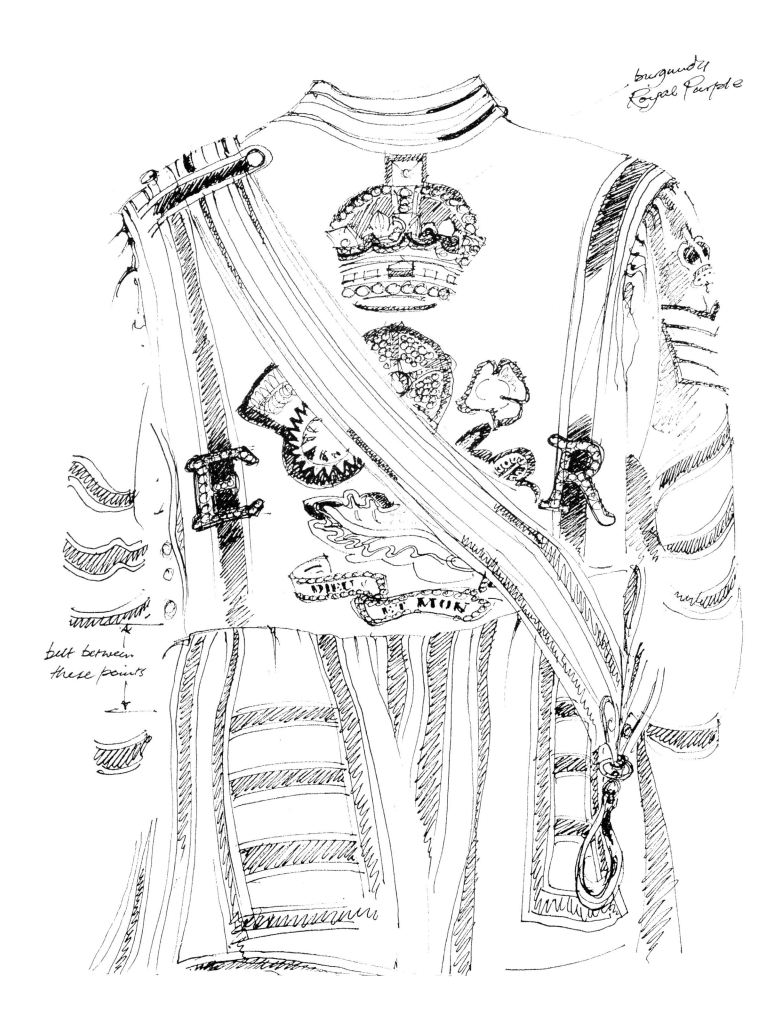

burgundy
Royal Purple

belt between
these points

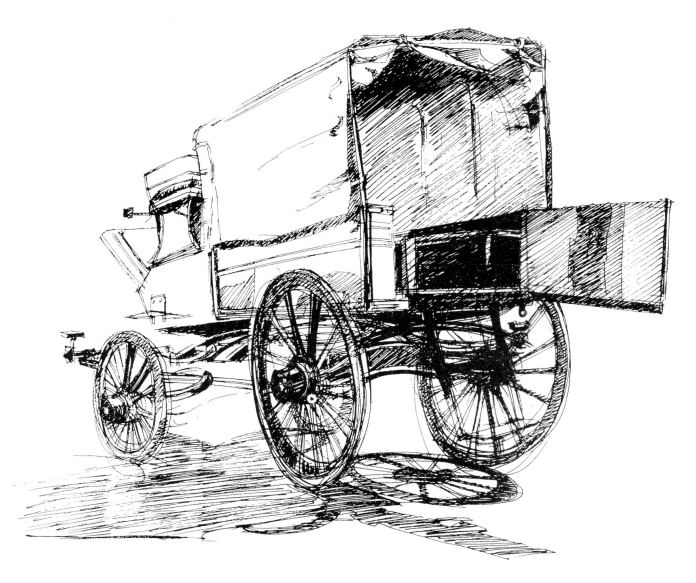

In 1826 the Duke of Wellington became Constable of the Tower and reformed some of their practices. The position of Yeoman Warder had previously been bought for life with the perquisite of an apartment in the Tower walls. It was said that one Warder had for sixteen years had an apartment in the Tower while being an innkeeper in another part of town. When this was discovered the miscreant presented the Warders with a large pewter bowl as a penance which is still used at the swearing-in of new Warders.

Since Wellington's day, the post of Warder is only filled by 'deserving, gallant and meritorious ex-sergeants of the cavalry, footguards and infantry'. Today ex-Royal Marines and Royal Air Force personnel can be made Warders. As with the Yeomen of the Guard, each is selected for his distinguished record and each must have two medals, those for long service and good conduct. The day dress or 'undress' of the Yeomen Warders is blue and red and this is what they wear as they act as guides round the Tower. Only at the Coronation, when they form a guard outside Westminster Abbey, do they wear their superb full 'state dress'.

The Royal Body Guard of the Yeomen of the Guard has its headquarters at St James's Palace and appear on most State occasions with the Sovereign.

FAR LEFT: Sketch of the uniform of the Messenger Serjeant of the Yeomen of the Guard

LEFT: The Yeomen's 'wagon'

They were so close to the monarch that they kept guard outside the royal bedroom at night and tasted the Sovereign's food in case of poison. Even today food-tasting is still carried out symbolically at State banquets. An Exon-in-waiting stands behind the Sovereign's chair throughout. There are two Exons among the Yeomen, the name deriving from the French and indicating that they were exempt from regimental duties while serving with the Guard.

The uniform of the Yeomen of the Guard is very similar to that of the Warders of the Tower, but is distinguishable by the red and gold cross belt which used to hold a sword. They carry a partizan which derives from a French word meaning spear. The staff is made of rosewood surmounted by a steel spear and double-edged axe. It bears the Queen's Coat of Arms and the cipher, EIIR. The Tudor doublet of scarlet and gold is embroidered with the initials of the monarch, a Tudor crown, the York and Lancaster roses, the motto *Dieu et mon Droit* (God and my Right), the thistle of Scotland and the shamrock of Ireland. They wear red breeches and stockings, black-buckled shoes with rosettes, and a black-velvet hat with red, white and blue ribbons. The uniform is completed with rosettes just below the knee. The embroidery on the doublets has changed over the centuries, the current pattern dating from 1901.

The Colour of the Yeomen is kept in St James's Palace. It is a new Colour presented to them by King George VI and is the first standard to bear the round tower signifying the House of Windsor. The original standard which flew at Bosworth Field was destroyed in a fire in 1809.

Yeomen on duty. The Epiphany service, Chapel Royal, St James's Palace

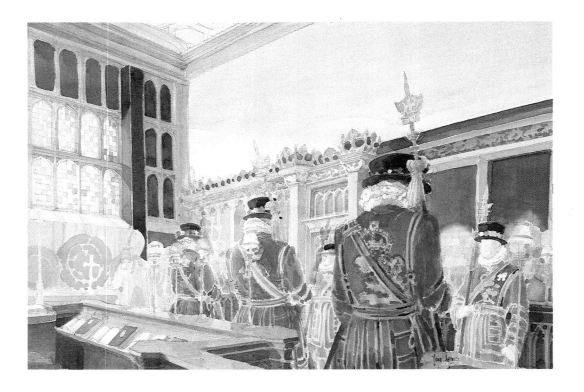

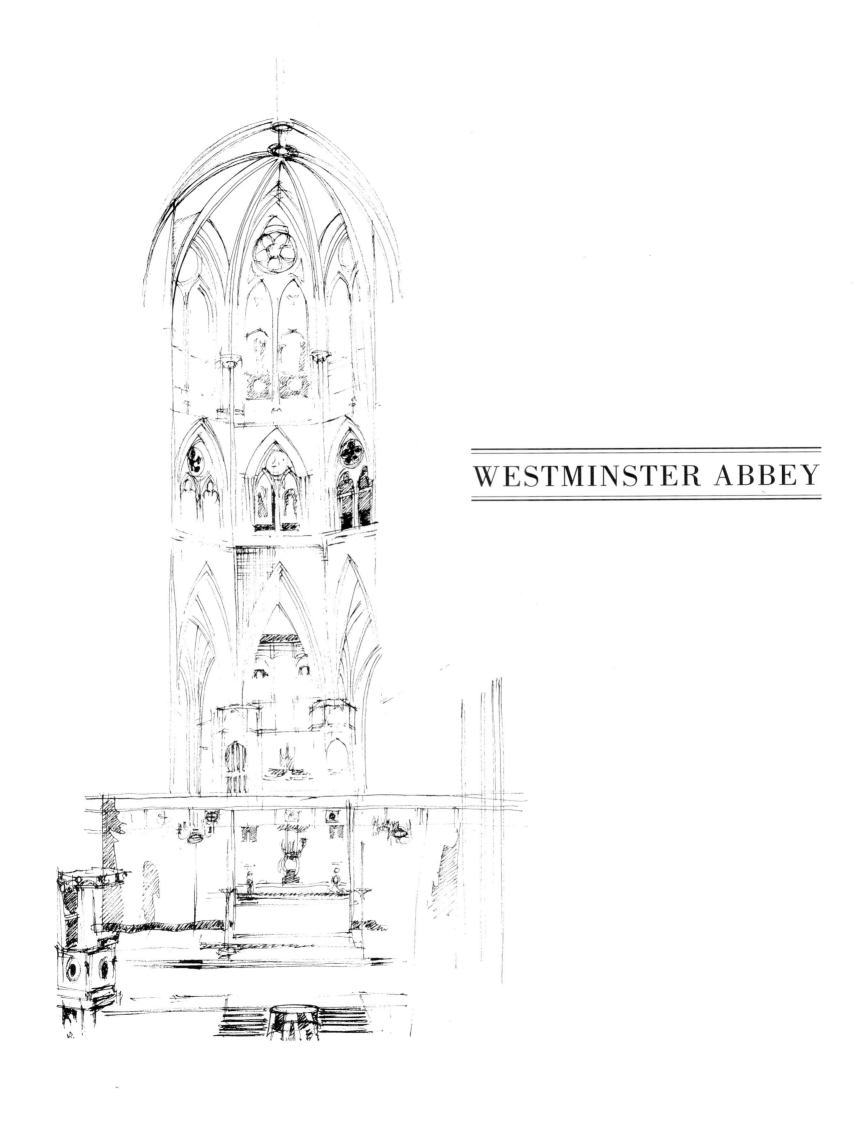

WESTMINSTER ABBEY

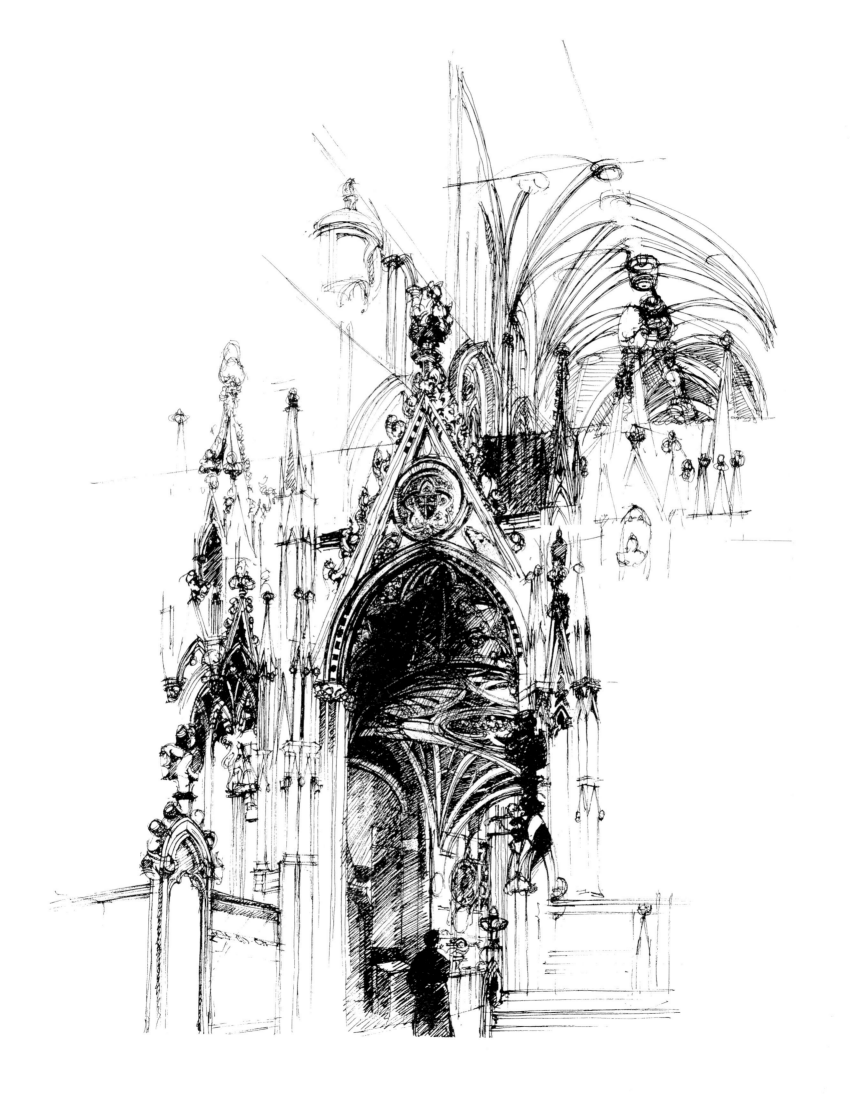

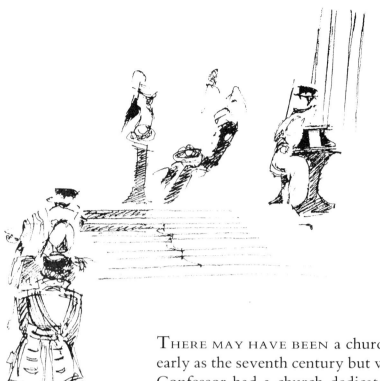

Sketches at the Office of the Royal Maundy, Westminster Abbey

THERE MAY HAVE BEEN a church where Westminster Abbey now stands as early as the seventh century but what we do know for sure is that Edward the Confessor had a church dedicated to St Peter built on the site, which was completed shortly before his death in January 1066. The King was too ill to attend the consecration ceremony in December 1065 but he had already arranged endowments to the Benedictine monastery which had been on the site for at least a century. The King was buried near the high altar in the church but his remains were transferred to a shrine on his canonization a hundred years later. Another hundred and six years later the dead king and saint was given an even more splendid shrine in a new abbey which was the basis of that which we know today.

The monastery at Westminster was dissolved by Henry VIII who established a new cathedral church there. Mary Tudor tried to resurrect the monastery, and Edward the Confessor's body, which had been hidden by the monks, was returned to his shrine. Queen Elizabeth I gave the church a new charter making the abbey into the Collegiate Church of St Peter in Westminster.

It is the procession of this Collegiate Church which forms the first part of the procession proper at the Royal Maundy Service when it is held at Westminster during which traditionally alms are distributed to the poor. This distribution of alms and the washing of feet on the Thursday of Holy Week is a ceremony even older than the foundation of Westminster Abbey with records of Maundy dating back to the time of St Augustine at the beginning of the seventh century.

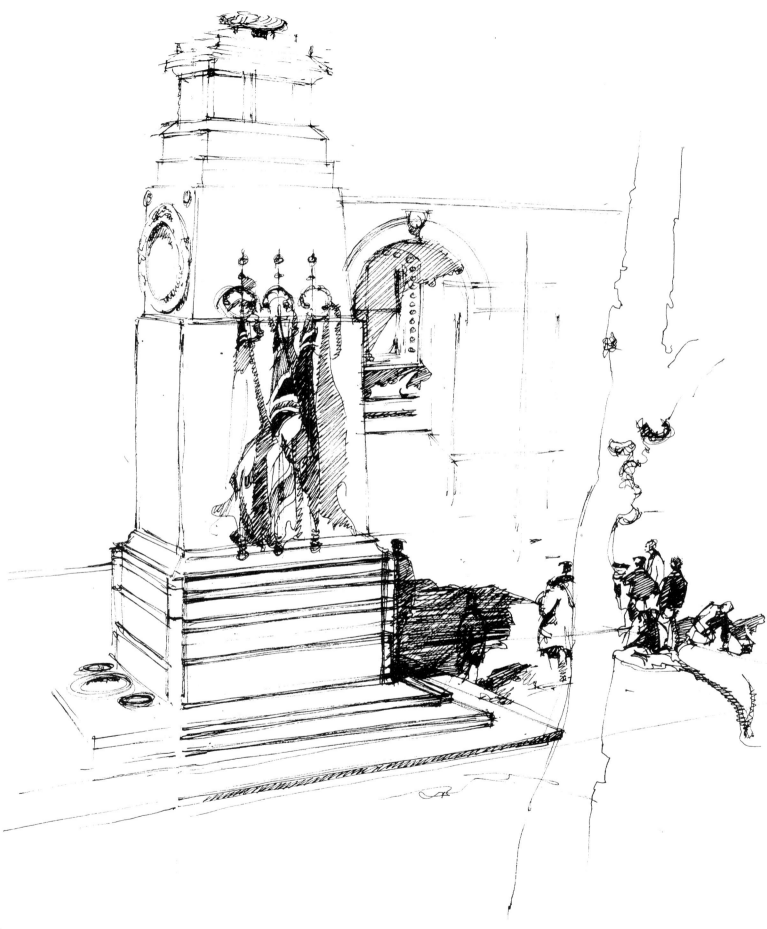

The service used to take place in the Chapel Royal at Whitehall, now the Banqueting Hall. From 1890 to 1951 the service was held in Westminster Abbey but since then the Queen, travelling with Yeomen and the Chapel Royal, has visited many dioceses for the service.

Although no longer practised today, the washing of feet recalling Christ's washing of the disciple's feet at the Last Supper, is symbolized by the Lord High Almoner processing with his assistants girded with linen and carrying nosegays of scented herbs. These latter must once have been helpful in disguising the stink of poverty.

When the service takes place in Westminster Abbey, representatives of other churches form the first section of the procession, then follows the procession proper led by the Beadle. Immediately following the Cross of Westminster are members of the Brotherhood of St Edward the Confessor. The Chapel Royal choirboys lead the choristers of Westminster Abbey who are followed by the Gentlemen of the Chapel Royal.

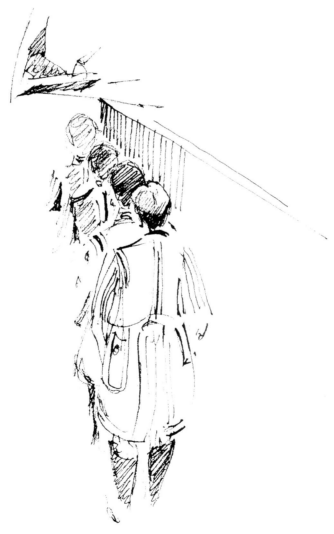

Sketches.
LEFT: *Preparation for a service at the Cenotaph*
RIGHT: *Entry of the Royal Choir*

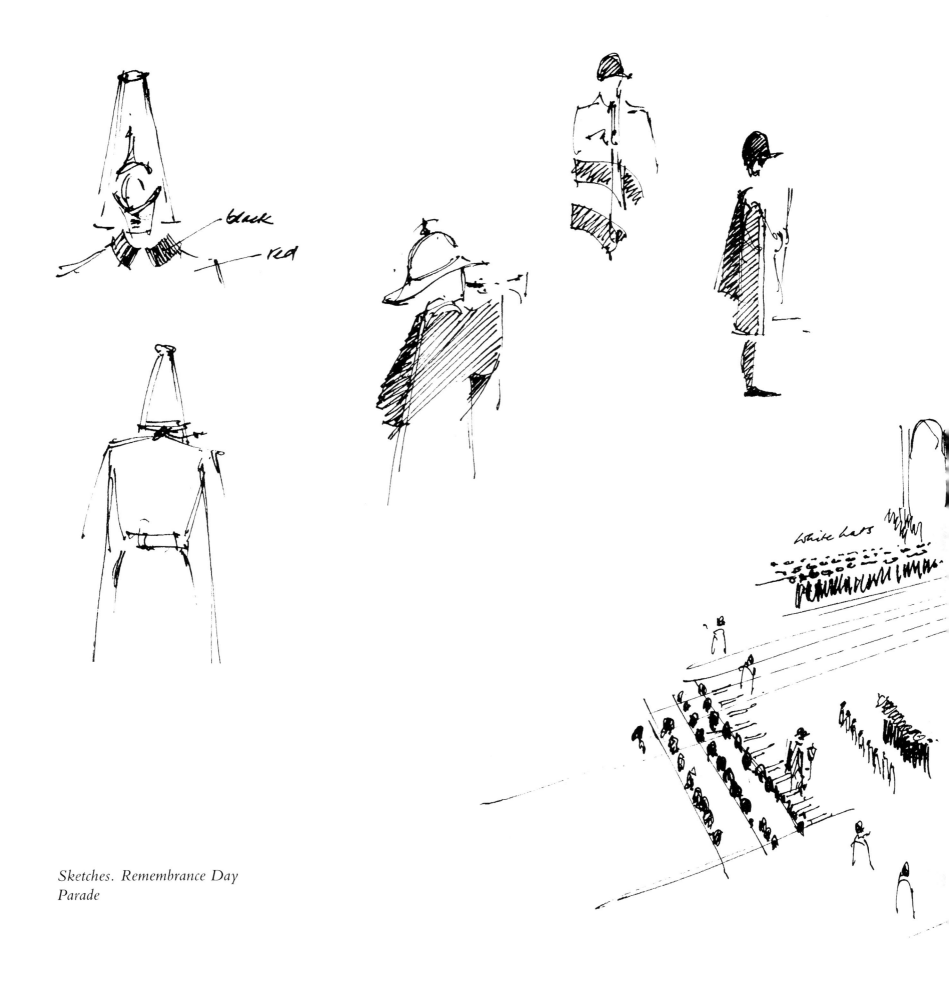

black

red

white hats

Sketches. Remembrance Day
Parade

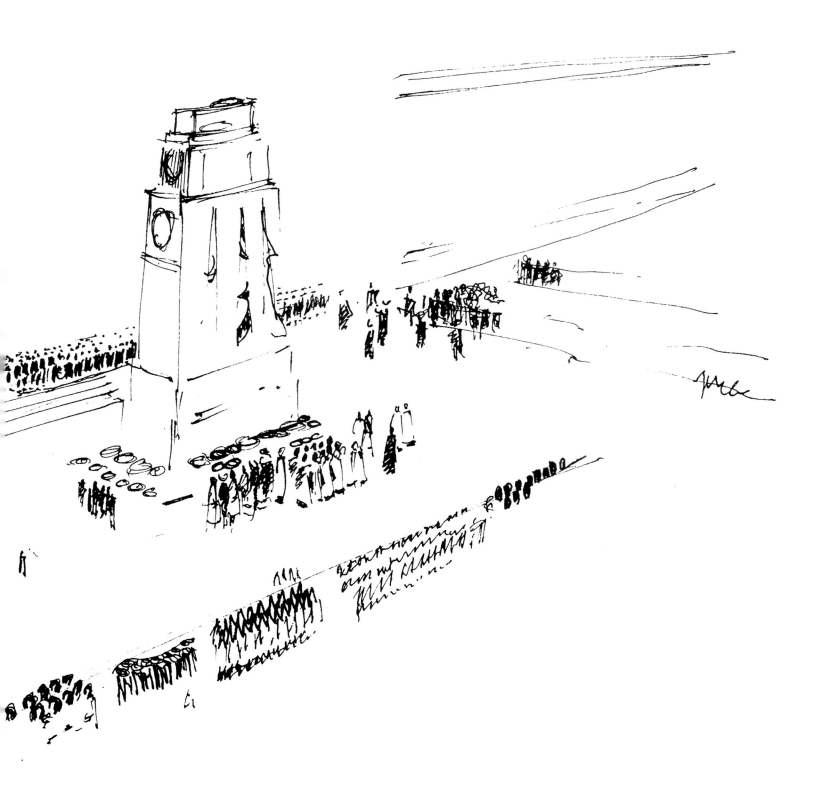

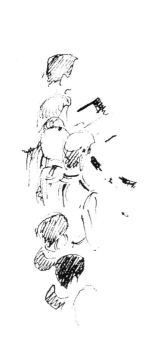

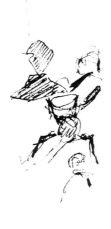

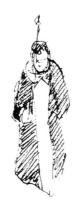

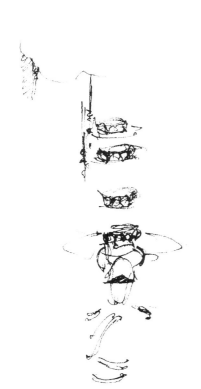

After the Organist, Choirmaster and Composer of Her Majesty's Chapel Royal comes that of Westminster Abbey, important members of the clergy, the Queen, Prince Philip and the Queen's Suite. Finally, there comes the Royal Almoner with the Yeomen, the Sovereign's personal bodyguard, carrying the Maundy money in golden dishes above their heads. The Lord High Almoner processes last.

The Maundy, like the procession, is in two parts, a red purse and a white purse. Although today the ceremony is symbolic the Maundy is highly prized. The red purse contains a clothing and provisions allowance while the white contains Maundy coins – pennies, twopences, threepences and fourpences. The total number of pence equal the Sovereign's age and are legal tender. The Maundy is distributed to pensioners selected for their Christian work for the Church and the community. Once, they had to be the same sex as the Sovereign but nowadays they are of both sexes.

Within the body of Westminster Abbey, there is an area specifically for the Sovereign's use. The ANZAC service after the wreath-laying ceremony at the Cenotaph to mark the seventy-fifth anniversary of the landings of the Australian and New Zealand Army Corps on the Gallipoli Peninsula on April 25 1915 was one event when the Queen used this special place. From there she watched the Parade of Flags of Australia and New Zealand – a most moving occasion.

The Remembrance Sunday parade on the second Sunday in November each year is another solemn event for Westminster Abbey and the whole nation. The First World War ended on the eleventh hour of the eleventh day of the eleventh month of 1918. The Bishop of London and the Chapel Royal lead the Queen and many thousands of her subjects in a moving service and march past at the Cenotaph commemorating the dead of two world wars and many smaller conflicts in which British and Commonwealth soldiers fought.

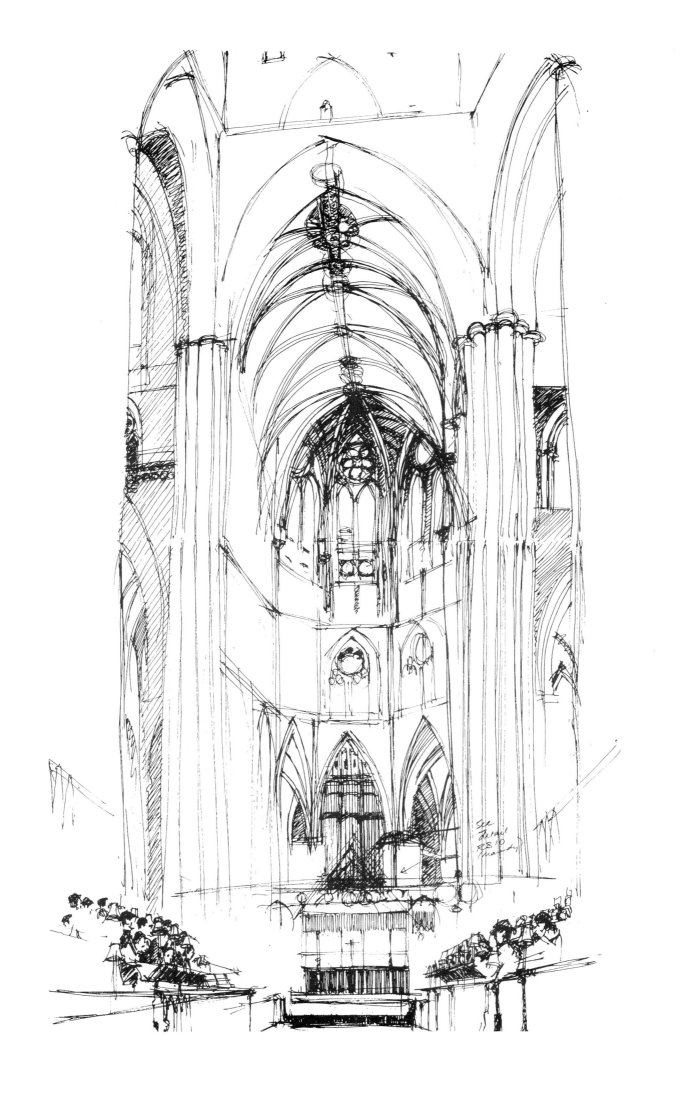

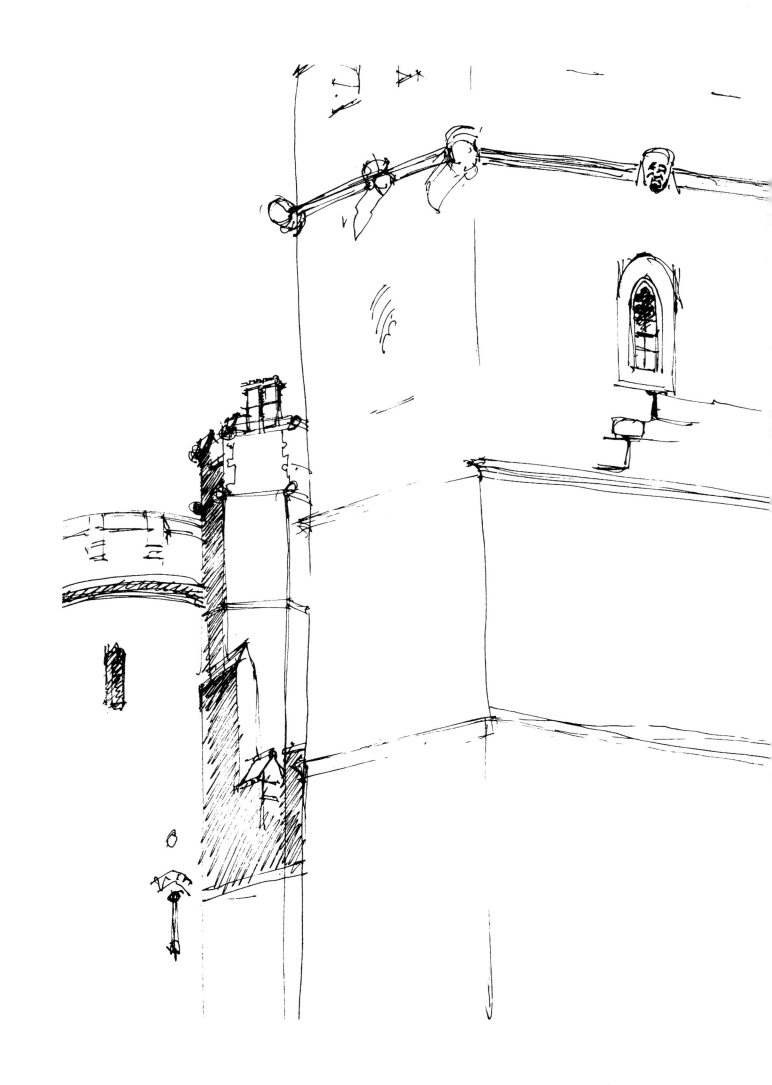

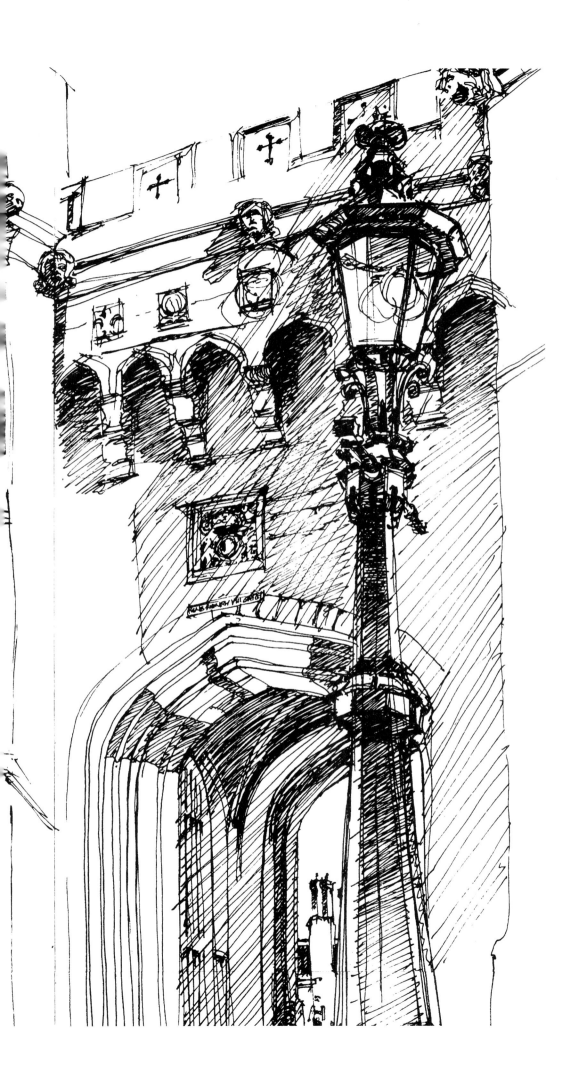

WINDSOR CASTLE

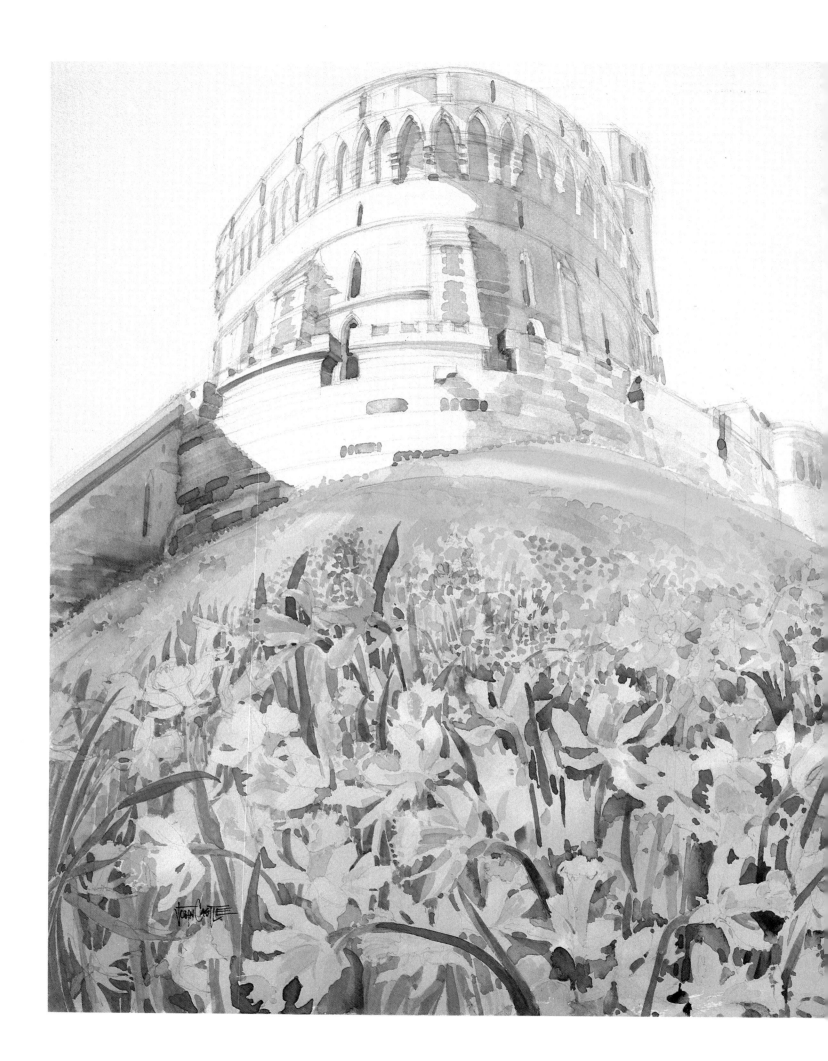

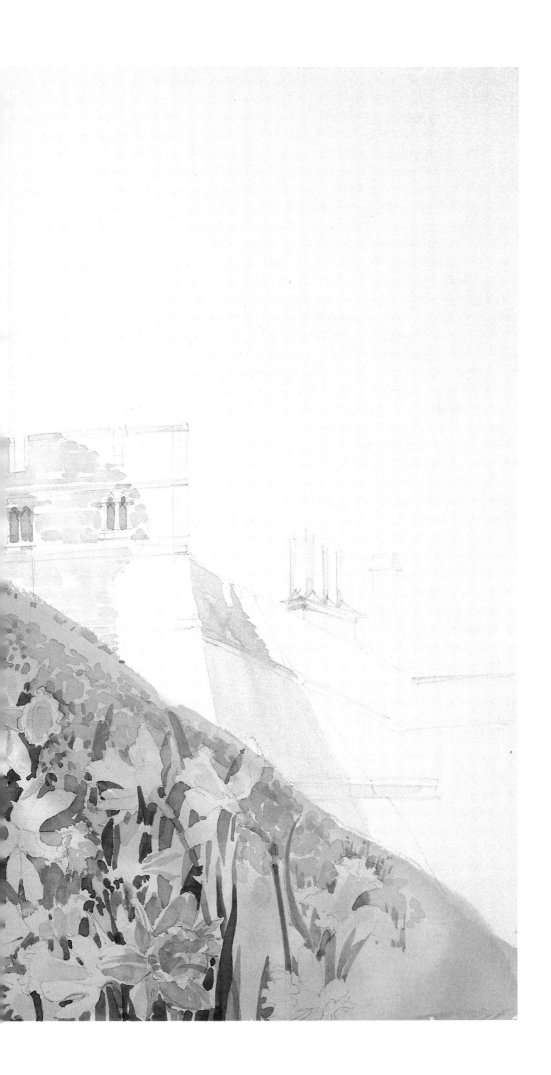

Out of a mountain of daffodils rises the Round
Tower. Each year at Easter this spectacular view is
seen from the Upper Ward of Windsor Castle

A view of Windsor Castle and St George's Chapel

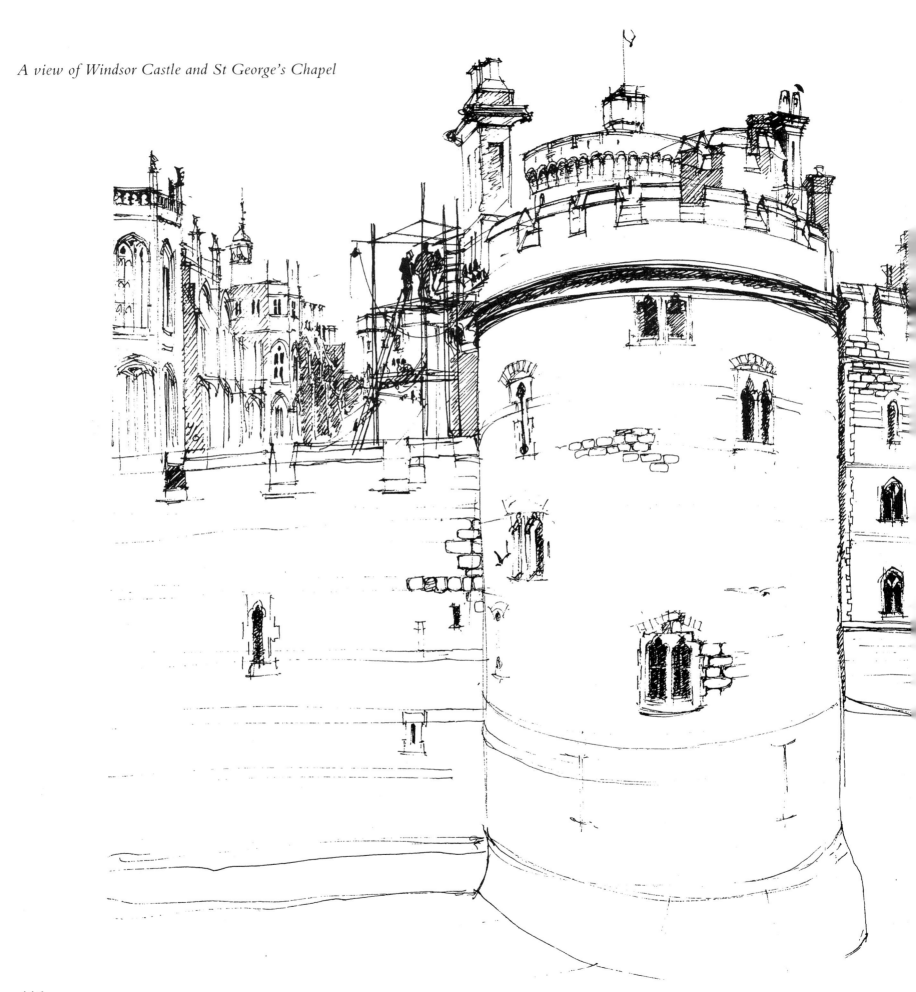

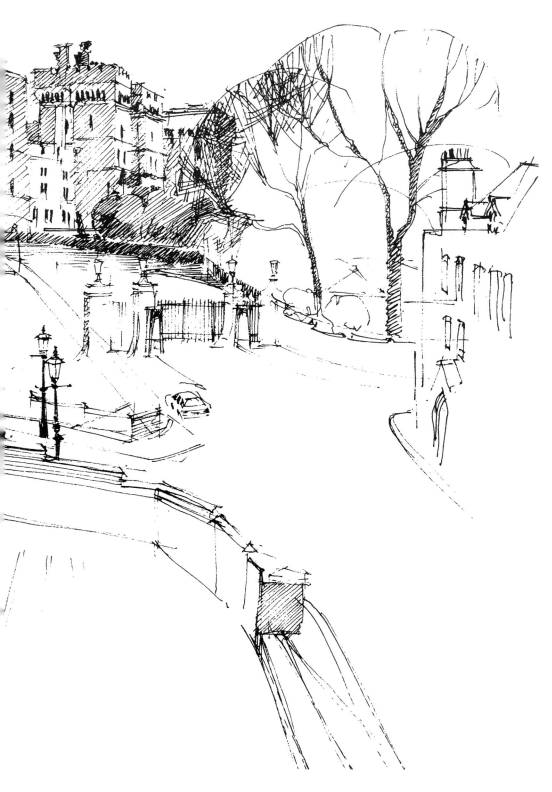

Long before William the Conqueror chose Windsor as a place on which to build a castle after his invasion of England in 1066, there had been fortifications on this thirty-five acre site. Windsor Castle is now one of the monarchy's best-known symbols. Queen Elizabeth II is the fourth sovereign of the House of Windsor, a name adopted by King George V in 1915 replacing the German name Saxe-Coburg & Gotha.

A hundred years after William the Conqueror built his wooden fort at Windsor, Henry II substituted one of stone, keeping the walls and round tower in the same positions. For more than nine hundred years, successive monarchs have had their private rooms in the Upper Ward. St George's Hall was built in the mid-fourteenth century when Edward III extended the royal apartments. He also added the tower and gateway. In the Lower Ward he had the Deanery built.

St George's Chapel was built over fifty years in the late fifteenth century. Henry VIII built the main gateway and further alterations to the State Apartments were made by Charles II who also laid out the Long Walk from the castle to Windsor Great Park. However, it was George IV's alterations early last century which have given it the appearance we know today.

Windsor Castle contains the Royal Archives, the Royal Library, the Print Room and much of the Royal Collection. Windsor Castle Royal Mews has stabling for a hundred horses, several coaches and a riding school.

It is the official residence for the Queen for a month at Easter when a whole hill of specially planted daffodils bloom, and for a week during the Knights of the Garter ceremony and Royal Ascot. Until recently, the Royal Family spent Christmas there but, while the Round Tower was being reconstructed, they spent the holiday at Sandringham House in Norfolk. The Queen often spends weekends at Windsor and sometimes entertains foreign dignitaries there.

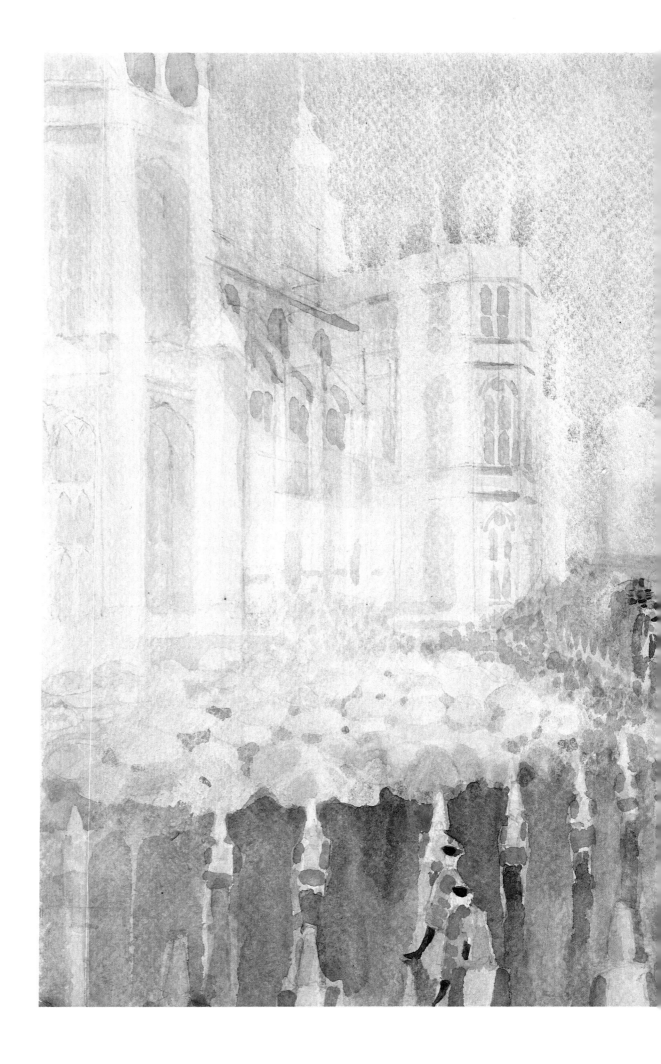

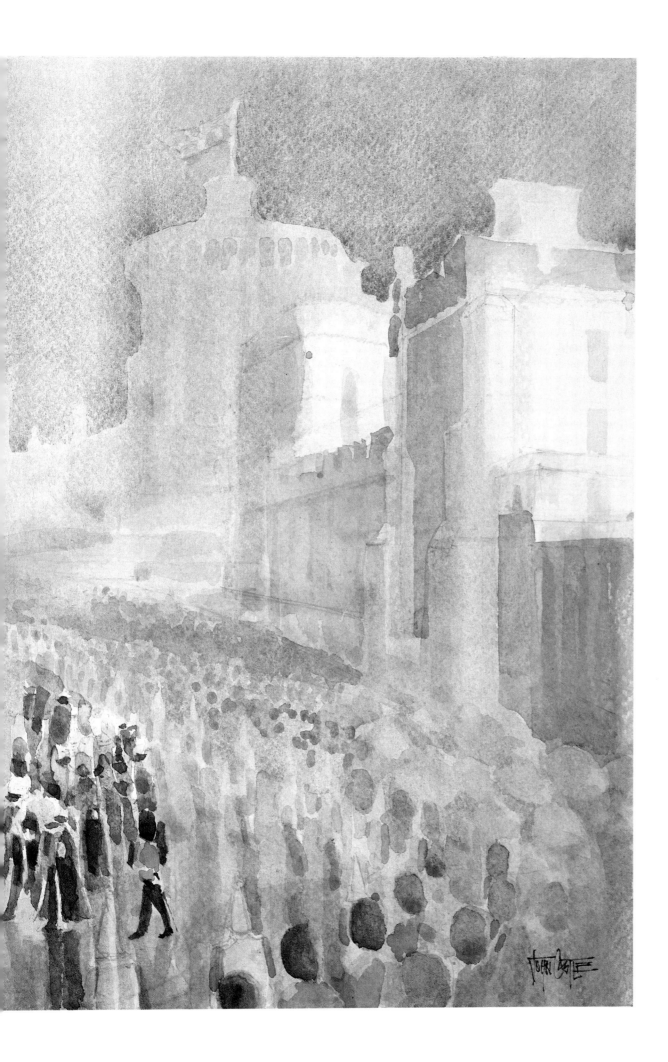

A view of the Knights of the Garter procession. Unusually, the rain did not result in it being cancelled

Paintings, however good, can hardly do it justice and then there is the problem of whether to include the cranes and scaffolding which seem to be a permanent part of keeping the castle in good repair. The weather is another problem and a painting of the procession of the Knights of the Garter proves that 'waterproof ink' still requires improvement.

The Most Noble Order of the Garter was formed by Edward III in the fourteenth century. The founder members were the King, his heir the Black Prince and twenty-four Knight Companions. The chosen patron saint was St George after whom the chapel at Windsor Castle was named. His coat of arms, a red cross on a white background, surrounded by a belt bearing the words *Honi Soit Qui Mal Y Pense* (Evil be to he who evil thinks), is worn on the left side of the velvet blue mantle of this most senior order of British chivalry. A blue garter is worn on the left knee or on the left upper arm in the case of ladies.

New appointments to the Garter are normally announced on St George's Day, April 23, although installations take place later – usually the Monday of Royal Ascot Week in June. After a private ceremony at the Castle, if the weather is fine, the twenty-six Knights of the Most Noble Order process down the hill to St George's Chapel where each member takes his or her own stall beneath his or her standard and the Garter service is held.

Compared to the formality of London, the atmosphere of Windsor is relaxed. From my vantage point on the guard-room roof, the procession turns into a sea of umbrellas and the band plays 'Don't rain on my parade' and 'Everything's coming up roses' . . . Perched in my eagle's nest, umbrella almost airborne in one hand and my pen in the other, elbows trying to anchor my paper, my task is rather more difficult than I had hoped.

The route is lined with troops of the Household Division standing to attention, swords drawn in salute. Two men in Tudor doublets and black berets carry rods of gold and silver before the Knights. After a small gap come the Royal Family Knights including the Queen and the Queen Mother, now aged ninety but still seeming to enjoy a mile-long walk in the rain. They are followed by the Gentlemen-at-Arms and the Yeomen of the Guard but my admiration and affection, as I am sure are the crowd's, stay with the diminutive, indomitable figure of the Queen Mother.

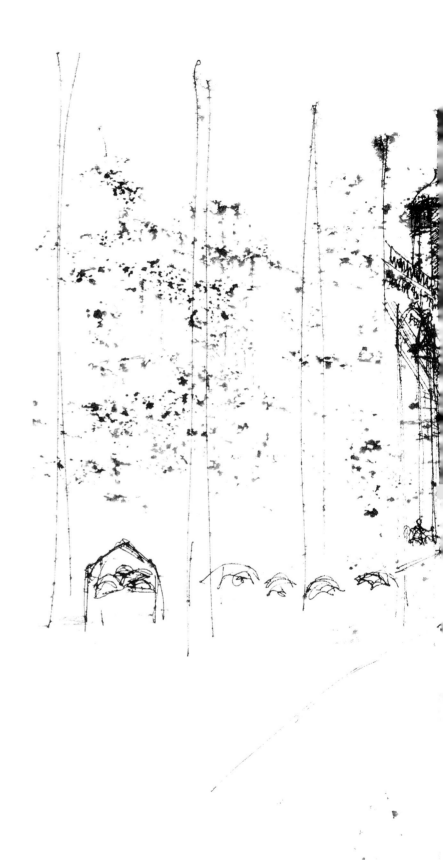

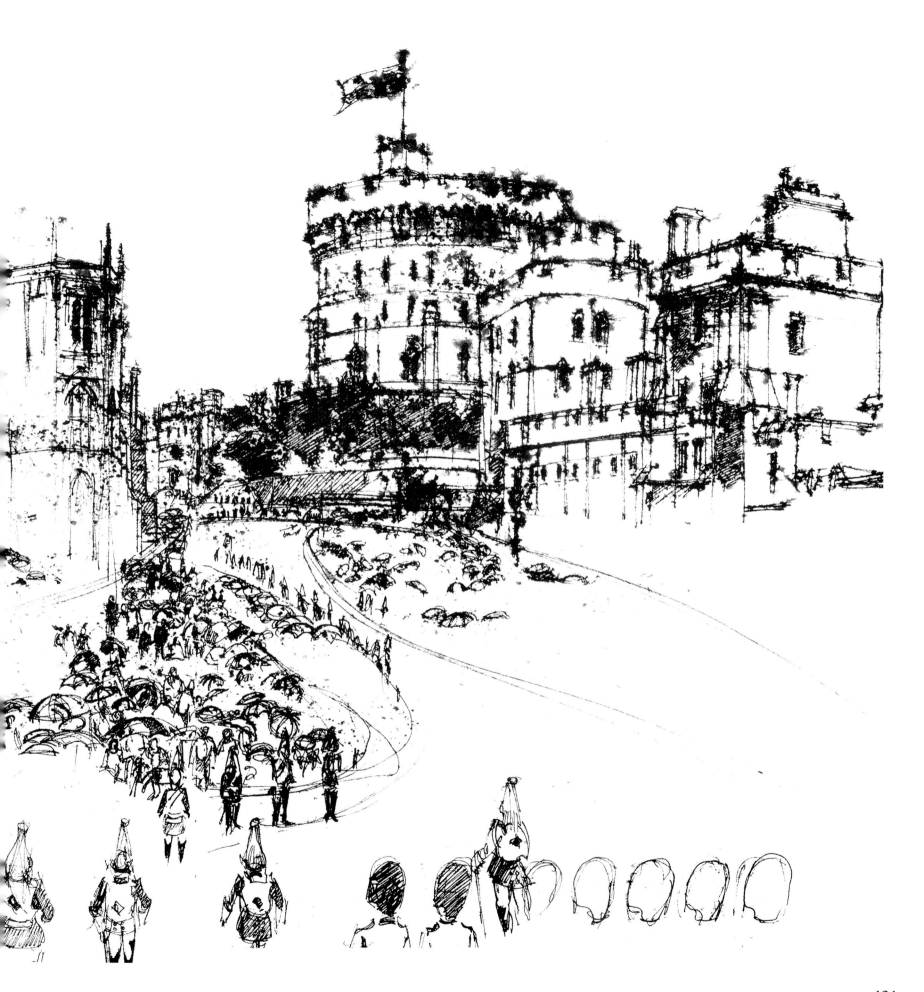

121

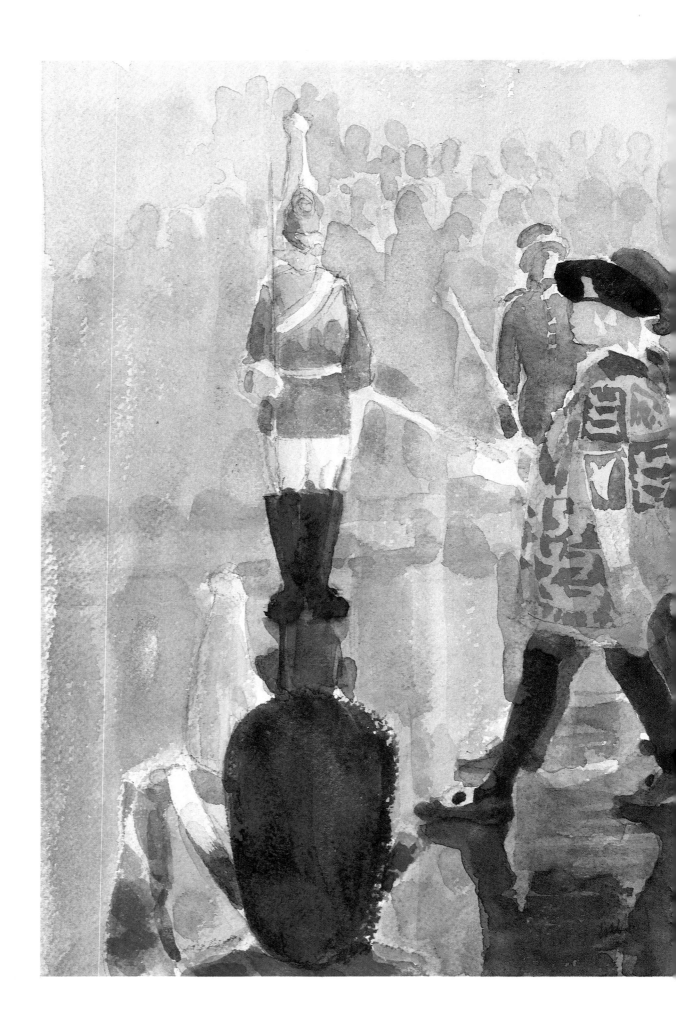

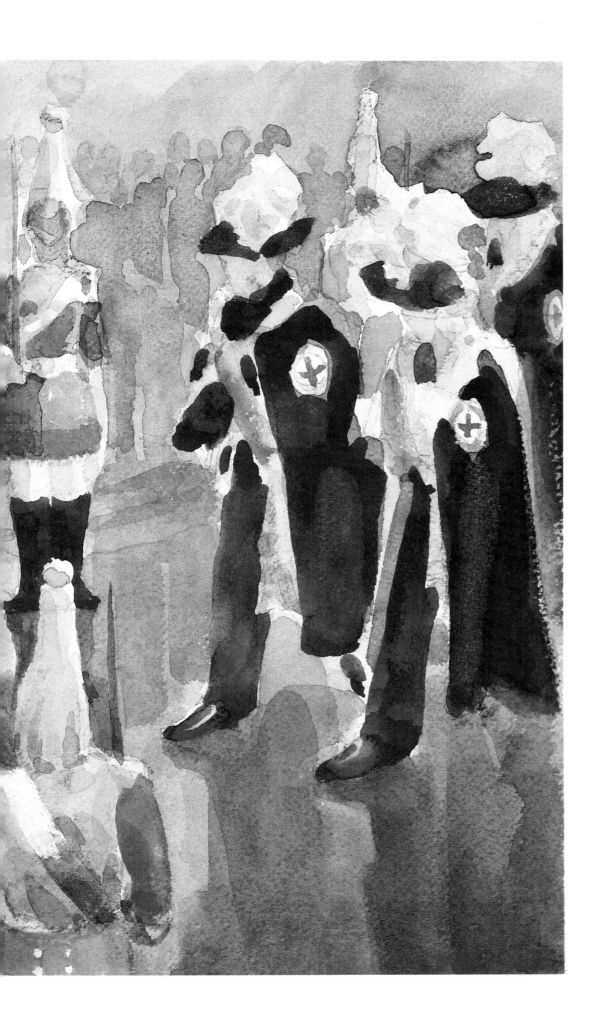

The Knights of the Garter procession –
detail

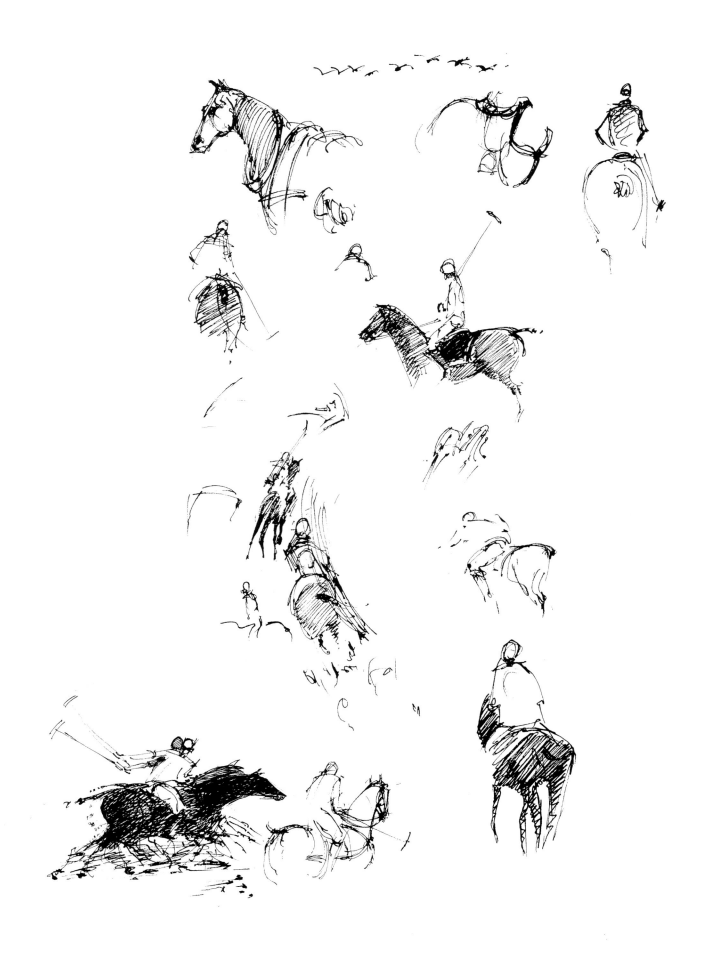

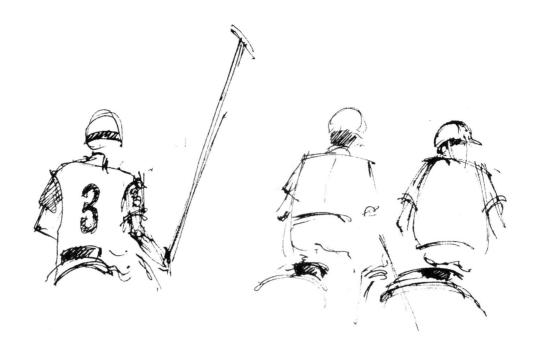

Tucked away in a quiet corner of Windsor Great Park's more than 5300 acres lies the historic polo ground of Smith's Lawn. During spring and summer each year polo players from all round the world gather here on the 160 acres of fields to play the best polo in the world.

For the uninitiated, polo is played on a field three hundred yards by sixty yards with four players aside. There are two umpires and six 'chukkas' or periods of play, each of seven minutes, though not all are always played. It is a game of speed, strength and skill and the hard helmets and kneepads are essential. It is also necessary that the goals should be collapsible on impact.

Polo is reputed to have its origins in Persia about two and a half millennia ago when the skulls of defeated enemies served for balls. Its popularity with Assam tea-planters and the Indian Army in the days of the British Raj ensured that it would be introduced into England. By the nineteen-twenties it was well-established, particularly among the Guards who had served in India. The Guards Polo Club adjacent to the Royal Box is the centre of much of the 'off-course' action.

The definitive book on polo was written by 'Marco' – in fact a pseudonym of the late Lord Mountbatten. It is therefore hardly surprising that both the Prince of Wales and the Duke of Edinburgh have been keen players, the former despite suffering a bad injury to his arm not long ago.

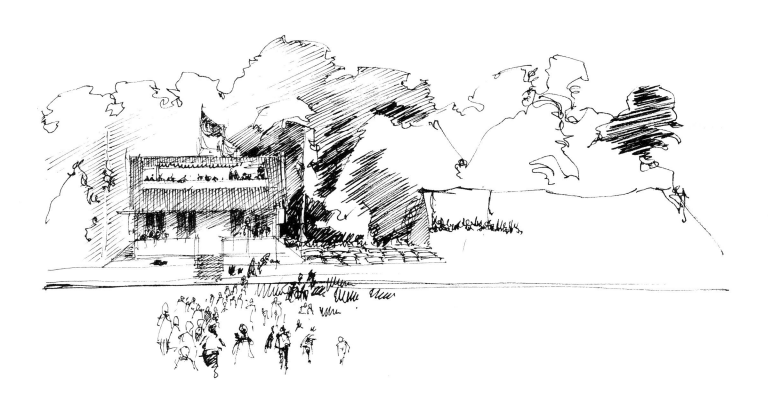

Sketches – Smith's Lawn

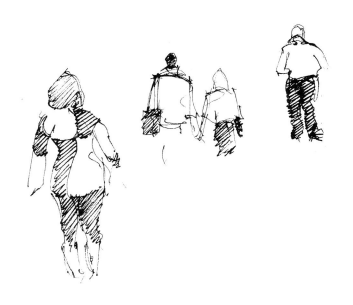

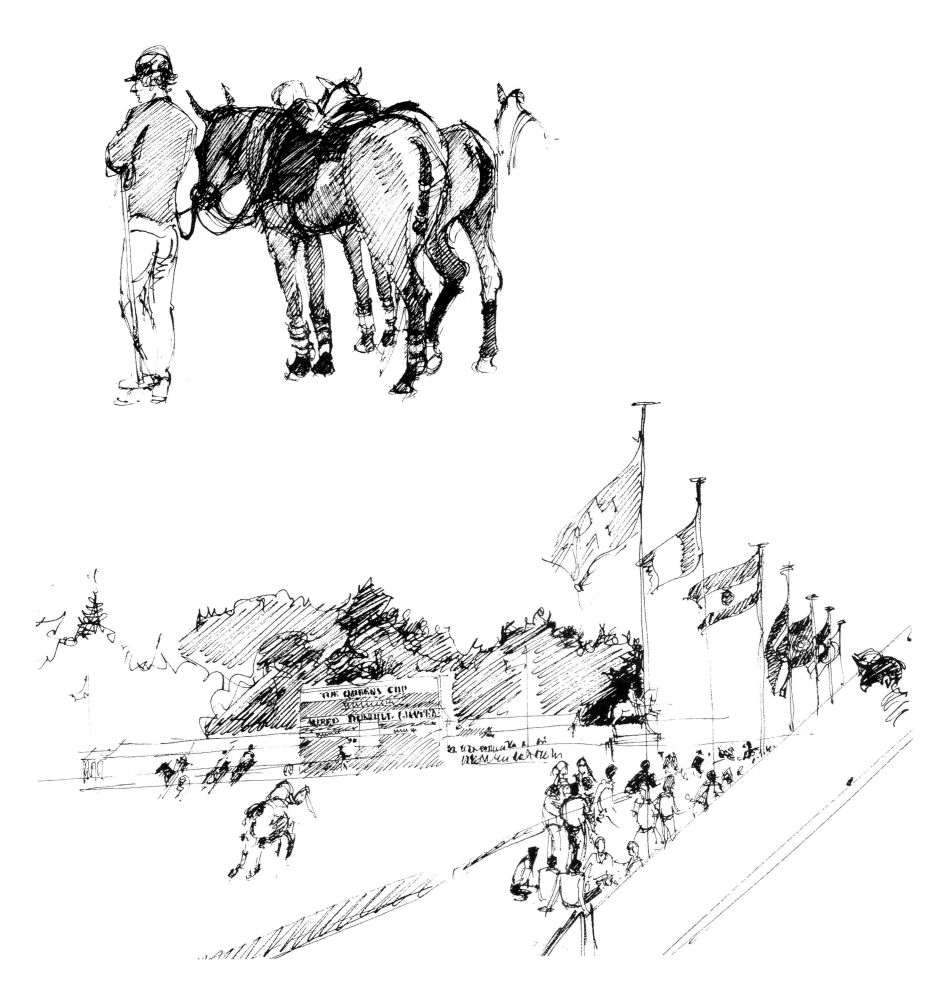

On the Sunday of the Queen's Cup final, Smith's Lawn is a hive of activity. Sponsors' hospitality tents prove that commercialism is now to be found even in the most aristocratic of sports. The paddock is surveyed by a statue of Prince Albert on horseback. Does he approve, one wonders, the picnickers eating their smoked salmon and drinking their champagne from the boots of Porsches and BMWs?

Lunch over, the Guards' band leads the players onto the field. Teams line up, the ball is rolled in and hooves thunder. The bamboo shafts of the players' mallets swish and bend. Hardwood clacks against hardwood and occasionally against a hard hat. The ponies pant and the commentator gets more and more excited.

At half-time the crowd is invited onto the ground to stamp in the divots while the players inspect their mounts and quench their thirst. At last the final bell rings and the trophies are presented, often by the Queen herself.

A final amble beside Virginia Water ends the day. By the lake there are Roman pillars, relics possibly of a Roman villa? Not so: these genuine Roman remains were brought here from Tripoli by George III. So many monarchs have taken pleasure in the Castle at Windsor and its Great Park, and it is not hard to see why that should be.

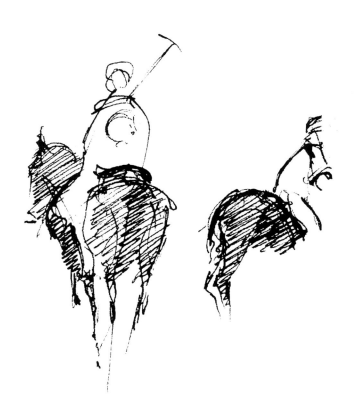

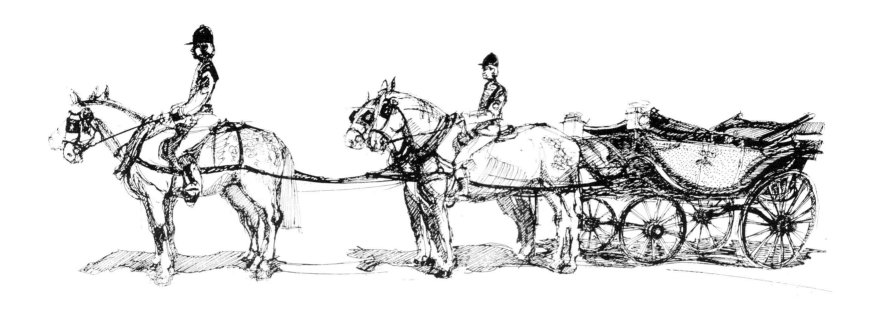

ROYAL ASCOT

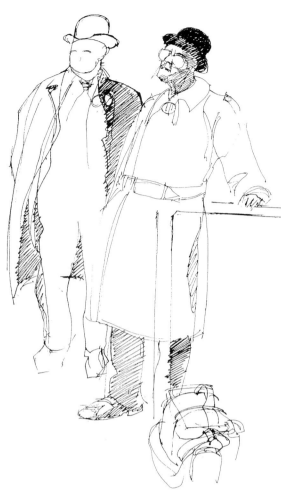

If, as they say, horse racing is the sport of kings, Royal Ascot is without question the race meeting where it is most obviously so. There are race meetings at Ascot throughout the year but in June, Ascot becomes royal. It is a tradition over several generations that members of the Royal Family attend and thus it is also one of the social and fashion events of the season. The Royal Ascot office is in St James's Palace and it is here that this particular week in the racing calendar is organized.

At the beginning of the eighteenth century, in the reign of Queen Anne, a racecourse was established at Ascot, the first meeting being held there on August 11 1711. From that date many monarchs have supported Ascot but it was Edward VII whose keen interest in racing led him to establish Royal Ascot week in the form in which it exists today.

The present Queen's enjoyment of Ascot is well-known and she usually plays host to a houseparty at Windsor during the week. But, of course, Royal Ascot is also hugely popular with the humblest racegoer. Traditional dress for Royal Ascot is morning suit for men and day dresses with hats for women. One year, lounge suits were permitted but this relaxation of standards was so unpopular that it was not tried again.

Guardians of the Owner's Enclosure

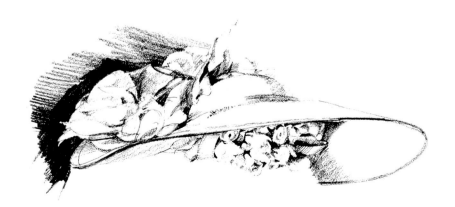

Many people's Royal Ascot begins in the carpark. There friends are met, picnics are eaten and a great deal of Pimms and champagne consumed. The traditional Ascot picnic leaves most other picnics far behind. Many are a match even for Glyndebourne. With lunch over, it is time to stroll over to the Royal Enclosure. Special arrangements have been made for me to sketch from a tree-hut where there is a good view of the paddock. The sensation of climbing up the slightly rickety ladder into my eyrie brought back memories of childhood hideaways. It was, perhaps, rather odd to be doing so in morning suit and top hat.

From my vantage point there was a view of a forest of fashion. Entry to the Royal Enclosure, the Royal and diplomatic boxes require special passes.

Picnic in the car park

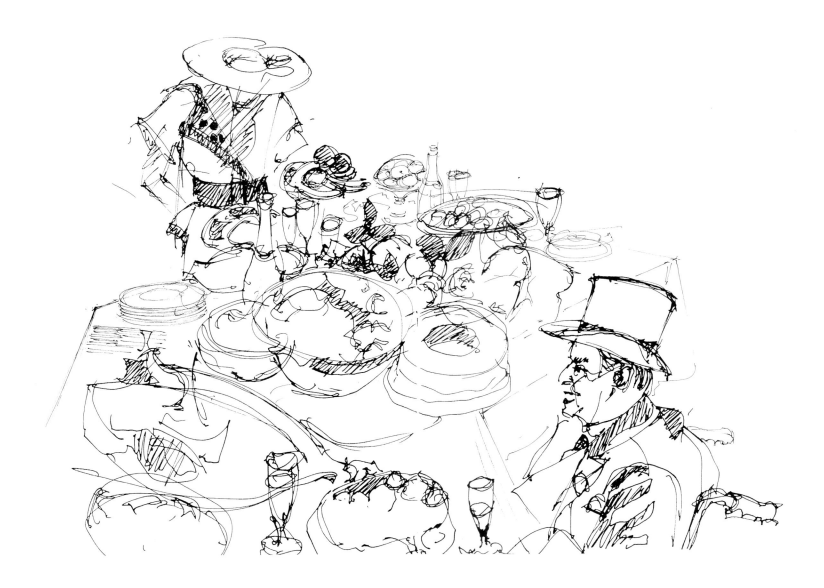

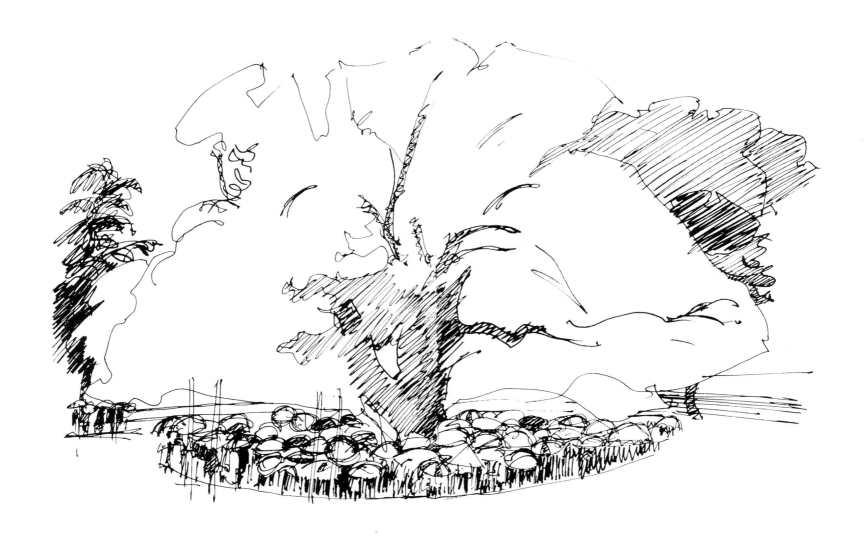

Sketches at Ascot

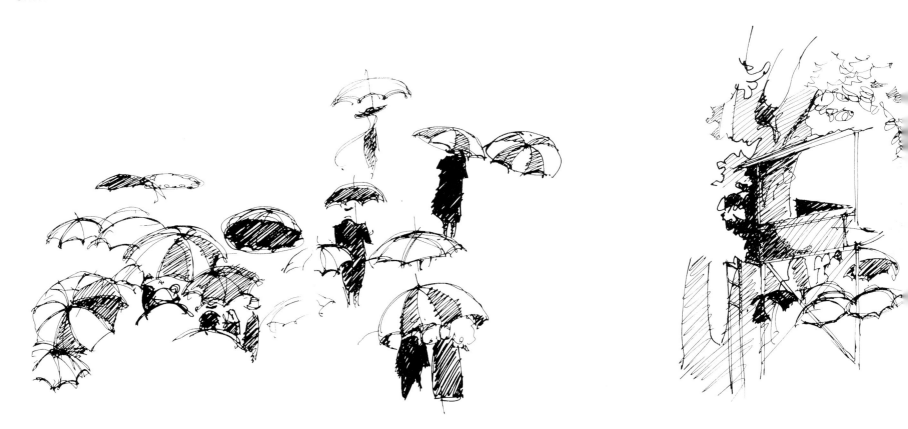

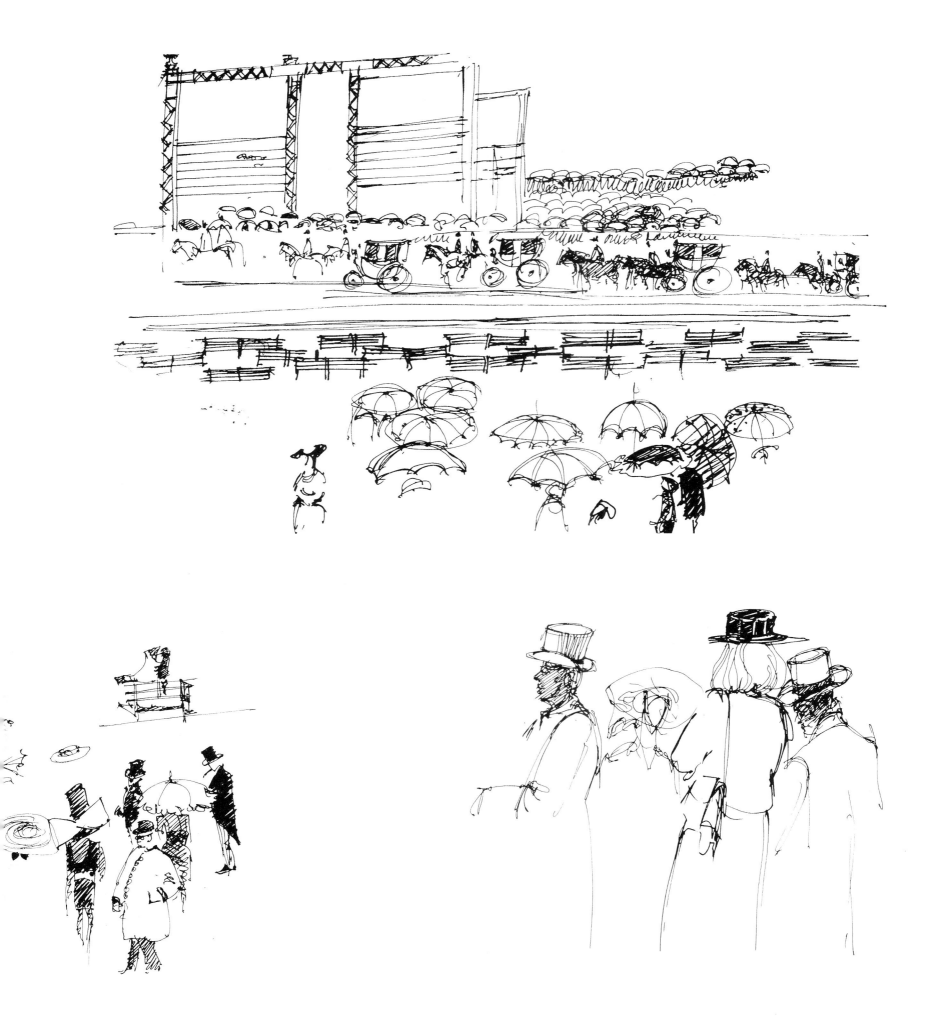

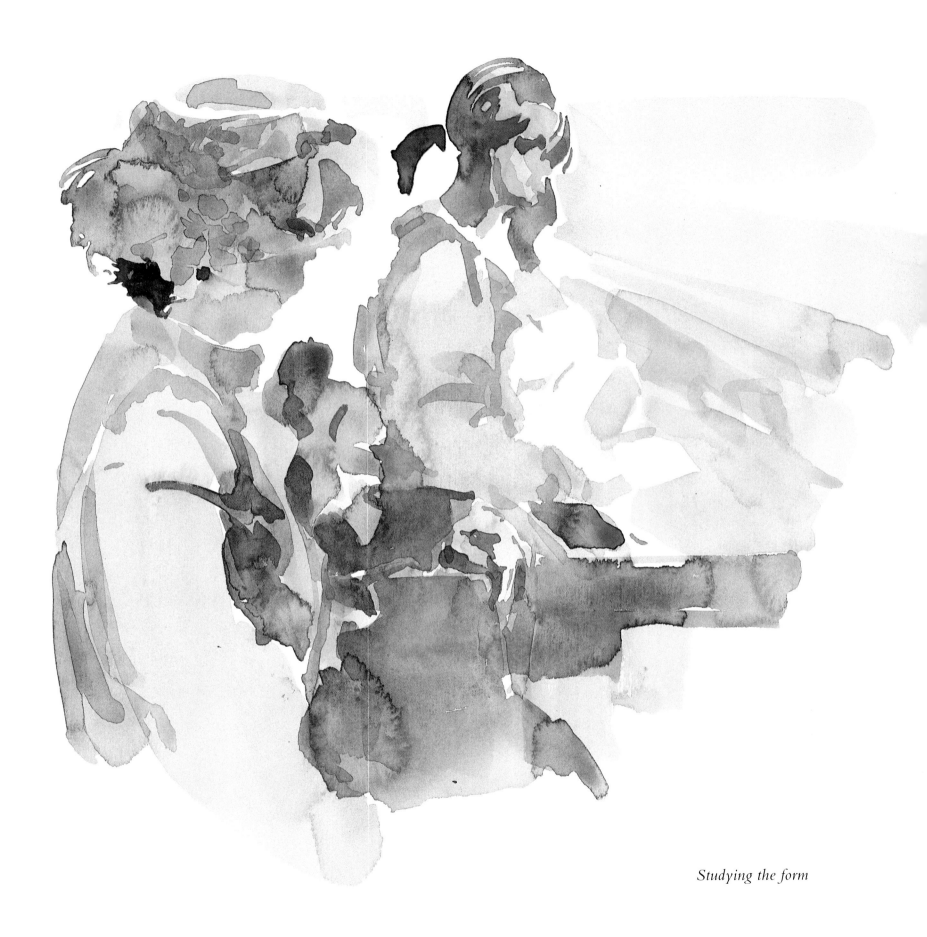

Studying the form

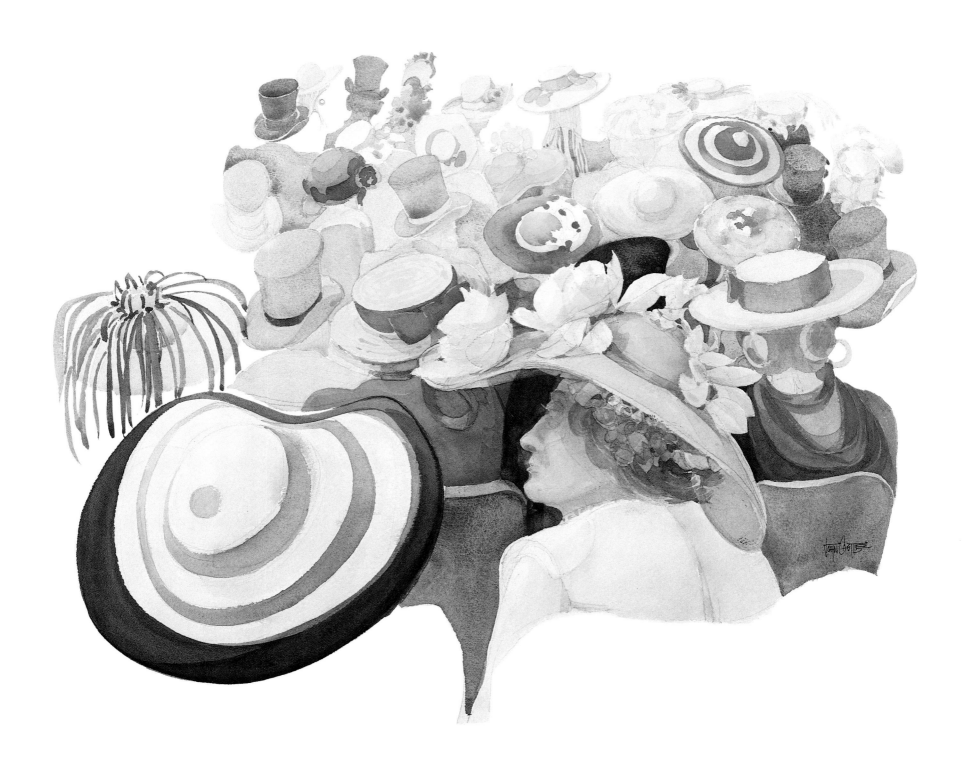

Ascot hats

A New Zealand racehorse stud owner recognized me – small world. Ladies Day is normally the Thursday of Royal Ascot and it is on this day that the fashion display reaches its climax. Unfortunately, on this occasion, the skies opened and rain drenched already scanty dresses and wilted some outrageous hats. Umbrellas and plastic bags were brought into service to protect expensive outfits. For the first time in twenty-five years the Ascot Landaus processed to the royal entrance totally covered.

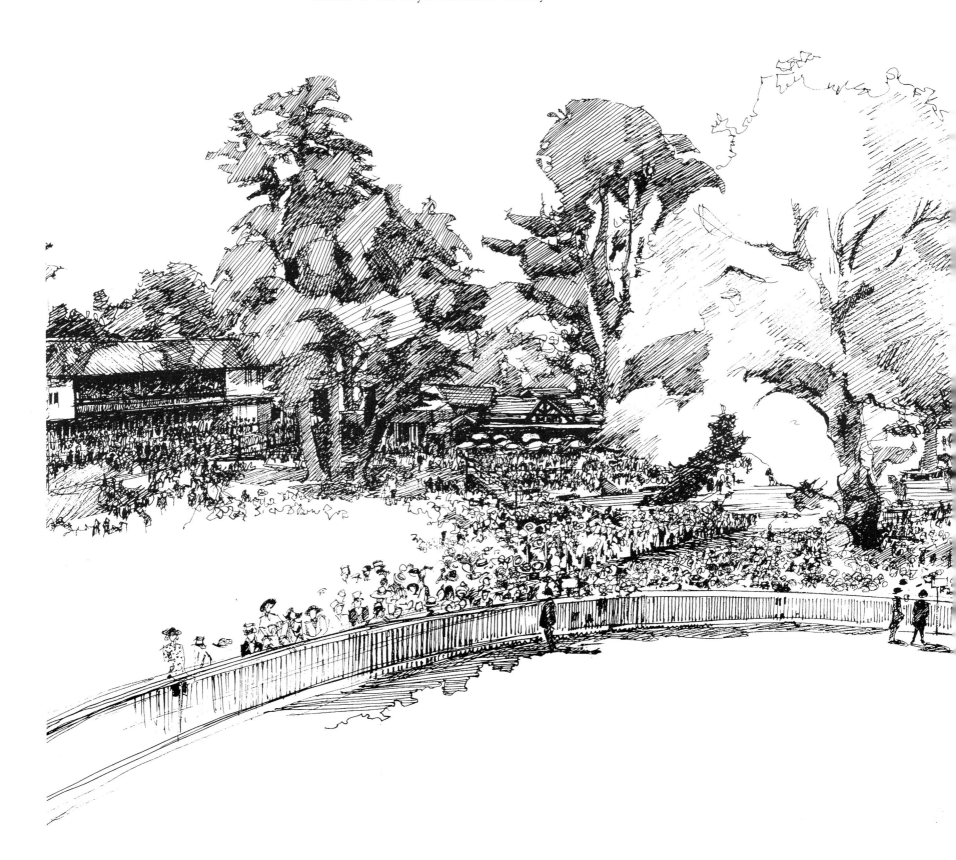

Ascot. LEFT: *The paddock.*
RIGHT: *The Royal Enclosure.*
BELOW: *Lunch*

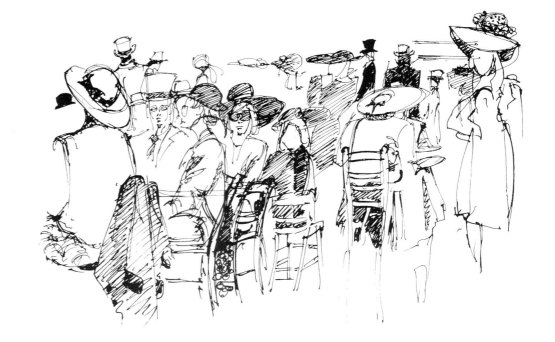

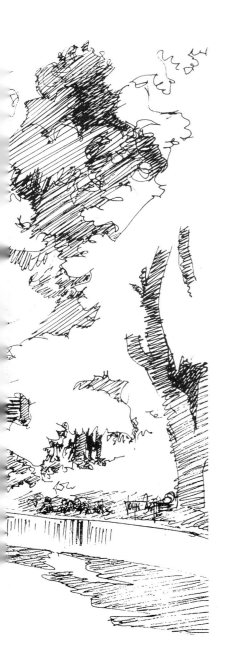

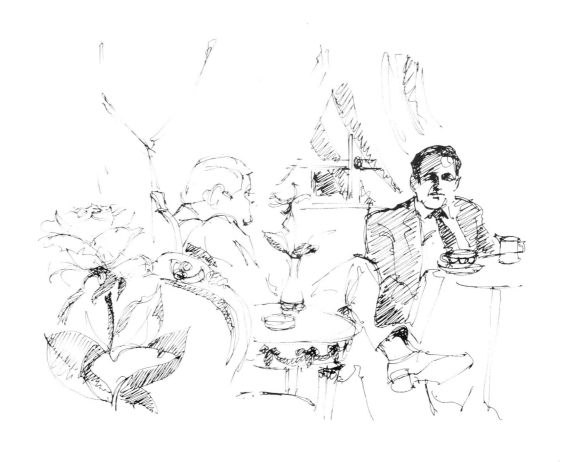

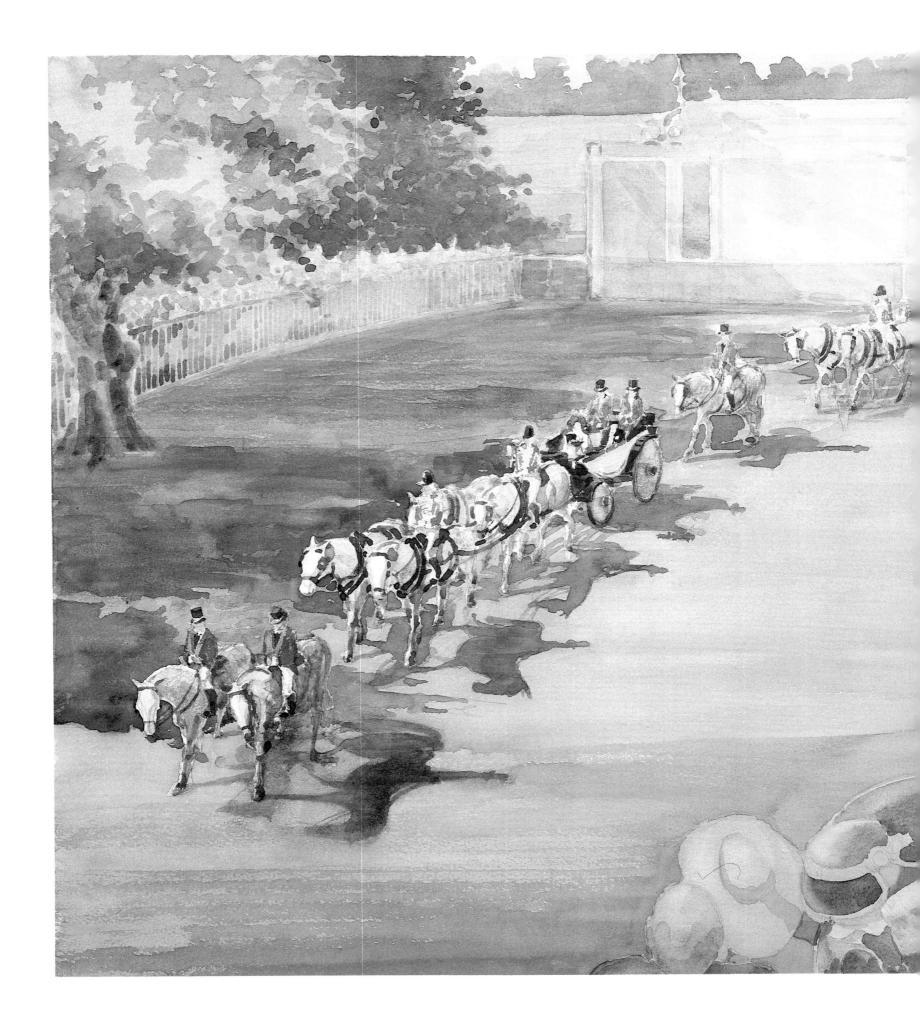

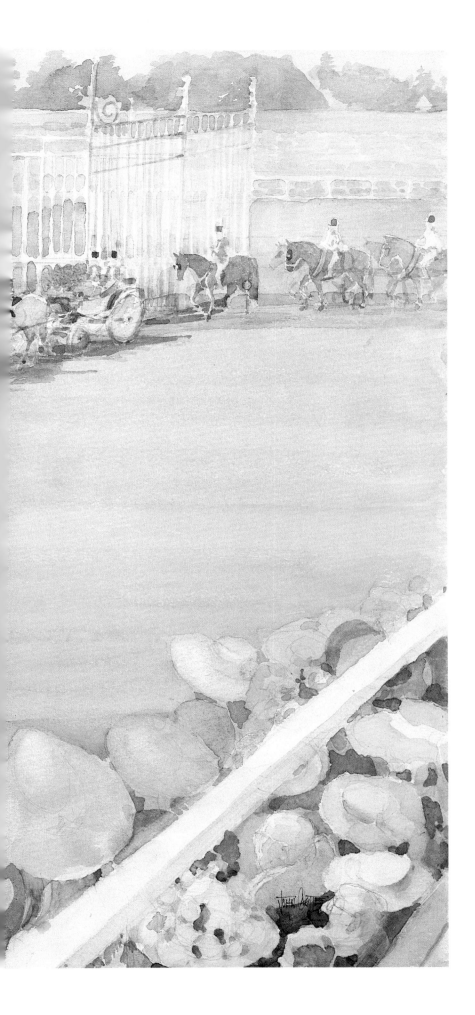

Among the more important races are the St James's Palace Stakes for three-year-olds, the Queen Anne Stakes covering the Royal Hunt Cup course and the Prince of Wales's Stakes over a mile and a quarter. This last was first run in 1862 over a mile and five furlongs. The last time this distance was run was in 1939. The race was revived in 1968 and has been run every year since on the first day of Royal Ascot. The Coronation Stakes, named in honour of the coronation of Queen Victoria, was first run in 1840 and is, with the exception of the 1000 Guineas, the most valuable race for three-year-old fillies. Several times the two races have been won by the same horse.

The Gold Cup was initiated in 1807 when it was worth a hundred guineas to the winner. On Tsar Nicholas's visit to Ascot in 1845 he presented a £500 plate and the race was known as the Emperor's Plate until the outbreak of war in the Crimea in 1854.

Perfectly organized, weather permitting, Royal Ascot is a highlight of the summer season both for followers of horse racing and those who enjoy a great party. The committed racegoer may regard the social side of Royal Ascot as a tiresome distraction but it brings together royalty and commoner in a shared enjoyment of the sport of kings.

Entrance of the Royal procession

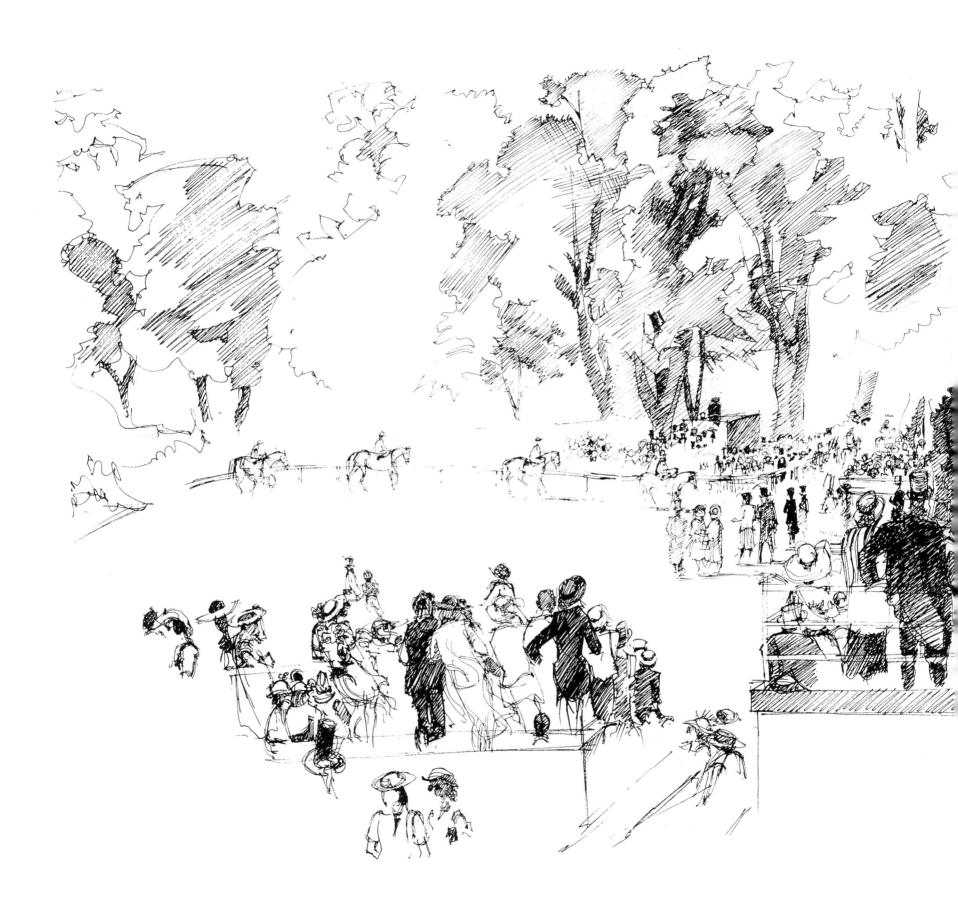

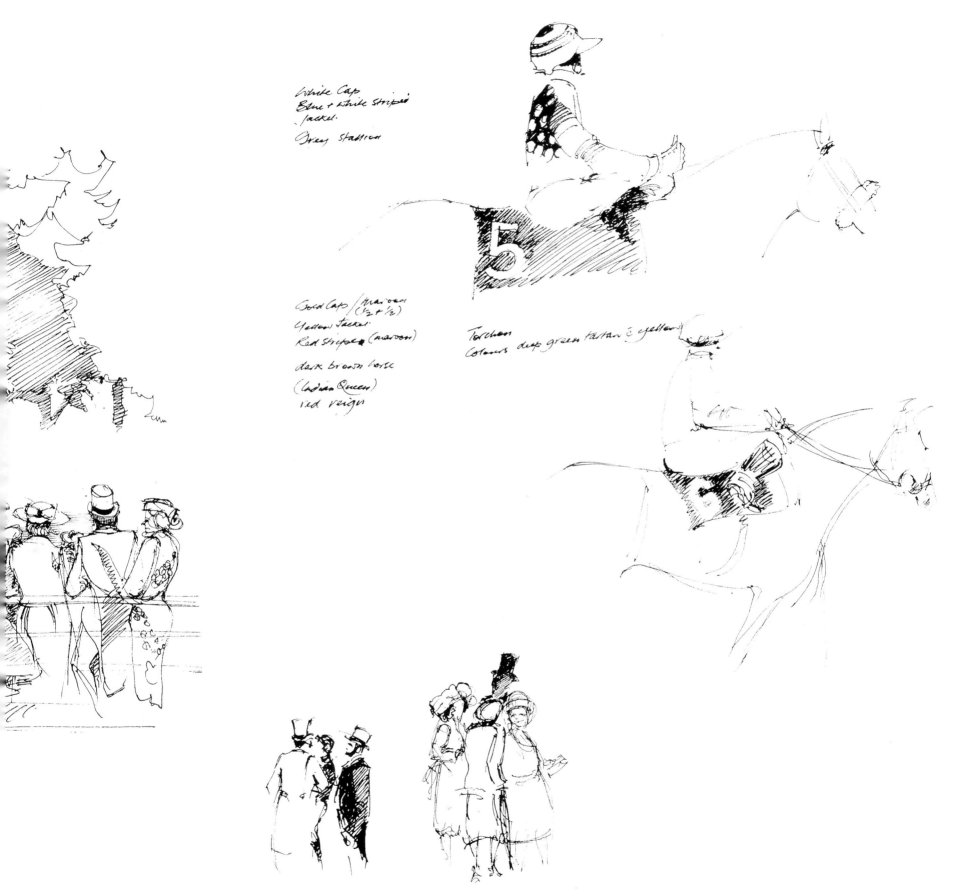

White Cap.
Blue + white striped
jacket.
Grey Stallion

Gold Cap / maroon
(½ + ½)
Yellow Jacket
Red stripes (maroon)

dark brown horse
(Indian Queen)
red reign

Torchear
Colours deep green tartan & yellow

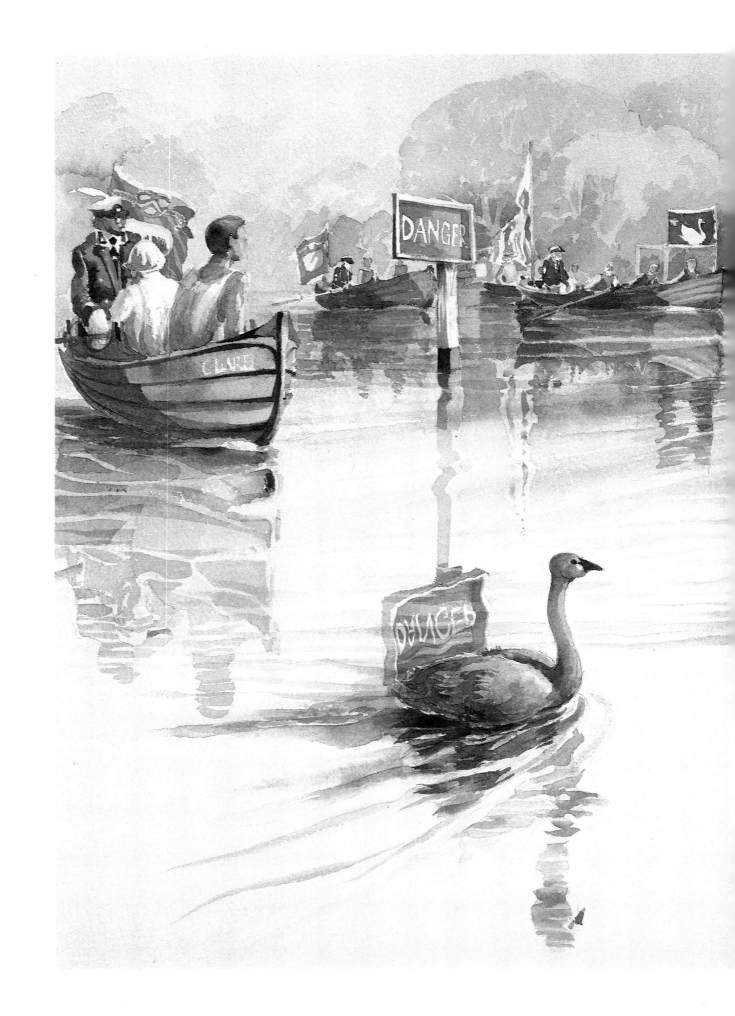

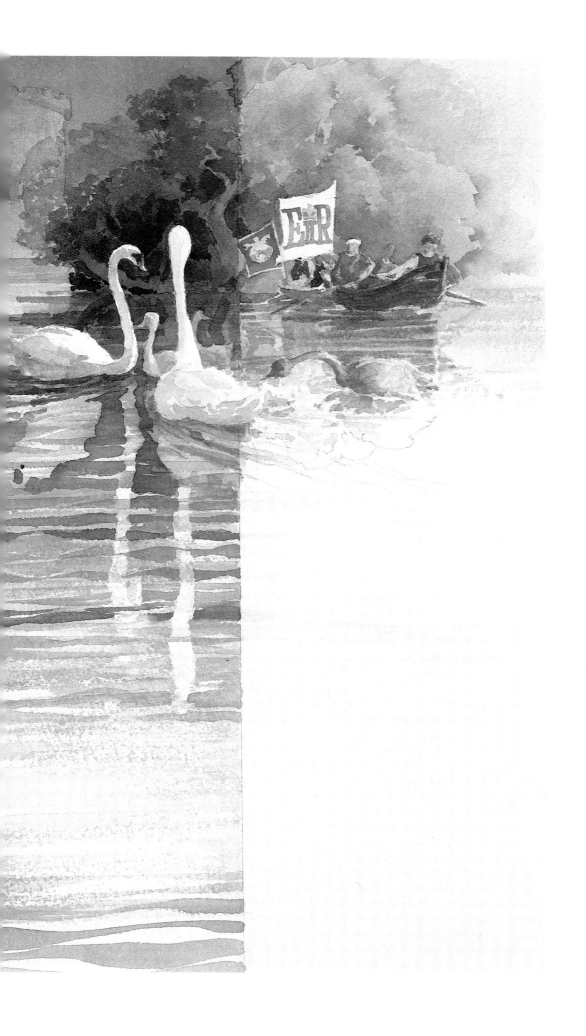

SWAN UPPING

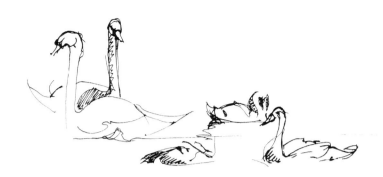

Hambledon Weir

EACH YEAR, in the third week of July, watermen representing the Queen and each of the two old-established livery companies, the Vintners and the Dyers, gather in traditional skiffs on the Thames to carry out the quaint and curious custom of 'marking' the swans. Now known as swan upping, it was originally called swan lifting or swan hopping and perhaps these names do better describe this colourful ceremony. The cygnets are lifted from the water and their bills painlessly marked with one nick for the Dyers and two for the Vintners as proof of ownership. Unmarked swans belong to the Queen.

The Adam and Eve of mute swans in England would appear to be two which formed part of Catherine of Aragon's dowry on her marriage to Henry VIII. As the mute swan was previously unknown in England, all in

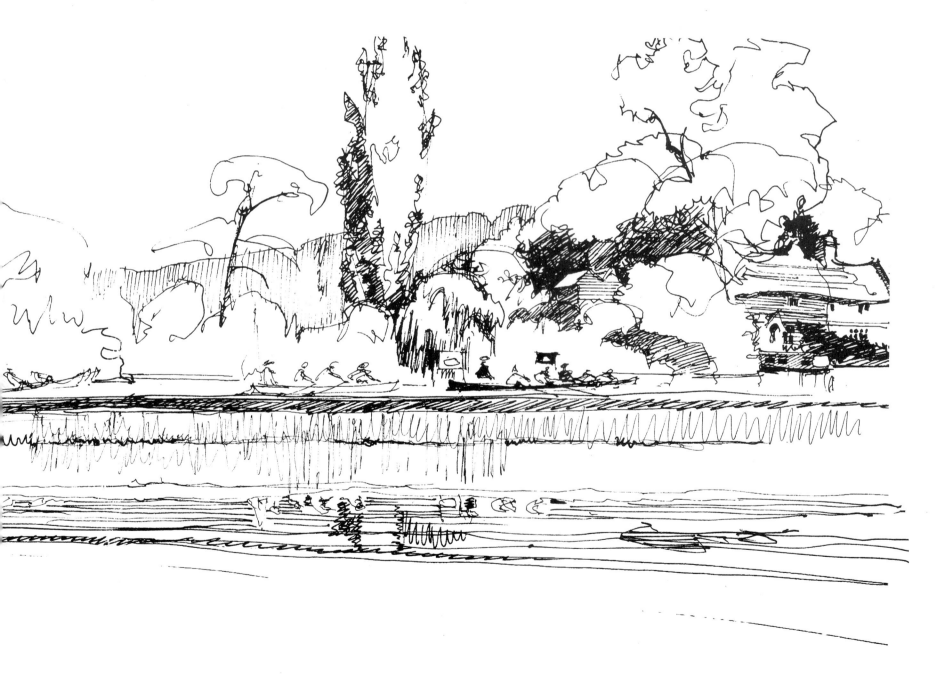

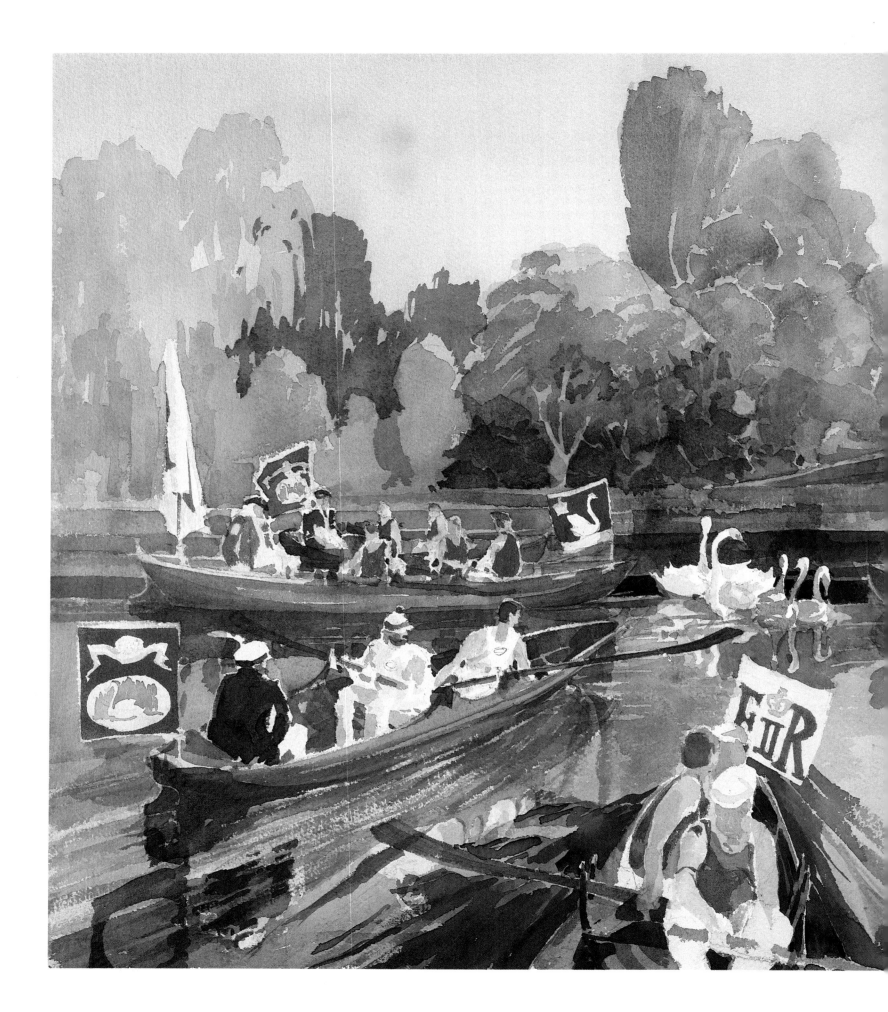

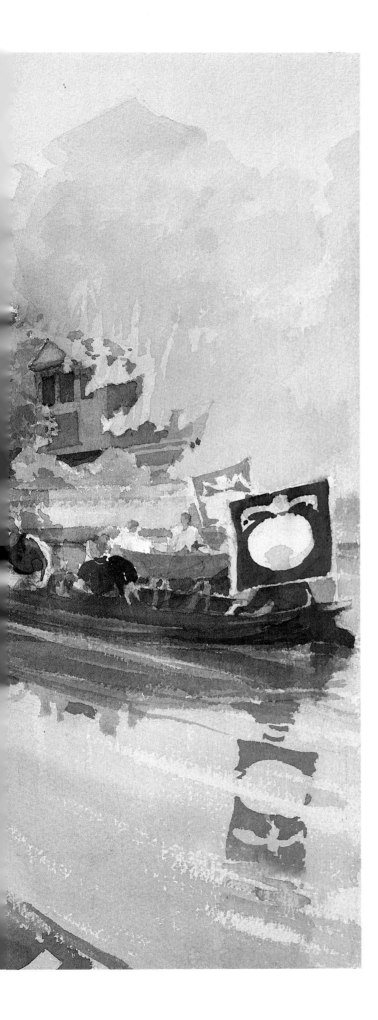

Rounding up the swans

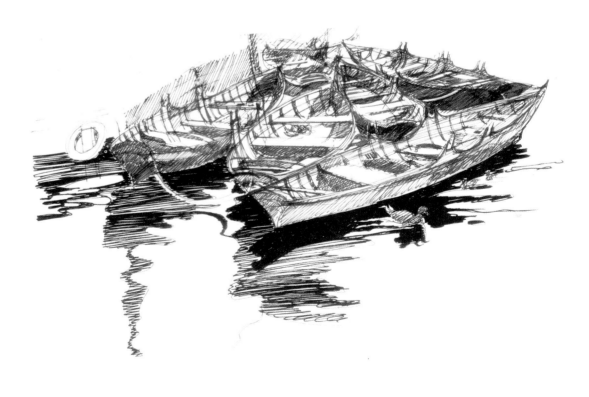

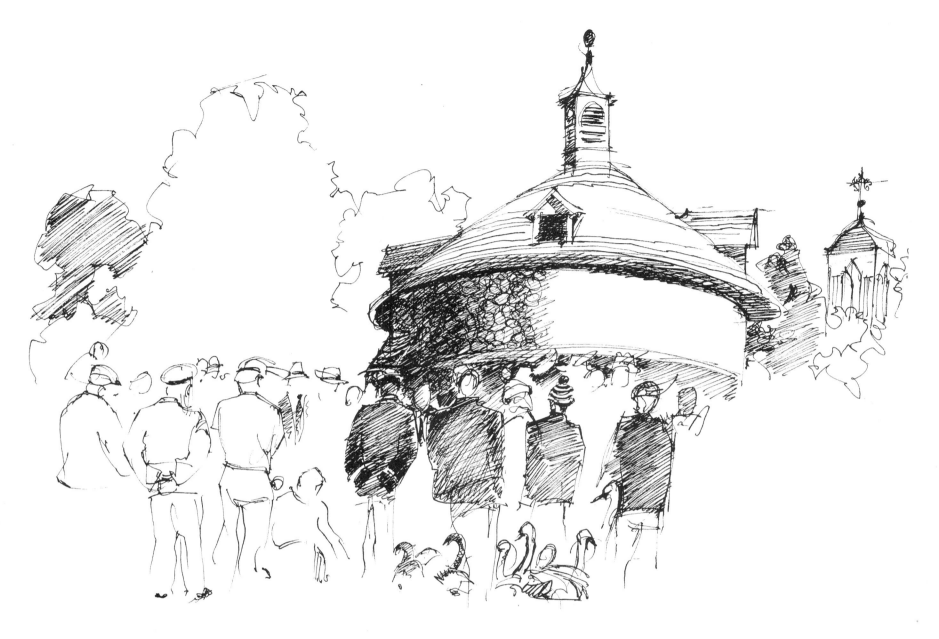

Dyers' Causeway

existence today are believed to be descended from this busy pair and hence belong to the Sovereign.

In the Middle Ages it was possible for landowners including livery companies to own swans with the king's permission but swans were regarded as ultimately the property of the Crown. In 1473 a royal charter was granted to the Worshipful Company of Vintners and a few years later to the Dyers, allowing them too to own swans on the river.

Swans are now protected and in 1971 an attempt to repeal the ancient statutes preserving swans for the Queen and, incidentally for the Vintners and Dyers, was fought off.

Swan uppers have the task of counting and marking all swans on the Thames between Sunbury and Pangbourne. The six Thames skiffs, ancient but in perfect condition, are lowered into the water and the flags of the

Companies are placed in the bows of five of them. The sixth is the Queen's Swankeeper's boat and it is larger than the others to accommodate two extra oarsmen and a representative of the Queen.

The flag of the Vintners has a swan on a red background and the Dyers' boasts a swan on a blue background. The uppers wear a uniform of white trousers and red, white or blue singlets depending on who they are representing. The Vintners' Swan Marker does his normal duty in a splendid black and silver Tudor doublet, black riding cap, silver badge and stave but this is replaced for upping with a dark green blazer with silver buttons and braid. The Dyer's Swan Marker wears a blue blazer. The Royal Swankeeper is simply resplendent in a bright scarlet jacket with gold buttons. On his arm he wears a large golden badge with his title on it.

Toward the end of the first day's work the swan uppers get a clear view of Windsor and stand erect in their skiffs and give three cheers for the Queen.

Swan upping: sketches

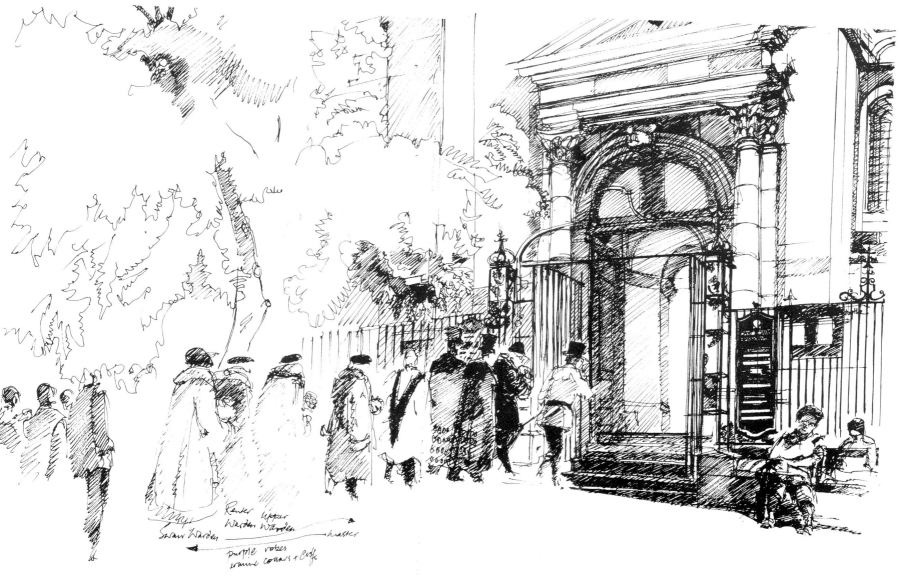

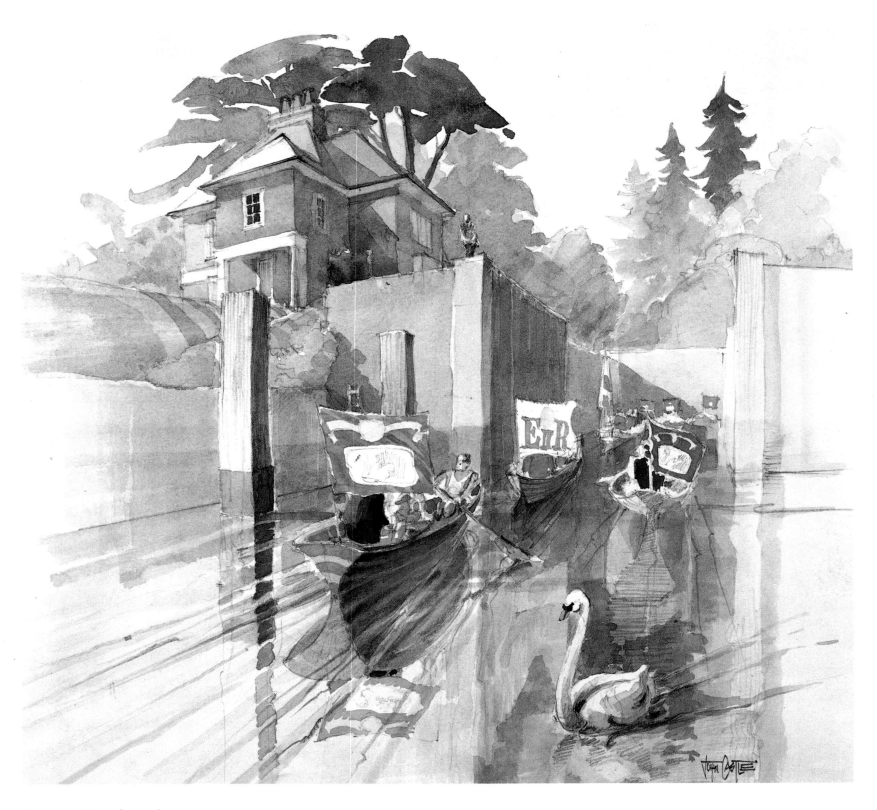

Entering Temple Lock

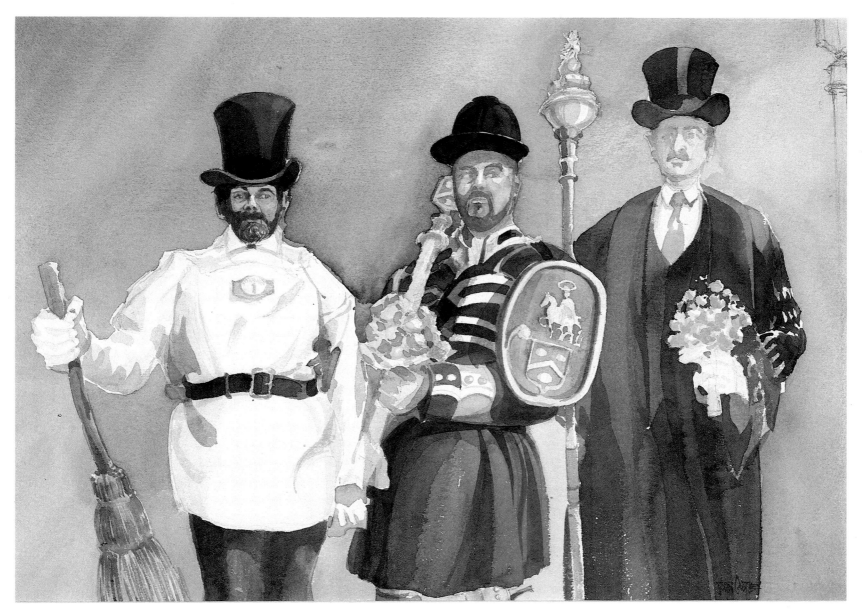

Overnight, the skiffs are stowed at Eton. Beyond Eton and Windsor the river becomes very beautiful and the uppers are joined by the barges of the Vintners and Dyers. The Masters of each Company are presented with swan families in short ceremonies. Speeches are made and the swans returned to the river.

Swan upping is a useful as well as a colourful tradition. It is a delight to witness and has given rise to much music and verse. It is this kind of royal ceremony which is a precious part of our heritage and worthy of record.

Vintners three. LEFT TO RIGHT: *The Road Sweeper, the Swan Marker and the Beadle*

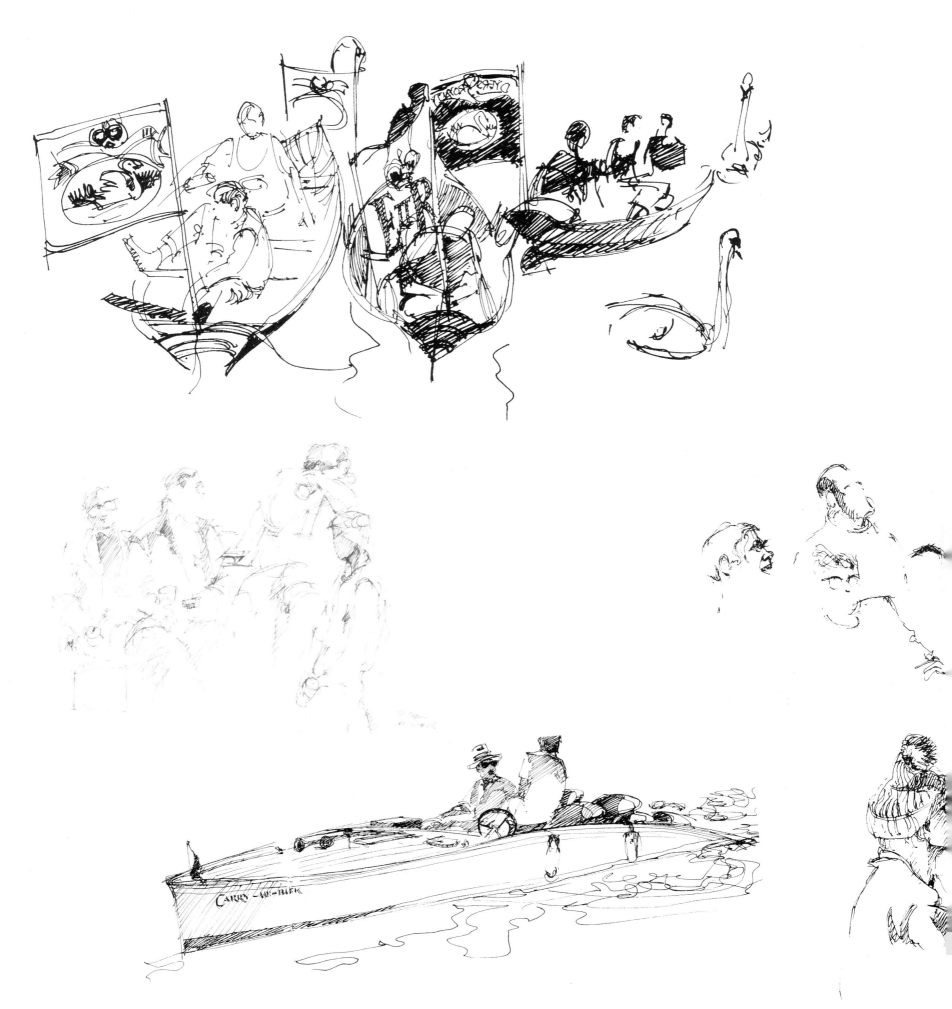

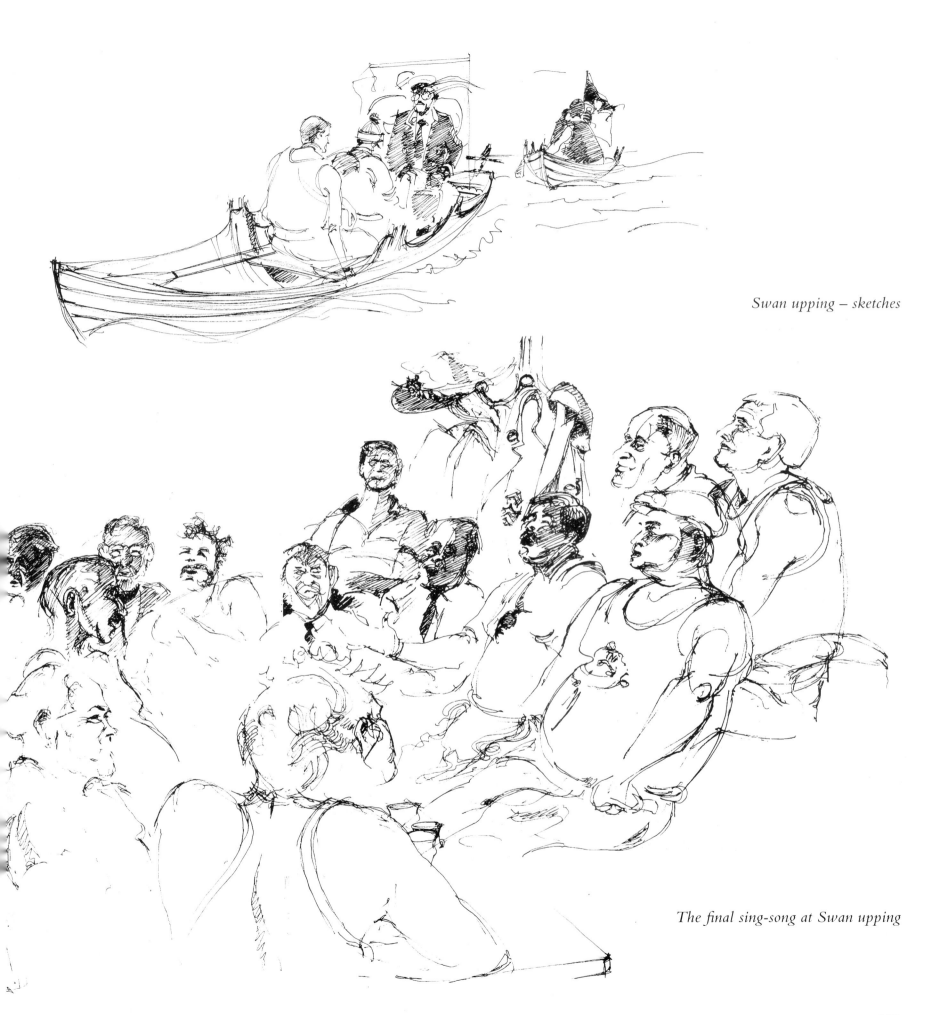

Swan upping – sketches

The final sing-song at Swan upping

153

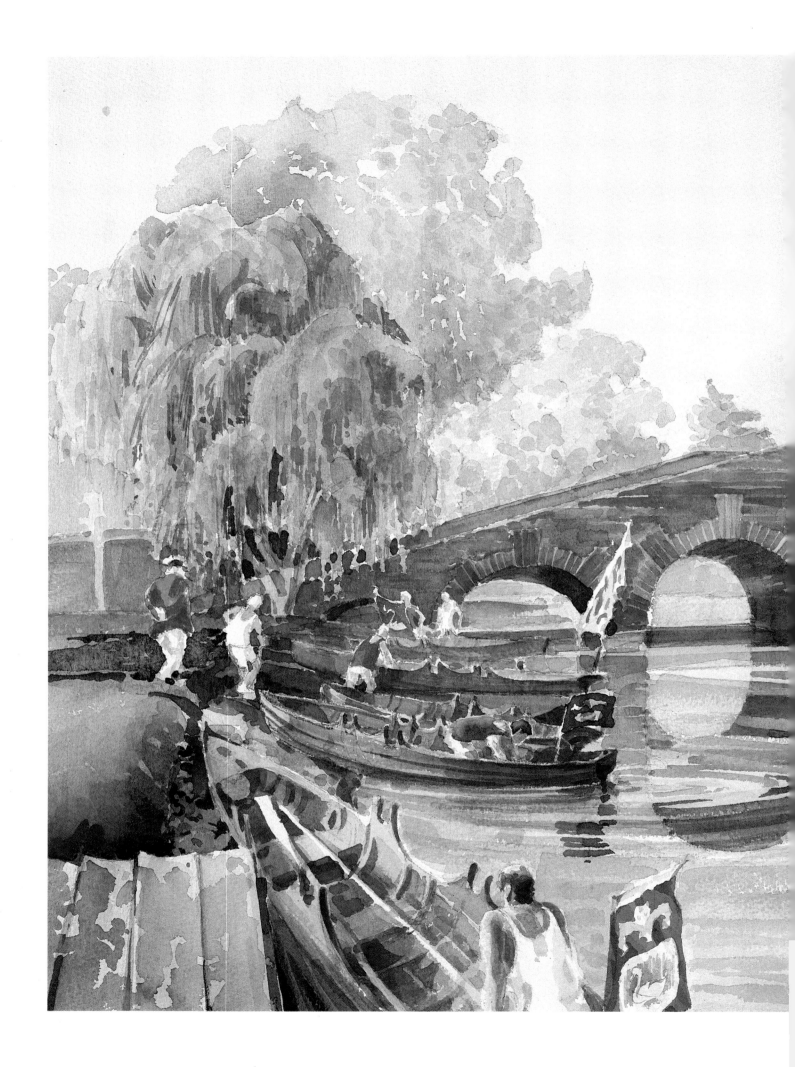

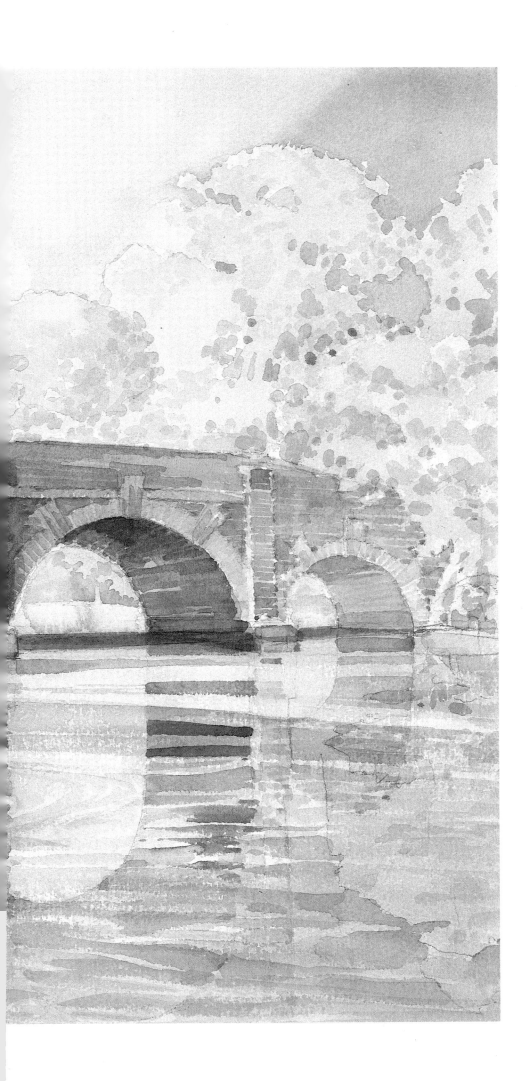

Swan uppers at the bridge at Sonning

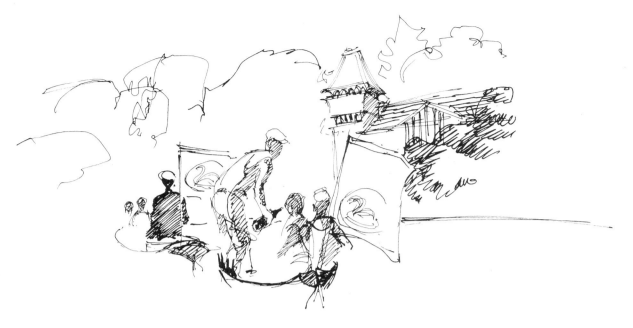

Swan upping is a complicated business replete with arcane rituals. The Vintners for instance, begin upping in mid-July with a church parade. The procession is led by the Swan Marker carrying his mace in one hand and a nosegay of perfumed roses as protection against the plague in the other. All traffic stopped, they walk the hundred and fifty yards from their hall in the City of London to the church of St James Garlickhithe. A Swan Feast is held in November, by which time the cygnets are big enough to eat, although of course they are not eaten nowadays.

Early on the first morning of swan upping, Sunbury is quiet. The skiffs in the river drift lazily in the breeze. The engine of the support boat buzzes. A family of swans look curiously at the preparations and glide on.

One shout of 'all up' and the tranquillity is transformed into tremendous activity. The swan uppers scramble into the boats and chase after the swans. Once the cygnets are caught they are boarded and marked and returned to the water unharmed.

'Rounding' the cygnets can be dangerous and involves making a ring of skiffs around the cygnets with the cob (the male swan) on the outside. The cobs do not like being parted from their brood and often end up chasing the chasers. 'Boarding' the cygnet is even more difficult. One oarsman stands in the boat nearest the hen and reaching out of the skiff tries to tie its legs with soft twine. If successful he can pick up even a heavy bird and put it in the skiff. Strangely enough, when landed, a mother swan sits contentedly in the boat admiring the view and not struggling.

First-aid is also administered to the swans during upping. Fishing lines, hooks and flies are removed. Fortunately, lead sinkers which poisoned so many swans have been made illegal. For a time, mute swans were in danger of becoming extinct but now numbers are increasing dramatically.

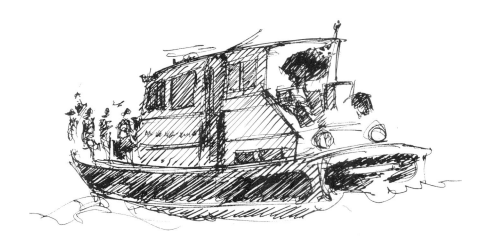

THE ROYAL WATERMEN

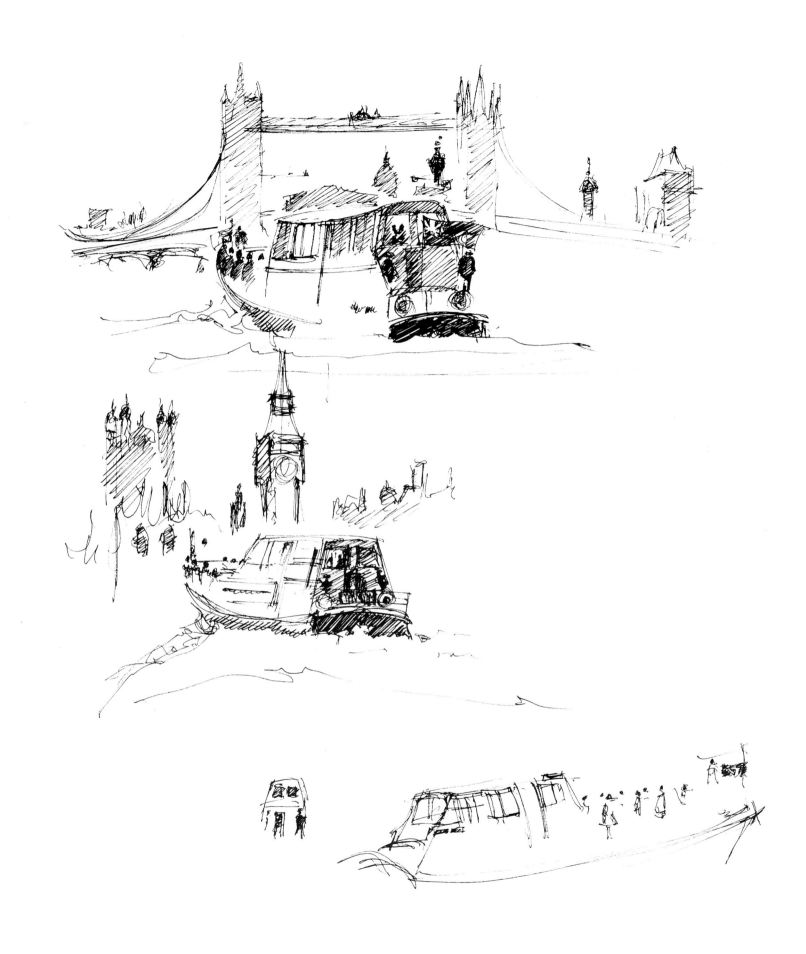

THE ROYAL BARGEMASTER and the Royal Watermen are among the most ancient of all appointments to the Royal Household and their headquarters is St James's Palace. Until the last century, the Thames was London's main highway and men of substance employed their own oarsmen to row their barges.

The Sovereign was no exception and employed some forty-eight Royal Watermen whose duty it was to row the royal barges up and down the Thames between the palaces of Windsor, Hampton Court, Greenwich, the Tower of London and Westminster. Then as now, it was a great honour to be chosen as Royal watermen. This appointment is different from others to the

Approaching Westminster Pier

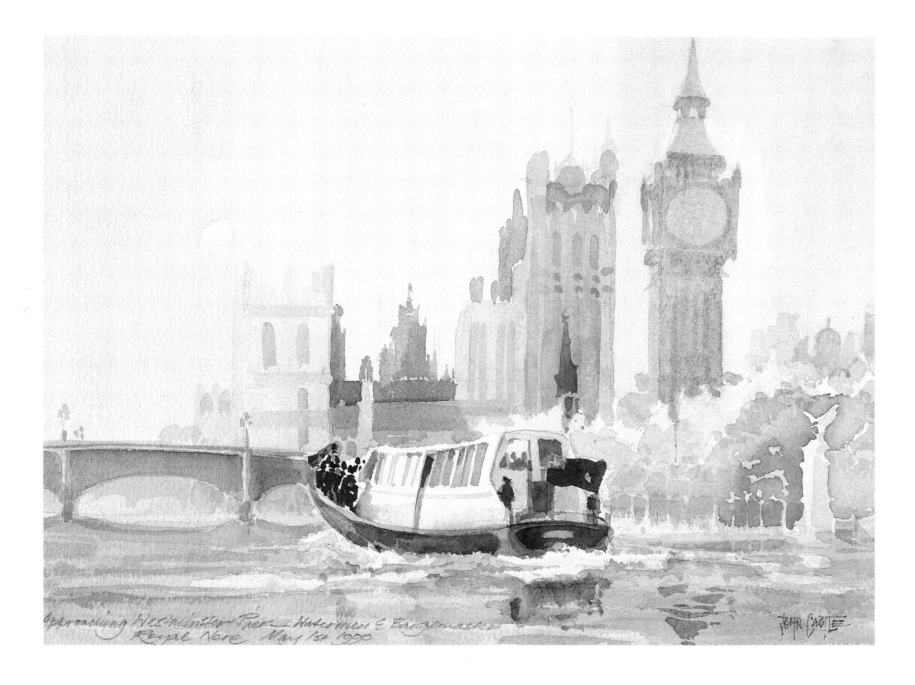

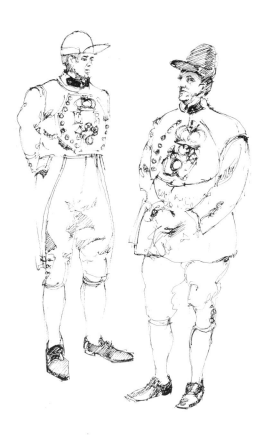

Royal Household in that they are not full-time appointments and Royal Watermen now have a purely ceremonial role. They are appointed from Thames watermen making their living on the river, in boatyards, manning tugs, lighters and launches.

There are two watermen's stones, one at Teddington and another at the Nore, between which any fare-paying passenger must be carried by a licensed waterman. However, the Royal Watermen are selected from any part of the river not just the licensed area. For instance, as many as eight of the Royal Watermen come from the upper river.

Apprentices to Thames' watermen working on the river are eligible to row in an annual race to win the Doggett's Coat and Badge. The race is administered by the Fishmongers, the ancient livery company. After the race, if the apprentice is of good character, he maybe invited to be a waterman to the Waterman's Company. The scarlet coat and cap of the Doggetts is similar in some ways to that of the Royal Watermen but is easily distinguishable by the large silver badge worn on the left arm.

The uniform of the Royal Watermen is a scarlet doublet with full skirts and scarlet collar with dark-blue velvet gorget patches in front with a small button. On the chest he wears a triangular plastron fastened with gold buttons. The stockings are scarlet, the shoes black calf and laced. There is a dark-blue velvet hunting cap and white cotton gloves.

In charge of the Royal Watermen is the Royal Bargemaster. His coat is scarlet cloth, single-breasted, edged with gold lace. There is a scarlet collar with a dark-blue velvet gorget patch and small buttons. The base of the collar

ABOVE: *Waterman and Bargemaster*

RIGHT: *Waterman's Wherry*

OPPOSITE: *Royal Waterman in regalia*

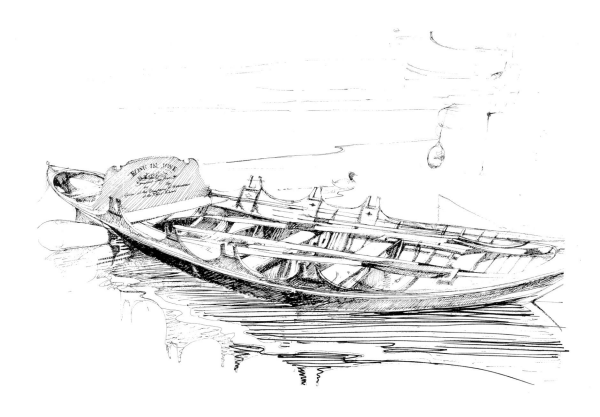

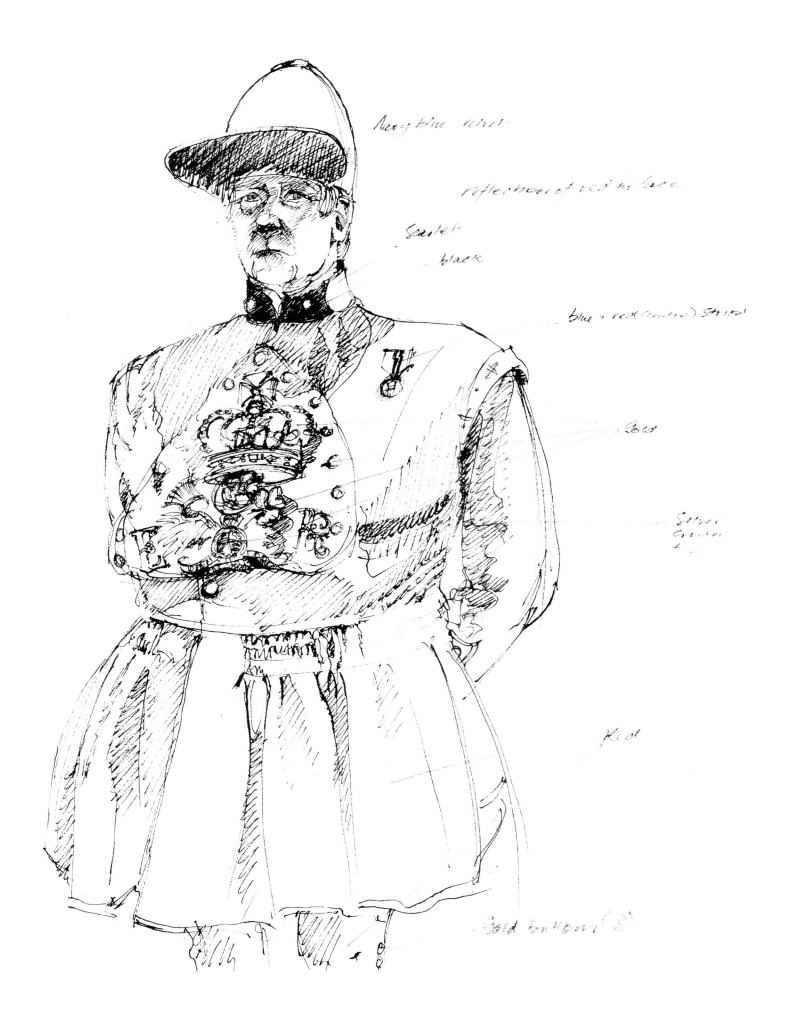

navy blue velvet

reflection of red in face

scarlet

black

blue + red (centre) stripes

gold

silver
Crown

Red

gold buttons (8)

161

and the pocket flaps are edged with gold lace. Octagonal plastrons with colour on the thistle and shamrock are worn on both back and front. Chased silver-gilt badges bear the royal arms encircled by a garter. His stockings are white and his shoes black patent leather with gilt buckles. He also wears a dark-blue velvet hunting cap. In his position as foreman of the Royal Watermen he takes his place at the bow of the *Royal Nore*, the state launch, holding the royal banner. Watermen line either side of the foredeck in the centre of which is a large crown on a plinth. The crown and banner are only present when the Queen is on board.

By contrast to the simple, modern lines of the *Royal Nore*, barges of yesteryear were ornate and individually designed. Known as shallops, examples can be seen in the Maritime Museum. Important passengers sat on a raised platform at the stern. Two shallops have been built in recent years at the boatyards of the Royal Watermen at Sunbury – *Man for all Seasons* and *Lady Mayoress*. Surprisingly lightweight considering their size, the latter made its first appearance at the start of 1991's Great River Race.

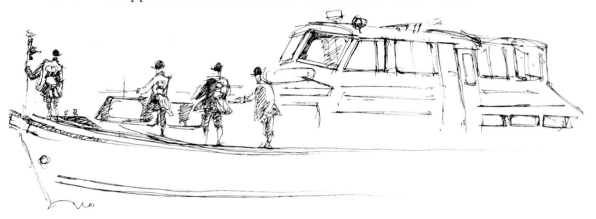

Watermen of the past were the taximen of their time using wherries similar to the one illustrated. Today, the role of the Royal Watermen even though ceremonial is important. They are on duty whenever the Queen and her guests travel on the Thames, always a memorable sight. The Royal Watermen are also present manning some carriages during state visits and at the State Opening of Parliament symbolizing their role in previous centuries when such ceremonies were river based.

At the State Opening of Parliament the Royal Bargemaster is responsible for transporting the crown from Buckingham Palace to Westminster and its return. This recalls the days when the Crown Jewels were kept at Hampton Court and on the day prior to the Opening of Parliament were brought to Westminster and delivered into the hands of the Comptroller.

The Royal Watermen and the Royal Bargemaster are reminders of the importance the Thames has always had for the monarch and her subjects and, in their magnificent uniforms are a significant part of London's royal ceremonial.

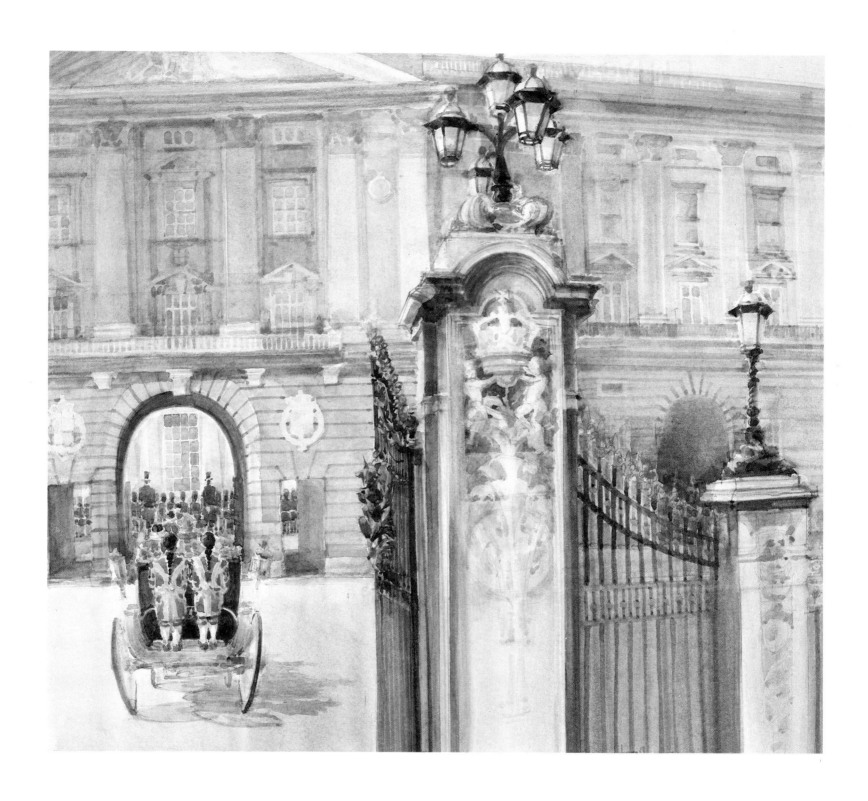

STATE VISITS

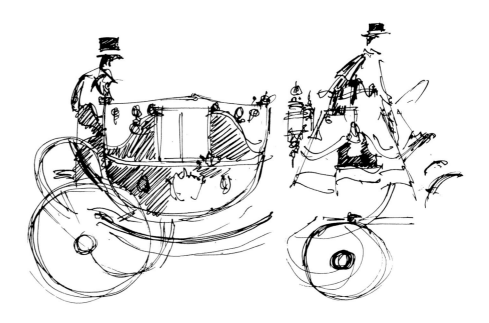

HEADS OF STATE making official visits to each other is an ancient tradition. (One of the first was in 1520 when Henry VIII invited Francis I of France to meet him at the Field of the Cloth of Gold.) Until relatively recently, state visits were confined to Europe and each sovereign paid one visit to the other's country in each reign.

With the decrease of monarchies and the increase of republics these conditions have been relaxed and more than one state visit can take place if heads of state so wish it. State visits to London last from a Tuesday to a Friday during which time the head of state and his or her spouse is a guest at Buckingham Palace. The planning for these visits is the responsibility of the Lord Chamberlain's office and will take about six months.

The visit usually begins with a member of the royal family meeting the head of state at Gatwick at 11.30am on the Tuesday. The party then travels by train to Victoria Station where the Queen and Prince Philip are there to welcome them. The Queen and the visiting head of state with their respective spouses are driven in the 1902 State Landau coach, escorted by the Horse Guards, to Buckingham Palace.

The procession, which includes six or more other carriages and bands playing, makes a splendid sight as it makes its way up Victoria Street, across Parliament Square, along Whitehall, through Admiralty Arch and down the Mall. The whole route is lined with flags and with Foot Guards. A gun salute is fired from Green Park as the cortège enters Buckingham Palace.

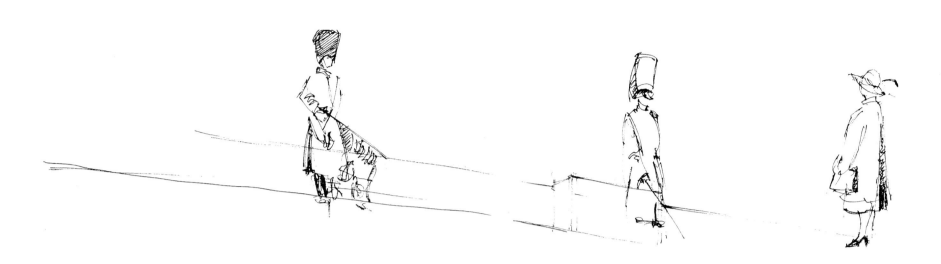

Sketches at Victoria Station

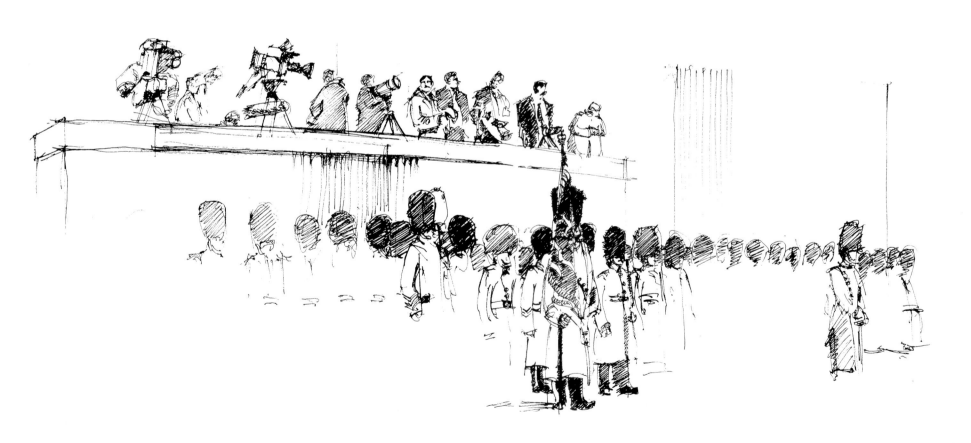

Entry through the Great Gates,
St James's Palace

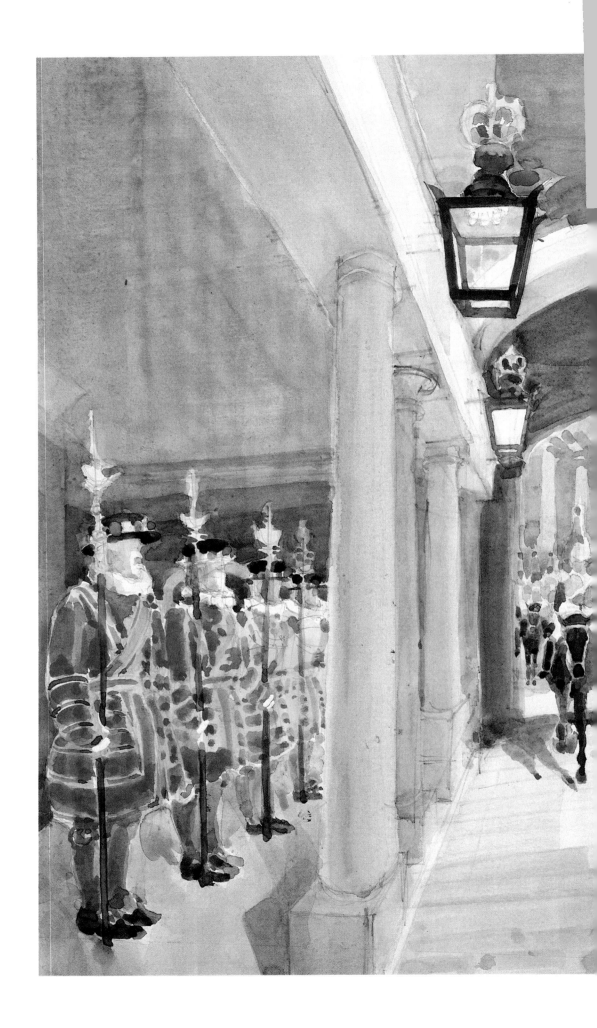

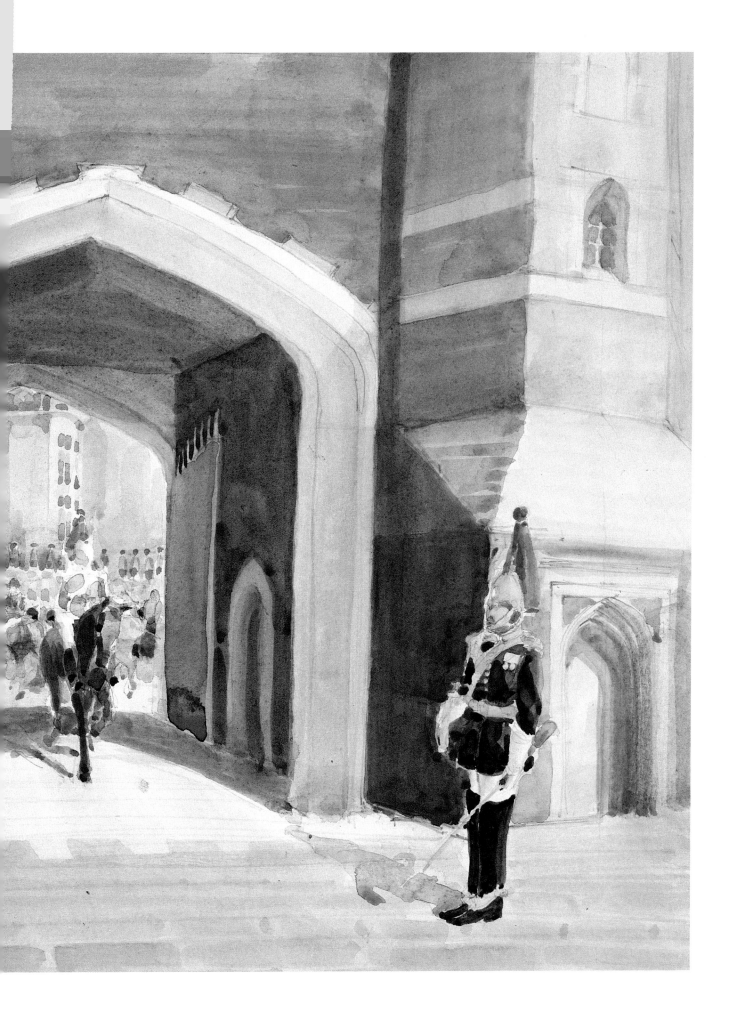

On Wednesday, the second day of the visit, there is a visit to St James's Palace for the head of state to attend a reception in the State Apartments for the Diplomatic Heads of Mission. Once again there is a colourful procession from Buckingham Palace up the Mall to Marlborough Road into Cleveland Row.

The Great Gates of St James's Palace are opened solely on these occasions to allow the Queen's State Landau coach to enter. As it clatters into Colour Court with all the panoply of state, the great court seems suddenly quite cramped. The Yeomen lining the colonnade and grand stairway, the Horse Guards, the postillions and liverymen all go to make the ancient palace seem fully alive. St James's Palace is doing what it has always done superbly – revealing the traditions and heritage of Britain's monarchy.

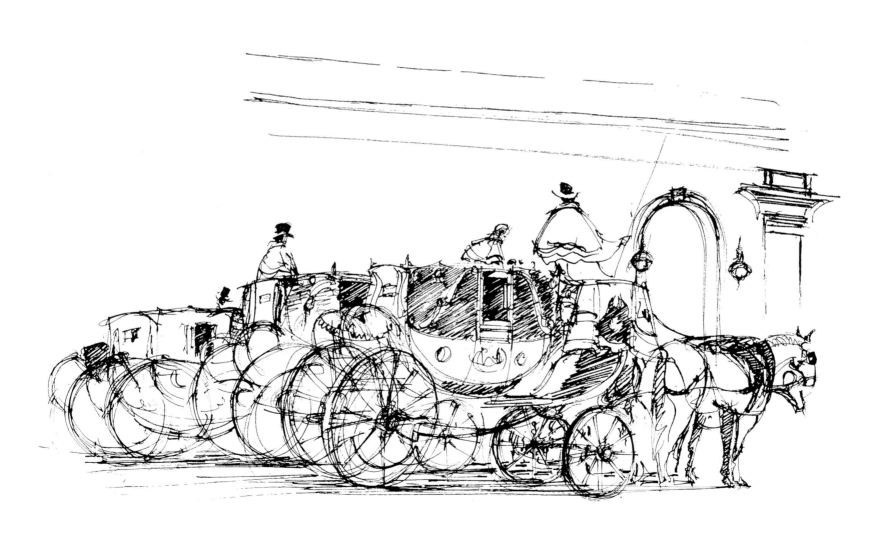

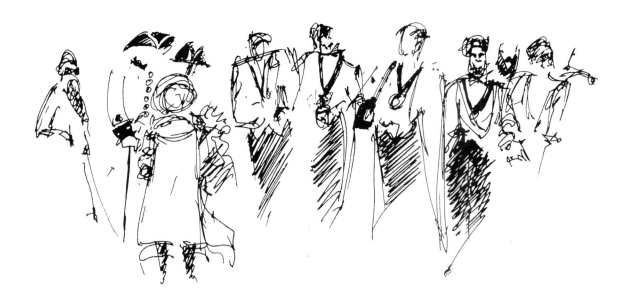

Sketches – Clarence House

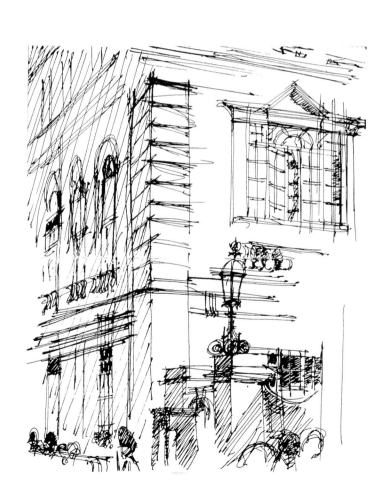

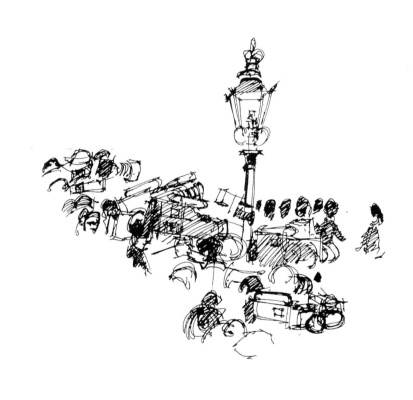

169

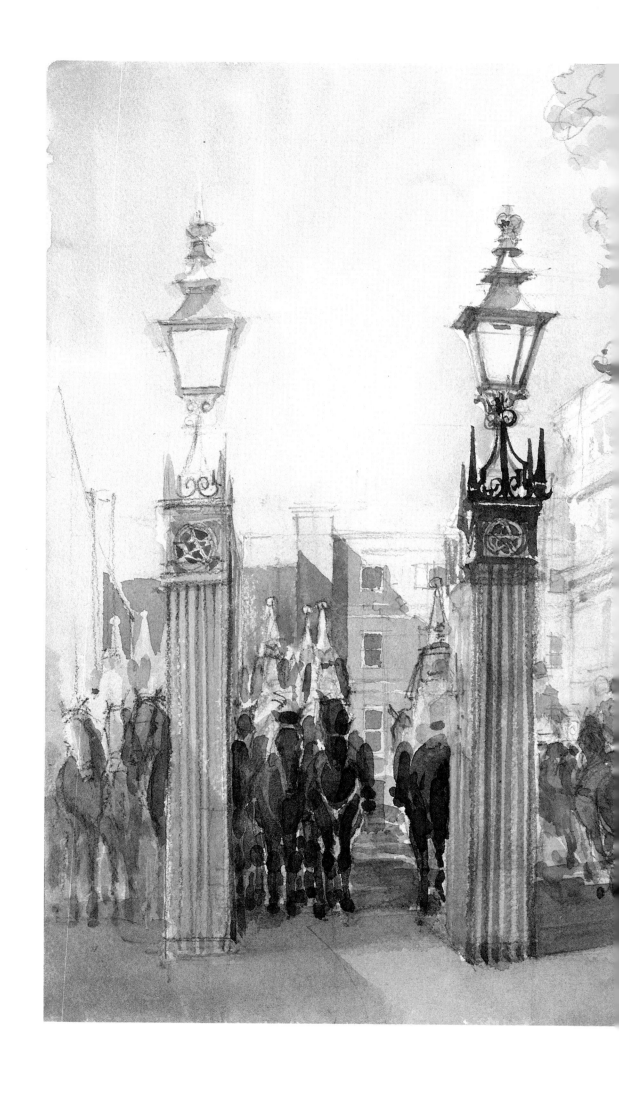

State visit: departing through
Clarence Gate

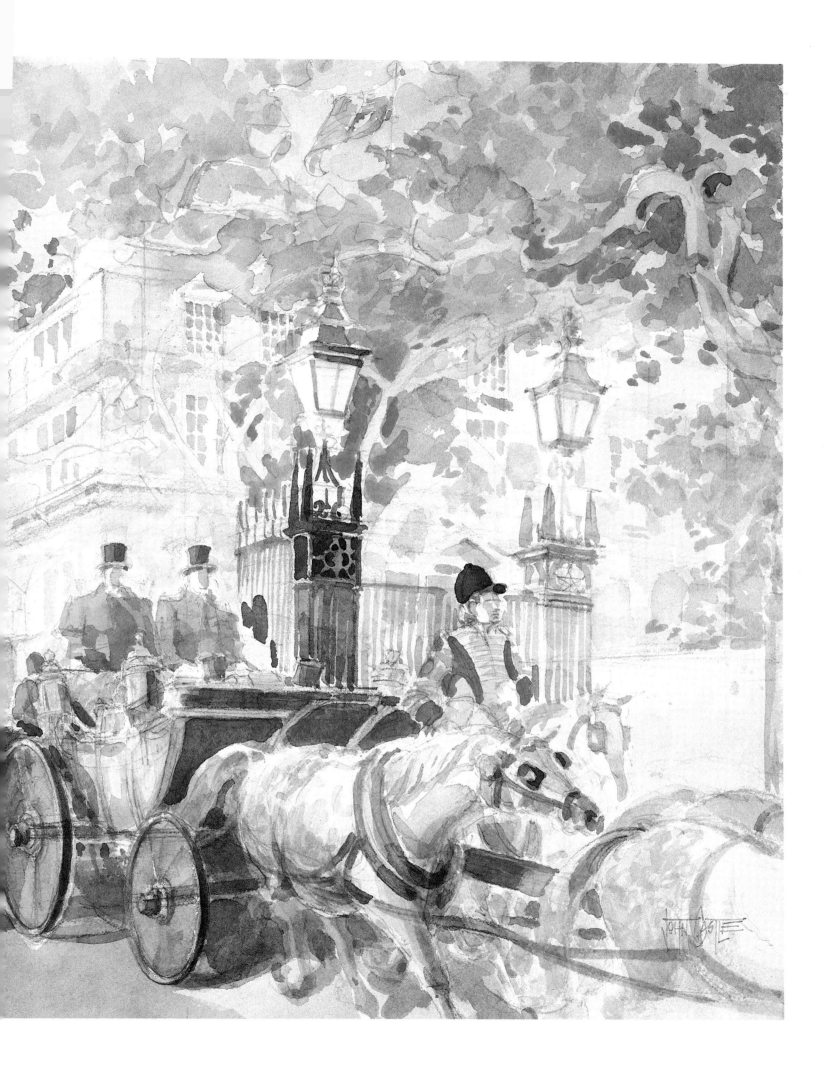

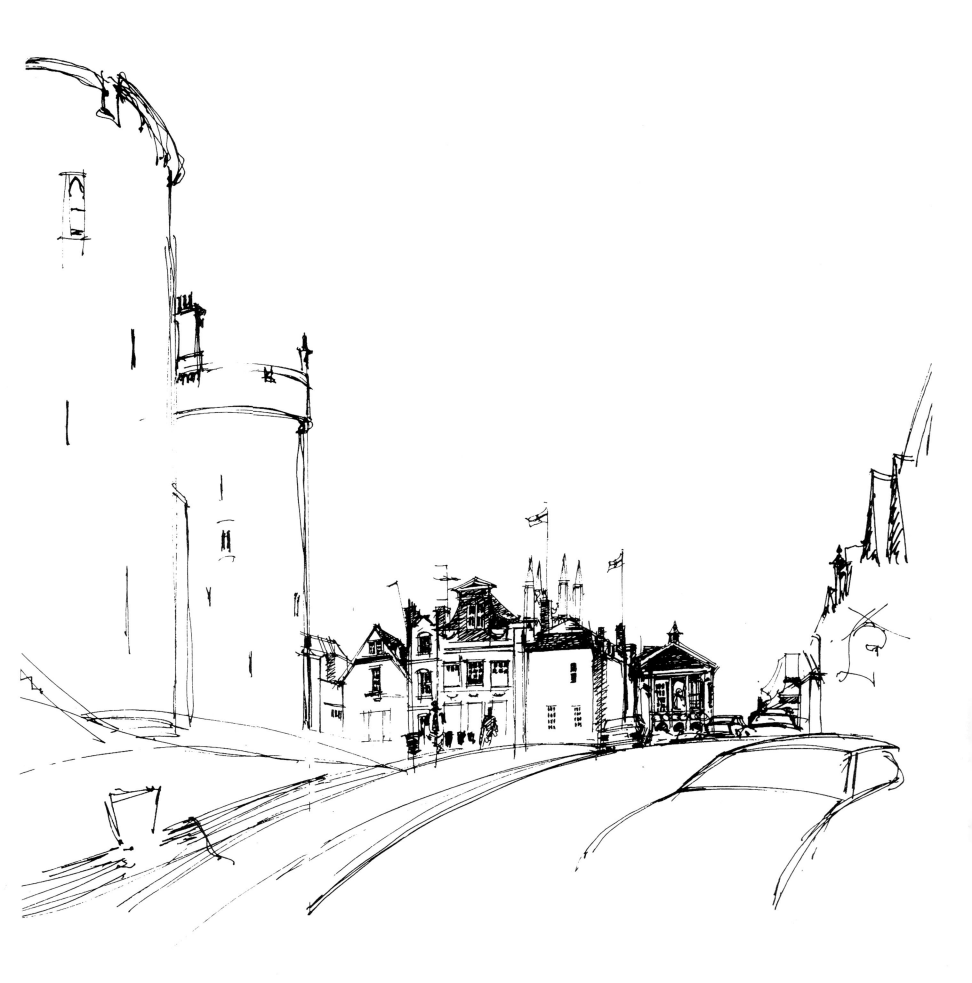

EPILOGUE

St James's Palace is the hub of royal ceremony. From this ancient and tranquil palace with its quiet courts and historic chapel there is fashioned modern monarchy. The pageant of soldiers marching in uniforms recalling the England of Marlborough or Wellington, of heads of state travelling in horse-drawn carriages and coaches, is a creation of a highly efficient administrative organization supervising hundreds of officials and skilled craftsmen.

It is easy to admire, with a view from behind the scenes, the hard work and professionalism that goes into the precision timing even of daily events such as Changing the Guard while an event such as Trooping the Colour makes enormous demands on the Palace organization.

My paintings can only show, if from a privileged vantage point, the colour and pageantry, but going behind the scenes revealed to me the immense amount of work involved in keeping the panoply of royalty, fresh. Almost all the traditions associated with royalty have real value and are not solely decorative. Just as the Household Cavalry are not toy soldiers but fully trained to use high-tech weapons so at the other end of the scale swan upping has a serious function conserving swans on our rivers.

If, in *Royal Occasions*, something is shown of the true nature of the ceremonies which tourists and Londoners so much admire then this book will have served its purpose.

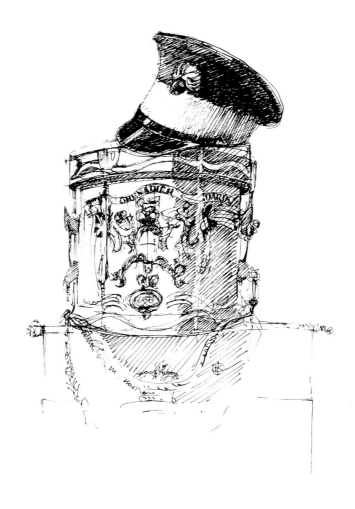

First published in 1992 by
Michael O'Mara Books Limited, 9, Lion Yard,
Tremadoc Road, London SW4 7NQ

Royal Occasions © 1992 by John Castle

A CIP catalogue record for this book is available
from the British Library

ISBN 1-85479-019-6

Designed by Simon Bell

Typeset by Florencetype Ltd, Kewstoke, Avon
Printed and bound in Italy by New Interlitho